A SourceBook of student writing guidelines, models, and workshops to accompany

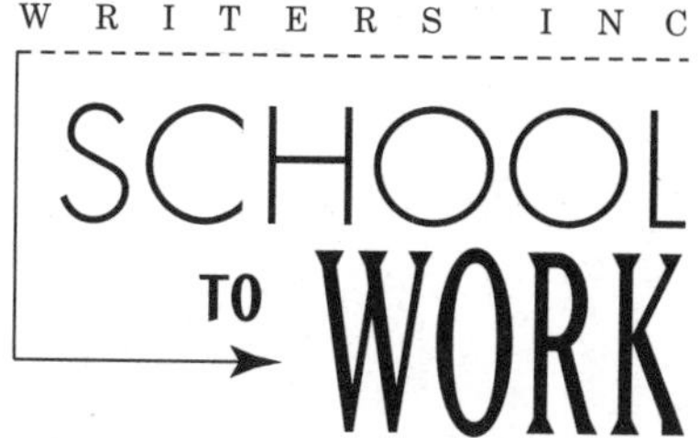

WRITE SOURCE

GREAT SOURCE EDUCATION GROUP
a Houghton Mifflin Company
Wilmington, Massachusetts

Before You Begin . . .

It is important for you to know a few things about your *School to Work SourceBook* before you begin to use it.

First of all, your *SourceBook* contains a wonderful selection of narratives and essays written by students and professionals from across the country. You will not find a more interesting and diverse collection of writing under one cover anywhere. To go along with these models, we have included clear, step-by-step guidelines that show you how to develop your own writing. The models stimulate you to write; the guidelines help you to carry out your work.

Second, your *SourceBook* contains a variety of letters, memos, reports, and other forms of workplace writing for you to study and practice. This section of your *SourceBook* should provide you with a number of valuable experiences you can take with you into the workplace.

Third, your *SourceBook* contains a collection of writing workshops covering all aspects of the writing process. The skills and strategies that you practice here will lead to real improvement in your writing.

Finally, your *SourceBook* is designed to be used with the *Writers INC: School to Work* handbook. Whenever you see a reference like this ("Refer to . . . ") in a *SourceBook* activity, you are being directed to the handbook for additional help. Together, these two books make quite a team.

Now, take a few minutes to page through your *SourceBook*, section by section. Stop, look, and read as you go. Once you've completed your quick tour, you will be **ready to begin.**

Written and Compiled by

Patrick Sebranek, Dave Kemper, Verne Meyer,
John Van Rys, Laura Bachman, Kathy Henning, and Randy VanderMey

Illustrations by

Kim DeMarco
Cover Illustration by Chris Krenzke

Printed in the United States of America

International Standard Book Number: 0-669-40877-8

6 7 8 9 10 -POO- 02 01

An Overview of the *School to Work SourceBook*

Part I The Forms of Writing

The forms of writing section offers a variety of real-life writing experiences. Student and professional models are provided for each form of writing, as are step-by-step guidelines.

Part II Writing in the Workplace

The writing-in-the-workplace section contains writing activities useful to anyone preparing to enter the world of work.

Part III Writing Workshops

The writing workshops cover all phases of the writing process—from selecting interesting subjects to organizing writing, from advising in peer groups to editing for clarity.

Part I The Forms of Writing

Personal Writing

Subject Writing

Academic Writing

Persuasive Writing

Part II Writing in the Workplace

Letter Writing

Writing to Get a Job

Writing on the Job

Part III Writing Workshops

Searching and Selecting

Generating Texts

Developing Texts

Reviewing and Revising Texts

Refining:
Sentence Strengthening

Refining:
Improving Style

Refining: Editing

Refining: Proofreading

The Forms of Writing

Level 2 Activities and Outcomes

The activities in the level 2 framework provide students with a wide variety of opportunities to re-create and connect past incidents, to describe other people and events, to develop essays and personal responses, and to form explanations and summaries.

Personal Writing:

Extended Reminiscence • Recall a phase or an important time of change in your life.

Personal Essay • Explore a subject of personal interest in a free-flowing essay.

Subject Writing:

Case Study • Develop an in-depth report about one person whose experiences typify the experience of a larger group.

Historical Profile • Share your findings about an interesting aspect from our past.

Venture Report • Offer readers an in-depth look at a business or profession.

Personal Research Report • Present your research findings on a topic of personal interest.

Academic Writing:

Problem/Solution Essay • Propose a solution(s) to a real problem.

Essay of Evaluation • Assess a policy, topic, class, etc., as to its value or worth.

Persuasive Writing:

Position Paper • Present your position on a significant issue.

Essay of Speculation • Explore a subject, noting what effect it might have in the future.

Overview of the Forms of Writing

Each form of writing is designed to be efficient and user-friendly for both the teacher and student. Each student-guidelines page is presented in a clear, step-by-step fashion. All models contain an introduction and helpful margin notes.

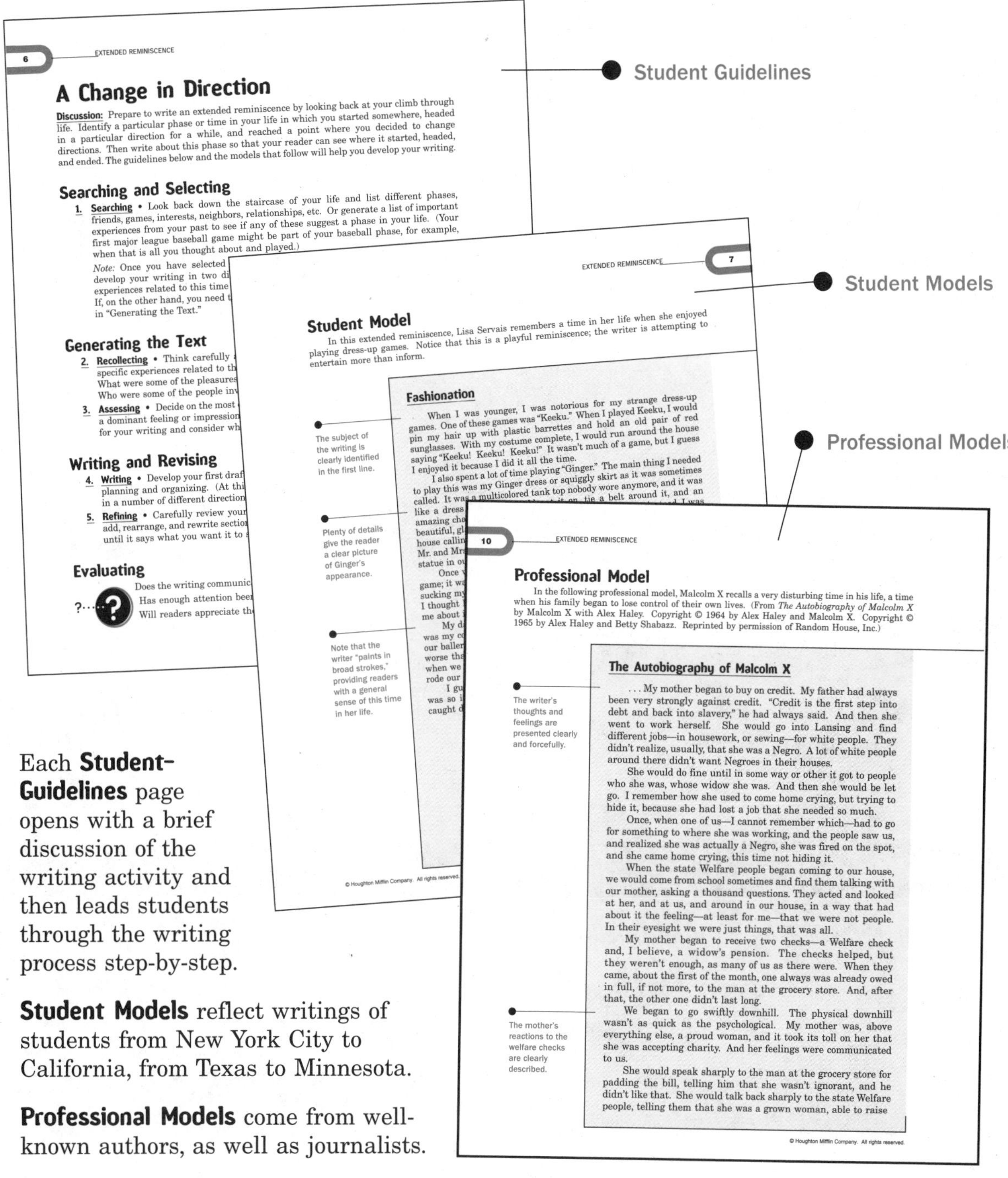

6 EXTENDED REMINISCENCE

A Change in Direction

Discussion: Prepare to write an extended reminiscence by looking back at your climb through life. Identify a particular phase or time in your life in which you started somewhere, headed in a particular direction for a while, and reached a point where you decided to change directions. Then write about this phase so that your reader can see where it started, headed, and ended. The guidelines below and the models that follow will help you develop your writing.

Searching and Selecting

1. **Searching** • Look back down the staircase of your life and list different phases, friends, games, interests, neighbors, relationships, etc. Or generate a list of important experiences from your past to see if any of these suggest a phase in your life. (Your first major league baseball game might be part of your baseball phase, for example, when that is all you thought about and played.)

Note: Once you have selected develop your writing in two di experiences related to this time If, on the other hand, you need t in "Generating the Text."

Generating the Text

2. **Recollecting** • Think carefully specific experiences related to th What were some of the pleasures Who were some of the people in
3. **Assessing** • Decide on the most a dominant feeling or impression for your writing and consider wh

Writing and Revising

4. **Writing** • Develop your first draf planning and organizing. (At thi in a number of different direction
5. **Refining** • Carefully review your add, rearrange, and rewrite sectio until it says what you want it to

Evaluating

Does the writing communic
Has enough attention bee
Will readers appreciate th

EXTENDED REMINISCENCE 7

Student Model

In this extended reminiscence, Lisa Servais remembers a time in her life when she enjoyed playing dress-up games. Notice that this is a playful reminiscence; the writer is attempting to entertain more than inform.

Fashionation

When I was younger, I was notorious for my strange dress-up games. One of these games was "Keeku." When I played Keeku, I would pin my hair up with plastic barrettes and hold an old pair of red sunglasses. With my costume complete, I would run around the house saying "Keeku! Keeku! Keeku!" It wasn't much of a game, but I guess I enjoyed it because I did it all the time.

I also spent a lot of time playing "Ginger." The main thing I needed to play this was my Ginger dress or squiggly skirt as it was sometimes called. It was a multicolored tank top nobody wore anymore, and it was like a dress

The subject of the writing is clearly identified in the first line.

Plenty of details give the reader a clear picture of Ginger's appearance.

Note that the writer "paints in broad strokes," providing readers with a general sense of this time in her life.

10 EXTENDED REMINISCENCE

Professional Model

In the following professional model, Malcolm X recalls a very disturbing time in his life, a time when his family began to lose control of their own lives. (From *The Autobiography of Malcolm X* by Malcolm X with Alex Haley. Copyright © 1964 by Alex Haley and Malcolm X. Copyright © 1965 by Alex Haley and Betty Shabazz. Reprinted by permission of Random House, Inc.)

The Autobiography of Malcolm X

. . . My mother began to buy on credit. My father had always been very strongly against credit. "Credit is the first step into debt and back into slavery," he had always said. And then she went to work herself. She would go into Lansing and find different jobs—in housework, or sewing—for white people. They didn't realize, usually, that she was a Negro. A lot of white people around there didn't want Negroes in their houses.

She would do fine until in some way or other it got to people who she was, whose widow she was. And then she would be let go. I remember how she used to come home crying, but trying to hide it, because she had lost a job that she needed so much.

Once, when one of us—I cannot remember which—had to go for something to where she was working, and the people saw us, and realized she was actually a Negro, she was fired on the spot, and she came home crying, this time not hiding it.

When the state Welfare people began coming to our house, we would come from school sometimes and find them talking with our mother, asking a thousand questions. They acted and looked at her, and at us, and around in our house, in a way that had about it the feeling—at least for me—that we were not people. In their eyesight we were just things, that was all.

My mother began to receive two checks—a Welfare check and, I believe, a widow's pension. The checks helped, but they weren't enough, as many of us as there were. When they came, about the first of the month, one always was already owed in full, if not more, to the man at the grocery store. And, after that, the other one didn't last long.

We began to go swiftly downhill. The physical downhill wasn't as quick as the psychological. My mother was, above everything else, a proud woman, and it took its toll on her that she was accepting charity. And her feelings were communicated to us.

She would speak sharply to the man at the grocery store for padding the bill, telling him that she wasn't ignorant, and he didn't like that. She would talk back sharply to the state Welfare people, telling them that she was a grown woman, able to raise

The writer's thoughts and feelings are presented clearly and forcefully.

The mother's reactions to the welfare checks are clearly described.

Each **Student-Guidelines** page opens with a brief discussion of the writing activity and then leads students through the writing process step-by-step.

Student Models reflect writings of students from New York City to California, from Texas to Minnesota.

Professional Models come from well-known authors, as well as journalists.

Personal Writing

"Once when I was playing 'Ginger,' I added something new to the game; it was my Ginger hairstyle. This delicate design was created by sucking my hair up into the vacuum cleaner hose until it stood on end." —Lisa Servais

Extended Reminiscence

In an extended reminiscence, you focus on a series of related personal experiences that make up a phase or unique period in your life. Then you explore how the experiences are related and why they're important. In the workplace, personnel managers, social workers, and educators use similar writing and thinking skills to write evaluations.

A Change in Direction

Discussion: Prepare to write an extended reminiscence by looking back at your climb through life. Identify a particular phase or time in your life in which you started somewhere, headed in a particular direction for a while, and reached a point where you decided to change directions. Then write about this phase so that your reader can see where it started, headed, and ended. The guidelines below and the models that follow will help you develop your writing.

Searching and Selecting

1. **Searching** • Look back down the staircase of your life and list different phases, friends, games, interests, neighbors, relationships, etc. Or generate a list of important experiences from your past to see if any of these suggest a phase in your life. (Your first major league baseball game might be part of your baseball phase, for example, when that is all you thought about and played.)

   Note: Once you have selected a subject for your extended reminiscence, you can develop your writing in two different ways. If all of the problems, pleasures, and experiences related to this time are clear in your mind, go straight to your first draft. If, on the other hand, you need to proceed more carefully, refer to the steps that follow in "Generating the Text."

Generating the Text

2. **Recollecting** • Think carefully about your subject. Can you remember a number of specific experiences related to this time? Discuss your initial ideas with a classmate. What were some of the pleasures, problems, causes, and costs of this time in your life? Who were some of the people involved?
3. **Assessing** • Decide on the most effective way to write about your subject. Think about a dominant feeling or impression that comes to mind. Also establish a starting point for your writing and consider which facts and details are essential.

Writing and Revising

4. **Writing** • Develop your first draft freely, as thoughts occur to you, or according to your planning and organizing. (At this point, don't be afraid to let your writing take you in a number of different directions.)
5. **Refining** • Carefully review your writing. Have a classmate review it as well. Cut, add, rearrange, and rewrite sections as necessary. Continue working with your writing until it says what you want it to say.

Evaluating

Does the writing communicate exactly what this particular phase was all about?

Has enough attention been given to important ideas and details?

Will readers appreciate the way the subject is presented?

Student Model

In this extended reminiscence, Lisa Servais remembers a time in her life when she enjoyed playing dress-up games. Notice that this is a playful reminiscence; the writer is attempting to entertain more than inform.

The subject of the writing is clearly identified in the first line.

Plenty of details give the reader a clear picture of Ginger's appearance.

Note that the writer "paints in broad strokes," providing readers with a general sense of this time in her life.

Fashionation

When I was younger, I was notorious for my strange dress-up games. One of these games was "Keeku." When I played Keeku, I would pin my hair up with plastic barrettes and hold an old pair of red sunglasses. With my costume complete, I would run around the house saying "Keeku! Keeku! Keeku!" It wasn't much of a game, but I guess I enjoyed it because I did it all the time.

I also spent a lot of time playing "Ginger." The main thing I needed to play this was my Ginger dress or squiggly skirt as it was sometimes called. It was a multicolored tank top nobody wore anymore, and it was like a dress on me. I would put it on, tie a belt around it, and an amazing change would take place. I was no longer Lisa; instead, I was beautiful, glamorous Ginger from *Gilligan's Island*. I'd walk around the house calling my sisters and brothers Mary Ann, Gilligan, Skipper, or Mr. and Mrs. Howell. The title Professor was reserved for the St. Agnes statue in our living room, which was just my size.

Once when I was playing "Ginger," I added something new to the game; it was my Ginger hairstyle. This delicate design was created by sucking my hair up into the vacuum cleaner hose until it stood on end. I thought I was pretty beautiful until the neighbor boys began teasing me about it. I gave up my Ginger hairdo.

My days of make-believe sometimes included my sister Mary, who was my constant companion. We played long dresses or dressed up in our ballerina outfits. Hers was blue, and mine was pink. They itched worse than poison ivy, but we'd wear them for hours. We wore them when we played house and store and restaurant . . . and even when we rode our Big Wheels down the driveway.

I guess all kids go through a pretending stage. Why dressing up was so important to me, though, I don't know. Today I wouldn't be caught dead looking like that.

Student Model

In this extended reminiscence, Jessica Thompson recalls the phase in her life when she lived in Iowa in a small town called Lake Mills. As you read this model, note the ideas and details that suggest whether or not this was a positive phase in her life. (Reprinted from the April 1992 edition of *High School Writer* with permission.)

In the first few sentences, the author identifies a specific time in her life.

She provides many details related to this time.

Growing Up in Town

"We are shaped and fashioned by what we love."
— Johann Wolfgang von Goethe

It was a somewhat prejudiced little town, but I didn't know that at the time. How could a child growing up in a small, all-white, all-Christian, midwestern town know about prejudice? All I know is that I loved growing up in Lake Mills, Iowa. The town was only one square mile in size and 2,200 people in population. We had one school; it held grades K-12, and 902 students. There was one swimming pool, always in bad need of repair; two grocery stores (we always went to Jerry's Foodland); and one doctor's office, where my mother worked. My father ran some businesses on Main Street, selling appliances and outdoor equipment, and also repairing them. We had a small video rental store at one time.

We lived in a big, white, two-story house on Lake Street. It was old and creaky, but I liked it. It had a large lawn with several towering oak trees, a swing set, and a sandbox. There were no fences to mark your property in Lake Mills; you could walk right through the middle of a block without getting barricaded in anywhere. While growing up there, my friends and I took advantage of this, playing tag and hide-and-seek throughout the neighborhood.

Oak Tree Park was a block from my house. It got its name because of the couple dozen oaks growing there. I remember when one of the trees fell during a tornado, crushing one of the shelter houses. Railroad tracks separated my house from the park. Sometimes when we were playing, a train would go by and we'd try to count the cars; there were usually more than 100. The man in the caboose would sometimes throw gum to us out of his window. The park and the school yard ran into each other, but the teachers kept a close watch on us during recess. Everyone knew everyone in Lake Mills, and everyone's business. There was never a problem of making friends for me. I knew practically everyone in my class since birth. We went to preschool together; we would play together when our mothers had coffee.

In the winter, you practically never saw the sun. I guess it was probably depressing for the adults, but all that my friends

The writer highlights what it was like to be a child in Lake Mills during winter and summer.

From a distance, the author reflects upon this time in her childhood.

and I saw was the four to five feet of packed white snow. (And occasional no-school snow days.) We'd make snowmen and have snowball fights, dig holes in drifts for forts, and slide down the ice-covered streets. It's strange, but I never remember being cold. At school, the yard workers would pile up all the snow from the blacktop into a huge "snow mountain." Then, during recess, we would slide down it. Sometimes we were allowed to go into the park to ice-skate on the frozen tennis courts. I must have gone through two or three pairs of snow boots every year.

In the summer, my friends and I would play *The Dukes of Hazzard* on our bicycles. We'd play in the mud and climb trees and go swimming. I don't remember ever being bored in the summer. There was a big whistle in the park that would sound off at noon and again at 6:00 p.m. every day; those were our signals to go home to eat. After we had shoveled down our fried chicken and watermelon, we'd go out to play again until the streetlights came on. That was sort of everyone's curfew.

Every Fourth of July week, the whole town would celebrate with the "July Jubilee." There were sidewalk sales, dances, picnics, rides, games, food. That was usually the best part of summer vacation.

School was a lot harder in Iowa than in Arizona, where I now live. I found it very strange to come to a new school having its halls outside. In Iowa, everything is inside. There were some portables, but they ended up being used for storage.

I learned good morals, values, and beliefs in Lake Mills that I possibly would not have being brought up in the city. I made some good friends that I miss a lot, and I miss my relatives; but I'm glad my family moved here to the city. My friends in Lake Mills do not have the opportunities that I have now; different things are expected of them. I used to think Lake Mills was huge. Now, when I go back to visit, I can't believe how small it is. I guess to see something for what it really is, sometimes you have to step away and look at it from a distance. They say you're shaped and fashioned by what you love; I loved growing up in a small town. ▣

Professional Model

In the following professional model, Malcolm X recalls a very disturbing time in his life, a time when his family began to lose control of their own lives. (From *The Autobiography of Malcolm X* by Malcolm X with Alex Haley. Copyright © 1964 by Alex Haley and Malcolm X. Copyright © 1965 by Alex Haley and Betty Shabazz. Reprinted by permission of Random House, Inc.)

The Autobiography of Malcolm X

The writer's thoughts and feelings are presented clearly and forcefully.

. . . My mother began to buy on credit. My father had always been very strongly against credit. "Credit is the first step into debt and back into slavery," he had always said. And then she went to work herself. She would go into Lansing and find different jobs—in housework, or sewing—for white people. They didn't realize, usually, that she was a Negro. A lot of white people around there didn't want Negroes in their houses.

She would do fine until in some way or other it got to people who she was, whose widow she was. And then she would be let go. I remember how she used to come home crying, but trying to hide it, because she had lost a job that she needed so much.

Once, when one of us—I cannot remember which—had to go for something to where she was working, and the people saw us, and realized she was actually a Negro, she was fired on the spot, and she came home crying, this time not hiding it.

When the state Welfare people began coming to our house, we would come from school sometimes and find them talking with our mother, asking a thousand questions. They acted and looked at her, and at us, and around in our house, in a way that had about it the feeling—at least for me—that we were not people. In their eyesight we were just things, that was all.

My mother began to receive two checks—a Welfare check and, I believe, a widow's pension. The checks helped, but they weren't enough, as many of us as there were. When they came, about the first of the month, one always was already owed in full, if not more, to the man at the grocery store. And, after that, the other one didn't last long.

The mother's reactions to the welfare checks are clearly described.

We began to go swiftly downhill. The physical downhill wasn't as quick as the psychological. My mother was, above everything else, a proud woman, and it took its toll on her that she was accepting charity. And her feelings were communicated to us.

She would speak sharply to the man at the grocery store for padding the bill, telling him that she wasn't ignorant, and he didn't like that. She would talk back sharply to the state Welfare people, telling them that she was a grown woman, able to raise

Time and experience helped the writer better understand his mother's actions.

her children, that it wasn't necessary for them to keep coming around so much, meddling in our lives. And they didn't like that.

But the monthly Welfare check was their pass. They acted as if they owned us, as if we were their private property. As much as my mother would have liked to, she couldn't keep them out. She would get particularly incensed when they began insisting upon drawing us older children aside, one at a time, out on the porch or somewhere, and asking us questions, or telling us things—against our mother and against each other.

We couldn't understand why, if the state was willing to give us packages of meat, sacks of potatoes and fruit, and cans of all kinds of things, our mother obviously hated to accept. We really couldn't understand. What I later understood was that my mother was making a desperate effort to preserve her pride—and ours . . .

Pride was just about all we had to preserve . . .

"You may think that because your car looks like trash nobody is going to steal it, but you're wrong. Many people will steal a car for any reason."

—from "Confessions of a Teenage Car Thief"

Personal Essay

In a personal essay, you do more than report details of a past experience—you look at the experience closely, and evaluate why it's important. Nearly all workplace writing involves some reporting and evaluation; but reports on research, professional conferences, and continuing-education classes are probably most like the personal essay.

The Way I See It . . .

Discussion: Write an essay about a subject you find personally interesting or important. Your goal should be to produce an essay that is based on personal experiences, thoughts, and feelings—an essay that informs or entertains or gets your readers thinking. Refer to the guidelines below and the models that follow for help with your writing.

Searching and Selecting

1. **Reviewing** • Review your journal entries for ideas, or list ideas that come to mind as you review the model essays. (Anything that is part of your life—and you care about—can become an effective writing idea.)
2. **Searching** • Still stuck? Check your wallet or purse for ideas. What about the ticket stub or receipt stuck in the corner? What about a picture, your driver's license, a membership card? Also think about any concerns, observations, and questions you may have right now—issues you may like to explore.

Generating the Text

3. **Collecting** • Free-write about your subject (for at least 10 minutes) letting your ideas take you where they will. One of the following open-ended sentences could serve as a starting point for your writing:
   - (*The subject*) makes me remember . . .
   - (*The subject*) causes me to . . .
   - (*The subject*) concerns me because . . .
4. **Assessing** • Examine your free writing carefully to help you get a feel for your subject. Look for parts of the writing that you like and want to explore further. Also look for any main idea or feeling that could serve as the focus for your essay. Continue gathering and focusing your ideas until you feel ready to write a first draft.

   (Your final essay may turn out to be a free-flowing exploration of ideas, or it may evolve into a tightly structured essay.)

Writing and Revising

5. **Writing** • Write your first draft freely, allowing your own personality to come through in your writing. Don't strain for a voice or try to make your essay sound too formal. Write what you are thinking and feeling.
6. **Revising** • Review, revise, and refine your writing. (As you work with your essay, try to maintain its original freshness while improving its impact.)

Evaluating

?...?

Is there a personal attachment between the writer and the writing?

Does the writing move smoothly from one point to the next?

Will readers appreciate the treatment of the subject?

Student Model

The student writer of "Confessions of a Teenage Car Thief" uses his own experience to discuss the methods and motivations of young car thieves. (Reprinted from *YO! (Youth Outlook)*, the Journal of [San Francisco] Bay Area Teen Life [Spring 1992], published by the Center for Integration and Improvement of Journalism at San Francisco State University and Pacific News Service.)

Confessions of a Teenage Car Thief

Editor's note: The 16-year-old writer of this essay has been arrested four times for auto theft for joyriding. Convicted once after pleading guilty to a misdemeanor, he is now studying auto repair.

The essay's style is very matter-of-fact, contrasting with the shocking criminal activity of the young writer.

You may think that because your car looks like trash nobody is going to steal it, but you're wrong. Many people will steal a car for any reason.

I was 13 when I stole my first car, and it wasn't very easy. The car was a piece of junk—dirty and all crashed up—but it was the kind of car everyone was telling me to steal: a 1986 Honda Accord DX. The first time was hard, but after that I got to where I could steal a car in under a minute. Some of the other thieves were doing it in 15 to 30 seconds.

When I started stealing cars, I did it just for fun, but after a while it got boring. I started doing it for money, but as soon as I got the money, I would go out and spend it. Before I knew it, the money was gone. So then I'd go out to steal another car—I just kept on doing the same thing over and over. Sometimes I stole a car for the dumbest reasons. "I'm bored with nothing to do"—that's how I was thinking at 13 and 14.

A couple of years ago, it seemed like kids were stealing cars just for fun—to drive around, show off, or learn to drive. These days most car thieves only break into cars for items of value, or if they need parts for their own car. So if your car looks good, the thieves will notice, and they'll think you've got some good stuff inside.

Personal experience leads into objective statements about auto theft and the experiences of one car thief in particular.

Even if your car doesn't look good, it's still at risk. Some people need money, so they steal your car to sell it and the buyer strips the car totally naked. Some car owners might get into an accident and look for a car that's the same as theirs to replace the parts that got wrecked. Or someone from the younger generation might steal your ugly car just for fun and driving lessons. . .

I know one guy who's got a family business in auto theft—his dad steals cars with him. They take the car home, and the mother helps them strip it. They aren't poor either. They drive a 1989 BMW 325i and a Toyota MR2, and they own a condo in the Sunset. But this kid has been in trouble with the law on six counts of auto theft, and after his sixth arrest he got six months at Log Cabin, a camp for juvenile offenders.

A strong sense of irony is evident in the concluding paragraph.

You might think that just because I'm a car thief I can avoid getting my car broken into, but I can't. My car got broken into in broad daylight, even though it had nothing worth taking. And lots of my friends have had their cars broken into for stereo equipment. Right afterwards they'd go out thieving to get their lost parts back.

Student Model

San Marcos High School student Lili Yee won first place in the University of California at Santa Barbara's Creative Studies Essay Contest (1991) with the essay "Swallowing Sorrow: Legacies of My Past," from which the following excerpt is taken. In her essay, Ms. Yee writes about the legacy of hope and sorrow that she carries as a first-generation Chinese American. In addition, the essay establishes a comparison between Ms. Yee's life and the life of the Chinese American daughter in Amy Tan's novel *The Joy Luck Club*.

Swallowing Sorrow: Legacies of My Past

The opening quotation stirs the reader's curiosity.

"In America, I will have a daughter just like me. But over there nobody will say her worth is measured by the loudness of her husband's belch. Over there nobody will look down on her because I will make her speak only perfect American English. And over there she will always be too full to swallow any sorrow!" Thus begin the legacies of four Chinese immigrant women and their four American-born daughters. *The Joy Luck Club* by Amy Tan kindles many memories and stories of China and Hong Kong that my relatives still tell me, of a childhood long gone, of the hardships of being poor, of the excitement, confusion, and fear of leaving home forever for America. My mother still tells me of her youth . . .

I grew up in a cold, grey stone house as a child in Hong Kong; everyone called it "The Stone House." Five families lived here, each sharing an individual room . . . A seven-by-eight-foot room housed seven of us. We slept on hard, wooden, three-tiered beds, staring at the bleak stone walls, dreaming of the future . . .

Unbeknownst to them, the future meant coming to America, the land of opportunity. For my mother, it was the experience of a lifetime. She was the first member of her family to immigrate to America. To her, America was an entirely different world where inhabitants spoke in a language she did not know.

During her first few months in Santa Barbara, my mother stayed home and watched television all day while my father worked at a hotel. She remembered watching *Gilligan's Island* and *The Flintstones* without any idea what the characters were saying. The television was, in many ways, her English teacher. Now, my mother occasionally tells me about those few months of living in Santa Barbara and the trauma of leaving her loved ones . . .

The shift from the mother's story to Ms. Yee's story signals the beginning of the heart of the essay.

Now it is time to tell my own story. I am a first-generation Chinese born in America just like the four daughters in *The Joy Luck Club*. I was raised by my aunt and grandparents, who arrived four years later in 1973, while both my parents worked. I looked like those cute, chubby, little, round-faced Chinese girls in travel magazines and films wearing pretty dresses and Chinese outfits. I spoke only Chinese then, but once I went to kindergarten I underwent a dramatic change. Gradually, I became the "daughter who grew up speaking only English and swallowing more Coca-Cola than sorrow." My relatives would speak to me in Chinese, and I would respond in English. Whenever I tried to talk in Chinese, especially to my grandparents, my American accent interfered, so they laughed at me. I never learned how to read and write in my native language, but I loved hearing stories about "The Stone House" and the hill on which the house was situated. I still remember the time when . . .

The italicized sections signal a departure from the basic development of the essay.

My mother, uncle, grandfather, and I took a trip to Hong Kong during Christmas of 1987. They took me around the city, and I was fascinated by the tall buildings, busy streets, and atmosphere of Hong Kong. Then my mother took me to another part of the city and showed her "Stone House" to me. I stood there right in the dim light of the porch. The building was dilapidated. Faded wintergreen paint was peeling off the cold stone walls in curly strips. Cracked, red wooden shutters hung on rusty hinges. The house was one of many bunched together on a side of a hill. Corrugated metal sheets placed on the rooftops between each house kept out the rain and strong sunlight. This was where my mother grew up . . .

Like Jing-Mei Woo, one of the daughters in *The Joy Luck Club*, I entered mainland China and became Chinese during my trip to Hong Kong. I met relatives that I never knew existed. I communicated with them as much as my American-accented Chinese could permit, and they tried to respond in their limited Chinese-accented English. It was wonderful how we could communicate with such limited means. We laughed and smiled at each other. They would correct my Chinese, and I would correct their English. We had a grand time together.

The essay ends on a reflective note as the writer comes to terms with her personal legacy.

Before my journey, I thought that I was "always too full to swallow sorrow." I grew up in a different culture and time, and I did not fully appreciate what my mother and all my relatives went through in order to get where they are now. I consider myself to be different from them, a "Coca-Cola-swallowing American," but looking into the browned faces and holding the calloused hands of my great-grandmother and my multitude of cousins, aunts, and uncles, never before did I realize how important my roots were to me. If it were not for them, I would not be where I am now. As I think back, I understand their suffering, their pain, their happiness. I realize how lucky I am to be an American, for what I am is what they dream of being: to be in America, a dream that probably will never be fulfilled. I recognize the sorrow that is ever present in my native homeland, a sorrow that I'll never forget and that will always be a part of my life. ▣

Professional Model

This personal essay by T. J. Gilding contains a little bit of everything: action, conflict, drama, reflection, and real feelings. As you will see, the writer's ideas are presented in the form of an internal dialogue that relives a most important cross-country meet. (This essay won second place in a 1993 writing contest sponsored by the *Milwaukee Journal*. It is reprinted with permission of the author.)

Passing on a Hill

The next red flag at the far end of the golf course signaled a hard right turn ahead. Reaching for a burst of energy, I lengthened my stride and positioned myself just enough ahead of the runner, a half step behind me, to safely make the turn around the bend. The conference cross-country meet was the last meet of the year, and the last race of my high-school career.

Looking out at the field ahead, I thought, "Seven runners to pass, with two miles to go. This race was my last and my only chance."

The essay begins right in the middle of the action, with two miles to go in the race.

Running was always my "ticket out." It was what I needed to do—to sort out my life, to build strong thoughts and strong words. Also, it was a way of building a record of wins, and winning a college athletic scholarship. I needed that, now, more than ever.

But my purposeful thoughts kept giving way to disturbing thoughts at the very time I needed to concentrate most. I couldn't get them out of my head—thoughts of my dad's words and my mom's speech. And the more I tried, like trying too hard to get to sleep, the harder it was to push them out. I knew I needed to concentrate on this race. Yet the thoughts kept screaming back and the infernal, internal dialogue in my head continued.

Angry at myself, with clenched fists, I knew what I had to do. I burst ahead of a runner, feeling no sympathy . . . but my thoughts again turned back to the scene of my father sitting down in the den with me. His words echoed in my head, "I know you blame me for what is happening, but you don't know the whole story. And I don't expect you to understand, perhaps someday you will, but you need to know I'm sorry and . . ." His voice trailed off. I knew he loved me—his eyes that were directed to the floor, his shoulders that were hunched over, his hand that touched his cheek, not his words, had told me that. But I still did not understand.

What whole story? All I had known and had heard was the yelling and the accusations. And I knew what Mom had told me that next morning about Dad's "official" leaving. And I knew she—all of us—from then on, would have it tough.

Disturbing thoughts about the writer's family surface again and again throughout the essay.

I felt cheated as I angrily passed another runner who couldn't keep up because of a side cramp. I knew the feeling of running in pain. But I had my own pains to think about, and I took advantage of this break.

I paced ahead, my mind springing back into the race. I deserved this win. Every morning for two years, up before dawn, out on the back roads, running to win. I tried to keep focused on the race, but it was hard.

"It's not fair." (Think about the race.) "They owe me." (Put it out of your mind.) "I can't do this myself." (Think, think, think.) Inner conflict was striding, pacing right along with me, keeping up with my every step, every heartbeat.

I thought back to Mom's announcement telling me my parents' marriage was over, their business split, and the money all tied up—unattainable. I would be on my own to earn my way through college. All that money needed for college. Where would I get it? Mom couldn't have helped if she had wanted to. Dad was gone, out of the picture. Even the two jobs I had lined up wouldn't do it.

"Honey, I'm really sorry. But I . . ." And her voice had trailed off as the tears came. Yeah? Well, I was sorry myself! Sorry I had been suddenly forced to fend for myself. I had seen the pain my mother was going through. I felt compassion for her, but . . . Okay, okay, it was all going to be fine. She would be fine; I would be fine, if I just focused on this race. I had to build it back.

The pace of the writer's thoughts reflect the breathless pace of the race.

Thoughts were racing in and out of my mind; there was a gaining of physical and mental momentum. Water from my eyes streamed down my cheeks. I had to keep it going—the rhythm of mind and body moving forward. The footsteps and breathing at my back was the runner I just passed! Passed? I hadn't even realized it.

Remembering a strategy Coach had taught me, psyching out the other runner, I tried to look stronger, more confident, showing that there was no way I could be beaten. I passed another runner without competition. And digging my toes deep into the grass on the hill, I passed yet another runner as I reached the top.

Passing on a hill I knew was something Coach had told me not to do. He would be mad about that, I thought as I remembered his last words to me, "And don't you ever pass on a hill." I grinned, and I ran.

Two ahead now, and less than a half mile to the finish. I was in this race. I had to be. I had practiced too hard before and after school when I could have been making money like many of my friends. I always said my running came first and meant it. Sure, I saved my money, but I had known my parents would be there for me. And then, slam! Now I needed to win this race, not for the glory, but for the money. A victory here meant a great chance at a state scholarship. Coach said a list of first-place finishers from around the state, especially in a major conference such as ours, was an immediate "send" to all state university athletic scholarship review boards.

Drama and intensity build as the finish line draws nearer.

It was all mixed together: the past, the present, the future. All coming together as I passed the next runner and squared down on the final jersey still ahead. It was all coming to me at once—the finish line two hundred yards away, Mom's surprise announcement, Coach's words of a must win, and my dad's sad expression as he asked for my understanding.

My thoughts cleared. It was my race. I was on my own, to fend for myself. My fate was in my hands—actually my feet. Yeah, a pun. Funny. I had to reach back, do what was needed. I had to realize the future, pass the last runner, run straight ahead—toward that line, toward that goal. It was mine!

Subject Writing

"Erica is no different than any other teenager. She wants to run to her next-hour class if she is late or be able to dance the night away. And she's tired of crutches and wheelchairs. Everything she has been through has not soured her personality or dimmed her determination, however." —Heather Bachman

Case Study

When writing a case study, you read, interview people, and use personal observations to gather information about an individual. Your purpose is to help the reader understand (1) who your subject is, and (2) how this person is like others with similar experiences. Social workers, anthropologists, historians, and news reporters do this kind of writing.

Making a Case

Discussion: Develop a case study based on your careful and thorough investigation of someone whose experiences typify a particular group of people (displaced farmers, recovering heart patients, apprentices, etc.). Gather information for your study through interviews, observations, articles, letters, journals, and so on. Your finished work should be developed as a narrative report telling the story of your subject's experiences. Keep personal comments and conclusions to a minimum. Instead, let your story speak for itself. Refer to the models that follow and the guidelines below to help you develop your writing.

Searching and Selecting

1. **Selecting** • Think of individuals you know whose experiences in a particular area speak for the experiences of others. (You may know a farmer who has recently lost his land, or you may know someone just starting a business.) Also think about certain groups of people that you would like to know more about. (Perhaps you're curious about police officers or foster children or first-year teachers.)

Generating the Text

2. **Collecting** • Plan for and carry out your interviews, observations, readings, and so on. (The lifeblood of an effective case study is information, so gather a good supply of facts, remarks, stories, and observations.)
3. **Focusing** • Carefully review all of the information you have collected. Make sure you understand how or why your subject's experiences speak for similar individuals. Also determine what it is about this person that you would like to emphasize in your writing—a specific turning point, a particular experience, an extended period of time, etc. And make some initial decisions about the structure of your writing. (What are you going to say first, second, third, and so on?)

Writing and Revising

4. **Writing** • Develop your first draft freely and naturally, working in ideas according to any planning you have done. (You may want to experiment or play with the sequence of events in your subject's story. The writer of "Health Care?" begins by describing how her subject passed away, drawing the reader's attention into the rest of the study.)
5. **Revising** • As you review your first draft, ask yourself two important questions: Have I addressed my subject's story in enough detail? Have I presented the details in an effective manner? Revise and refine accordingly.

Evaluating

Does this study read like a narrative report, effectively detailing an individual's story?

Is it clear how the subject speaks for, or represents, a larger group?

Will readers appreciate the treatment of this subject?

Student Model

In this model, student writer Rohan A. Dewar shares the story of one streetwise young man who eventually makes some smart choices. Dewar's case study typifies the experience of many young people who have turned their lives around. (This article first appeared in *New Youth Connections: The Magazine Written By and For New York Youth*, May 1992. It is reprinted with permission.)

In the first few paragraphs, the writer introduces his subject and offers some background information about him.

Notice how effectively the writer incorporates many of his subject's direct comments into the text.

A Street Kid Goes Straight

As a kid growing up in the Bronx, Troy Morrell, 23, was quiet, kept to himself, and never went outside much. He was a teacher's pet and a mama's boy, always getting picked on but never wanting to fight.

Troy lived a model life in the Bronx for 13 years. But then he moved to Brooklyn, changed schools, and started hanging out with the wrong crowd.

Troy rarely went to school and constantly disobeyed his mother. He got involved with a gang, started blowing up cars with "cocktails" (homemade firebombs), and began forging other people's signatures to cash checks.

At 15, Troy was arrested for injuring a couple with a firebomb and imprisoned in Spofford Juvenile Detention Center. He spent five months there before being released. But going to Spofford didn't help. Troy says it only made him worse.

When he got out, the neighborhood youths gave him the street name "Psycho." "I had that name," Troy said, "so I had to live up to it."

He went on a rampage. He threw TVs from roofs, wounding people below, hit people with hammers, burned people's eyes with paint remover, and carried a large butcher knife.

HE FELT ASHAMED

That was eight years ago. As Troy grew older, he started developing a conscience. He remembered his days in the Bronx and realized how much he'd changed. He started feeling ashamed and vowed to better himself.

He transferred to Lafayette High School where a guidance counselor named June Feder pushed him to do better. She scheduled Troy's classes in order to ensure that he didn't cut. She'd schedule his gym classes for the beginning and end of the day and put the classes and teachers Troy liked best in between.

Feder also introduced Troy to Operation Success, a program that encourages kids to come to school by rewarding them for good grades. Participants go on trips, have contests, and belong to a co-op program where students go to school one week and work the next. She also helped him get his first job at a toy store.

With Dr. Feder standing by him, Troy became more active in school. "She really turned my life around," he said. "She was always on my back." Troy won awards for art and play writing and the President's Award for achievement and improvement in school. "But the best thing I got," said Troy, "was my diploma."

WORKING WITH KIDS

Now, at 23, Troy has a 3-year-old daughter he helps support. He is the head counselor at a Manhattan after-school program for young children. He watches over and interacts with them. "I would've never thought it would be my career," Troy confided.

But he enjoys his job. "It's cool working there," he said. "You keep the kids entertained and it brings out the kid in you . . . you almost believe they're your own."

While some people may think that working with children is a woman's job, Troy doesn't. He feels that he can do a great job with the children because he understands and can relate to them.

"All these kids are from the neighborhood," he said. "They're going through what I went through. I'm an inner-city kid just like they're inner-city kids."

Troy has another job at a supermarket where he works in the evening to better support his daughter. He works long hours but he can handle it. "At the beginning it was [hard]," said Troy. "But when you get used to a certain pace, it's no problem."

As Troy wanders through his old neighborhood, he sees that things have changed. Asked the whereabouts of his old gang, he said, "Some are down South. Some are married. Some are in jail. I walk around now and I hardly see anyone I know."

The essay emphasizes the importance of an individual's power to change the circumstances of his life.

In his teen years, Troy Morrell seemed like a lost cause—a boy who would never grow up to see manhood. All it took for him to realize his true potential was a little inner strength and a helping hand from someone who cared.

By using his life experiences, Troy is touching the lives of kids like himself and making sure they too live up to their potential.

Student Model

In this model case study, Heather Bachman shares the story of a freshman girl in her high school who has had to live with a rare, painful bone disease. This person's story speaks forcefully for all young people with disabilities who struggle to fit in, who want desperately to be like their peers.

Walking Tall

Erica Lovell acts like any freshman in high school. She's bubbly, energetic, and one of the sweetest people I know. She's in Honors Art Club and loves golfing. I was somewhat surprised the first time I saw her walking down the hall with what appeared to be a limp. But I didn't really think anything of it until recently when Erica entered the hospital for major surgery.

Background information about the subject's disease is provided.

I discovered that Erica has *leggs perthees*, a disease that is rare among boys and almost unheard of among girls. Leggs perthees causes the portion of the femur that fits into the hip socket to deteriorate and grow into a rigid oblong shape. In Erica's case, this portion of bone grew to double its normal size and caused intense pain in her hip and left knee. And due to her condition, her left leg stopped growing, making her legs noticeably uneven. "I tried to make up the difference by walking on my tippy toes," Erica says. Although the cause is unknown, doctors know how to correct the unevenness caused by leggs perthees once the bones have stopped growing.

At one time Erica had to wear awkward braces on her legs. Around her waist was a belt from which two metal bars went down the sides of her legs. Plastic, velcro-secured cuffs around her calves were attached to the end of the bars. Finally, a rigid bar connected the two cuffs. This forced her to walk stiffly, cowboy style. She remembers, "My classmates would tease me and call me names." Their comments hurt, especially those made by her friends.

In July 1990, the pain became unbearable and doctors had to operate. Erica spent six and a half hours on the operating table while the doctors reduced friction between the hip bones and added pins and screws for support. Her recovery time included five weeks in a body cast, two weeks in bed, a month in a wheelchair, and a month on crutches. Erica started junior high on crutches. She had another operation in December 1990 to remove the pins and screws. The two surgeries relieved a lot of the pain, somewhat improved her bad hip, but did nothing to change her uneven legs.

Erica lost some friends during her years in junior high. "People would ask me what was wrong, and then they would stop being my friends." She couldn't participate in gym, sports, or dances. And the pain persisted, especially in her knee.

Finally on February 11, 1993, the doctors felt that Erica was ready for corrective surgery. The three-and-a-half-hour operation involved taking out a 1.25-inch section of her longer right femur and securing the bones together with plates and screws.

Direct quotations are used effectively throughout the case study.

As Erica says, "I can't wait to try out my legs," but she faces a long recovery period. The femur takes the longest to heal of all the bones in the body. She must be in bed for four weeks (which means missing school), in a wheelchair for two to three weeks, on crutches for two to three weeks, and finally, by May of 1993, she hopes to be walking again. She is not supposed to move or bend her legs for the first month after surgery. Then physical therapy will begin for her leg and will entail a lot of weight lifting, leg risers, and careful bending of the knee. Some of the exercises will be done with a therapist while others will be done at home.

Throughout the essay, the writer describes how leggs perthees has affected the subject's life.

Erica's list of "can't do's" has been rather lengthy: no soccer, no track, no cheerleading, no gym, no fast dancing, no twisting . . . basically anything involving heavy impact to the legs and joints has been out of the question. Erica roller-skates, ice-skates, walks, bikes, and lifts weights to stay in shape. She will still have to refrain from more strenuous activities in the future, because the pin that remains in her hip could detach from the bone and even possibly puncture her skin.

"Leggs perthees is like cancer in how it affects a family," Erica says. "It is very hard on my parents. My mother had to quit her job at one point to take care of me while I was in a body cast and confined to bed." It was hard on other family members too. "My sister was jealous of all the attention I got from my parents." Fortunately her family has very good insurance to help them cover the high costs of hospitals, doctors, and physical therapy.

Soon Erica will be able to wear something other than shoes with lifts. She can't wait to wear high heels. Golfing will be much easier since she won't have to compensate for her shorter leg while swinging. And tripping should no longer be the problem it was. "I once fell in a crosswalk in front of a line of cars right when the light turned green," she remembers.

The case study ends on a positive note, with Erica looking toward the future.

In her early twenties, Erica hopes to have a complete hip replacement. That would finally put an end to the pain and probably enable her to participate in more strenuous activities. Erica eagerly anticipates that surgery.

Erica is no different than any other teenager. She wants to run to her next-hour class if she is late or be able to dance the night away. And she's tired of crutches and wheelchairs. Everything she has been through has not soured her personality or dimmed her determination, however. Erica is, as always, upbeat and positive, someone who richly deserves our respect and our support.

Professional Model

Laura Bachman gathered the information for this case study from someone who was well acquainted with a dying man—someone who was at this man's side through his final, painful hours. Once you read this case study, you will see that it speaks eloquently for the experiences of all elderly men and women who have lost control of their own lives because of infirmity. (This essay was used at an in-service for resident physicians at Lutheran Hospital, La Crosse, Wis.)

Health Care?

The elderly gentleman being monitored in the cardiac intensive care unit lies buried in wires and electrical pads. When the monitor suddenly sounds an alarm and shows a straight line, his nurse, who happens to be out of the room at the time, as well as two or three others, comes rushing in. However, they make no attempt to revive him.

Lester and Esther DeBow celebrated their 60th wedding anniversary several years ago. In his later years, Lester kept active maintaining various gardens. He also made the rounds of his neighborhood taking the widows shopping, running errands, and doing odd jobs. Lester had been a master plumber and could often put those old skills to use fixing leaky faucets, clogged drains and even more serious problems. He took everything in stride with his indomitable sense of humor.

Background information not only places the case study in its larger context, but also brings the individual to life.

Three years ago, Lester's sense of humor served him well as he faced losing his right leg due to a blockage that cut off his circulation. He was insistent and, in fact, convinced the doctors not to take his leg above the knee. And unlike many amputees, he eagerly did everything necessary to speed the fitting of an artificial leg. He couldn't hide his amusement when he discovered the initial leg was simply a piece of pipe fitted with a shoe.

Having to use a cane didn't slow Lester down one bit. Although it was his right leg, he quickly learned to drive again. His widow friends never felt neglected. Though Lester and Esther never had children, they were constantly driving to communities across Wisconsin and Minnesota visiting their many friends and relatives.

Then Lester fell and cracked a hip, an injury requiring hospitalization. His nurses had to be on guard because he kept sliding out of bed, slipping on his leg, and sneaking off to the bathroom unassisted. Thinking they could solve the problem, the nurses took the artificial leg away. However, that didn't stop Lester, who simply used a chair for support and kept scooting around.

One of his favorite phrases, in or out of the hospital, was "It's a great life, if you don't weaken." At first, that naturally seemed to mean staying physically active; but on the fateful day when his bodily strength gave out, "not weakening" clearly referred to something different—his mind and spirit.

At age 86, with a failing heart that had been weakening him for a month or so, Lester was admitted to St. Mary's Hospital in the small community of Sparta (Wisconsin), on Thursday afternoon, March 17. The following afternoon he was moved to Lutheran Hospital in La Crosse.

From his bed in the cardiac intensive care unit, Lester said, "The doctor told me I'm going to die tonight." Later, still with a touch of humor, he said, "I'm not going to die tonight . . . maybe tomorrow, or maybe I'll wait a few days. . . ."

Meanwhile, the doctor continued serious efforts to monitor and control Lester's blood pressure. To do so required lowering the head of the hospital bed periodically. Earlier in the afternoon, Lester had been sitting up on the edge of his bed, despite having some trouble getting enough oxygen. His mind remained perfectly clear, and he just wanted to sit up and talk.

Instead, he spent the evening tossing in pain created by a catheter. Because any medication could interfere with his already weakened heart, pain killers were withheld. Eventually the catheter was removed—too late to significantly reduce the pain it had already caused.

The "buried" image in the introduction is reinforced by each added medical procedure.

Occasionally Lester's bed would be raised to a level position, but never elevated as he so fervently desired. Due to Lester's difficulty breathing, the doctor ordered an oxygen mask. Now conversation, already labored, became almost impossible. The best he could do throughout the night was mumble, "If I could only sit up for five minutes, five minutes, that's all I ask." Lester was not delirious. He was not crazy. He wasn't saying, just let me sit up and I'll be fine; I'll get out of here. No. He simply wanted to sit on the edge of the bed one last time.

And the nurse would respond each time, patiently, but firmly, "Your blood pressure couldn't take it."

At one point Lester admitted, "If this is what it's going to be like, then I just wish it would end."

Not only was Lester monitored constantly by the heart machine he was wired to, but he also had to contend with an automatic blood-pressure cuff on his arm, which pumped up and took his blood pressure every few minutes. This device required that the arm remain at a very exact angle. Otherwise a beeper went off, and then Lester had to be realigned. After numerous beeper alarms and painful realignments, Lester's arm was taped to a board to keep it properly positioned.

In the very early hours of the morning, efforts to reach the doctor succeeded, and permission was granted to give Lester some pain medication.

But Lester never got free of the blood-pressure cuff, never got his bed raised, never got to shed his oxygen mask, never got to sit on the edge of the bed and talk to his wife one last time. Because, less than 15 minutes after the final IV medication injection, he died.

The writer concludes by connecting the subject of this study to a larger group.

The nurse felt bad, but he was only following orders. All night, Lester endured being manipulated, maneuvered, and monitored. Painful, inconvenient, and even degrading efforts to control his blood pressure during his last hours were admittedly futile. Despite all the obvious concern expressed for Lester, this gentle man, who lived so long and so well, was forced to die, almost in self-defense. How many others spend their final hours subjected to procedures intended to prolong life (for a matter of hours), only to be robbed of their final peace and dignity? ▣

Professional Model

In the following model (an excerpt from an in-depth report), professional writer Gary Smith shares the story of a gifted high-school athlete named Jonathan Takes Enemy. As you read this model, notice how Takes Enemy's story speaks for the plight of other Native American athletes in Montana. (The following article is reprinted courtesy of *Sports Illustrated* from the February 18, 1991, issue. Copyright © 1991, Time, Inc. "Shadow of a Nation" by Gary Smith. All rights reserved.)

Shadow of a Nation

A dramatic, almost poetic introduction draws readers into this study.

. . . Young Indian boys formed trails behind him, wearing big buttons with his picture on their little chests. They ran onto the court and formed a corridor for him and his teammates to trot through during pregame introductions, they touched his hands and arms, they pretended to *be* him. The coaches had to lock the gym doors to start practice. Girls lifted their pens to the bathroom walls: "I was with Jonathan Takes Enemy last night," they wrote. "I'm going to have Jonathan Takes Enemy's baby." He was a junior in high school. Already he was the father of two. Already he drank too much. Already his sister Sharolyn was dead of cirrhosis. Sometimes he walked alone in the night, shaking and sobbing. He was the newest hero of the tribe that loved basketball too much.

Takes Enemy felt the bus wheels rolling beneath him. The sun arced through the Montana sky. The circle was the symbol of never-ending life to the Crows—they saw it revealed in the shape and movement of the sun and moon, in the path of the eagle, in the contours of their tepees and the whorl of their dances. As long as the people kept faith with the circle, they believed, their tribe would endure. Jonathan settled back in his seat. Sometimes it seemed as if his life were handcuffed to a wheel, fated to take him up . . . and over . . . and down . . .

The experience of another legendary Crow player puts Takes Enemy's own situation into perspective.

Somewhere behind him on the highway, his first cousin would soon be getting off his job on the reservation's road crew and joining the exodus to the ball game in Billings—*the* legendary Crow player, some people said; the best player, *period*, in Montana high school history, said others; the one who ignited his tribe's passion for high school basketball back in the 1950s and seemed to start this dark cycle of great players arising and vanishing: Larry Pretty Weasel. The one whose drinking helped drive him out of Rocky Mountain College in Billings and back to the reservation in 1958, just a few days before the NAIA's weekly bulletin arrived proclaiming him the best field-goal percentage shooter in the country.

Horns honked in the caravan behind Takes Enemy, passengers waved. In the long-ago days before white men had brought their horses or guns or cars or liquor, his people had chased buffalo in this same direction, across these same valleys, stampeding them over cliffs near the land where Billings would one day arise. This same creature whose skull the Crows would mount on a pole and make the centerpiece of their religious Sun Dance . . . they would drive over the edge of the cliff and then scramble down to devour.

The bus ascended another hill. Takes Enemy looked back at his people one more time.

. . . He knew the danger he was wooing. The night he learned he had made the varsity, a rare honor for a freshman, he and a few friends went out in a pickup truck to drink beer. A tribal police car pulled up to the truck. Alcohol was banned on the reservation, but Crow policemen sometimes looked the other way. "Go home," this cop ordered the teenagers, but the kid at the wheel panicked, jammed the accelerator and roared away. Suddenly, Takes Enemy, a boy who was afraid even on a sled, found himself hurtling down a curving country road at 100 mph, four police cars with flashing lights and howling sirens just behind him. One came screaming up beside the truck, trying to slip by and box the teenagers in. Instead of letting it pass, Jonathan's friend lurched into the other lane to cut the car off. The pickup truck skidded off the road, toppled onto its roof and into a ditch. Takes Enemy limped out, somehow with just a badly bruised hip.

Learning about the subject's past helps readers better understand where he is headed.

He vowed not to drink again. He remembered how uneasy he had been as a child, awakening on the mattress between his parents' beds to see the silhouette of his father stagger into the room. Even in an alcoholic haze his father was a gentle man, but still, that silhouette was not Dad—it was a *stranger*. Then, too, there was what alcohol had done to his cousin the legend, Pretty Weasel. So many fans thronged gymnasiums to watch Pretty Weasel play for Hardin High that his team had to crawl through windows to get to its locker room. He could shoot jump shots with either hand, fake so deftly that he put defenders on their pants and, at five-ten, outjump players half a foot taller. It was almost, an opponent would muse years later, "as if you were playing against a kind of enchanted person." Pretty Weasel's younger brother Lamonte got drunk and died in a car accident. Then Pretty Weasel partied his way out of a four-year college scholarship and onto a reservation road crew.

But Jonathan couldn't keep his vow. He felt as if he were locked up in a tiny room inside his body, and it was only when he was playing basketball or drinking that he could break out of it. The first time he was drunk had been in seventh grade at Crow Fair, the week-long celebration every August when the field on the edge of his town became the tepee capital of the world. Hundreds of tepees were erected, and Indians from far away came to dance and drink and sing with his people deep into the night. Jonathan slipped the bootlegger four dollars for a half pint of whiskey, poured it down—and out poured the talking, laughing Jonathan he had always yearned to be. His mother came and found him at the fair at 3 A.M. Dorothy, a sweet, passive woman dedicated to the Pentecostal Church, began yelling that he would end up just like his father . . . but that was all. In many homes across the reservation . . . that was all.

A feeling of entrapment underlies the entire essay—"the danger he was wooing," "his daydream of escaping snuffed out," etc.

His sophomore year he moved in with his girlfriend and her parents, to help her bring up their baby daughter. Four months after his girlfriend delivered, she had news for him. She was pregnant again. His whole life seemed hopeless, his daydream of escaping snuffed out.

Was it his fault? No matter how hard Jonathan thought about it, he could never be sure. So many things had happened to his people that *were* beyond their control, it had become almost impossible to identify those that were *not*. He watched three brothers go to college and quickly drop out. He watched all three of them take turns with the bottle.

There were no movie theaters or bowling alleys or malls on the reservation. When it became too dark to see the rim on the courts behind the elementary school, Jonathan and his friends would drive up and down the main street of Crow Agency—from JR's Smokehouse to the irrigation supply yard and back again—seeing the same people, the same mange-eaten dogs and rust-eaten cars, until the monotony numbed them. Then someone would say, "Let's go drinking." It was a ritual that had become a display of solidarity and shared values among his tribe, so much so that to say no was to mark oneself as an alien. None of the teenagers had enough money to buy liquor, but all of them had Indian wealth—relatives. Uncles and aunts, cousins and grandparents are as close to most Crows as parents and siblings are to a white child; a boy can walk into five or six houses without knocking, open the refrigerator without asking, eat without cleaning up the crumbs. Jonathan and his friends would each ask a relative or two for a buck, and all of the sharing and family closeness in which the Crows pride themselves would boomerang. Each kid would come up with three or four dollars to pitch into the pot, and off they'd go to the liquor stores that waited for them half a hiccup past the reservation borders. It wouldn't take long to see someone they knew who was of drinking age—the boys were related by blood or clan, it seemed, to *everyone*. They whisked their beer or whiskey back onto the reservation, where the statutes against juveniles drinking were less severe, and began gulping it as if they were racing to see who could sledgehammer reality quickest, who could forget his life first.

The writer obviously did a lot of interviewing and observing in order to present so many facts and details.

Jonathan's absences from school mounted. That was how he responded to trouble. He disappeared. His parents wanted him to get an education, but to make the house quiet for two hours each night and insist that he study, to pull him out of his bed when the school bus was rolling up the road—no, they couldn't quite do that. Each of them had dropped out after the ninth grade, but there was more to it than that. Almost every Crow parent had a close relative who had been forcibly taken from his home by white government agents in the early 1900s and sent off to a faraway boarding school, where his hair was shorn, his Indian clothes and name were taken away, and he was beaten for speaking his own language. How many Indians could chase an education without feeling an old pang in their bones?

On intelligence alone, Takes Enemy had made the honor roll in junior high, but now he fell behind in class and was too ashamed to ask the white teachers for help. He lost his eligibility for the first half-dozen games of both his sophomore and junior seasons, regained it after each Christmas and started dropping in 25 or 30 points with a dozen assists a game, leading his teammates flying up and down the floor. His coaches called it Blur Ball. His people called it Indian Ball. And his brothers, three of whom had also been stars at Hardin High, would whip the crowd to wildness, reaching back into imaginary quivers on their backs, loading their make-believe bows, and zinging invisible arrows at the other teams; vibrating their hands over their mouths to make the high, shrill *wooo-wooo* battle cry that once froze frontiersmen's hearts; shouting themselves hoarse, making Takes Enemy feel as if he could simply lift up his legs and let his people's ecstasy wash him up and down the hardwood.

He scored 49 points in a state tournament game his senior year and was named the tournament's MVP. The outside walls of his house literally vanished, swathed in posters of congratulation from his fans. "A great major college prospect," said then BYU coach Ladell Andersen.

As this case study steadily builds in suspense, so does the reader's interest in Jonathan Takes Enemy's special problem.

Do it, teachers urged him. Do it so they could once more believe in what they were doing, do it so all the Crow children whose eyes were on him could see how it was done. "Just one," they kept saying to him. "If just one great basketball player from here could make the break and succeed, it could change everything. College recruiters would start coming here, other kids would follow your example. You can be the one, Jonathan. You can be the breakthrough."

. . . Takes Enemy's head spun. There were just too many mixed signals, too many invisible arrows from the audience whizzing by. Like most Crows, he'd been brought up not to make autonomous decisions but to take his cues from his immediate family, his extended family, his clan and his tribe. If *they* hadn't decided whether to assimilate into the white man's world or to recoil from it, how could he? And then, his two little children—he couldn't just walk away from them. The small living room he grew up in, with its sixty-five photographs of family members on the wall—a warm, happy place that the people in those pictures would flow into with no invitation, sit around sipping coffee and exchanging the sly puns and double entendres that his people excelled at, talking until there was nothing left to talk about and then talking some more—he couldn't just leave that behind. "Why?" he remembers wondering. "Why do I have to do it the white man's way to be a success in this world?" Why did all the human wealth he had gathered in his life, all the close friends and relatives, count for nothing when he crossed the reservation borders; why did material wealth seem to be the only gauge? And then his eyes and whys would turn the other way: "Why am I so important to my people? Why do *I* have to carry the hopes of the Crows?" All he had really wanted to do, ever since taking apart a stereo in the tenth grade and staring in wonder at all the whatchamacallits inside, was to go to a vocational school and learn electronics. But no, the herd was rolling, the people were waving and shouting him on, his legs were pulling him closer and closer to the ledge. He drank to close his eyes to it. One night at a school dance an administrator found out he was drunk. The next day he was ordered to take a chemical-dependency class. . . . ▣

The stress and confusion experienced by the subject is captured in a series of "why" questions.

Postscript: *The report goes on to describe Jonathan Takes Enemy's life once out of high school. After a few difficult and aimless years on the reservation, Takes Enemy and his wife moved to Billings (Montana) and entered college. When this article was first published, he was the leading scorer on his college's basketball team.*

"In those days, lake passenger shipping was a very common practice. I remember that you could set your watch by the Christopher Columbus, which was a whaleback passenger vessel that ran between Chicago and Milwaukee."

—Leonard Palmer

Historical Profile

To write a historical profile, you gather accurate information about a person, a place, a time, or an event from the past. Then you report the information in an interesting manner. Historical profiles are similar to feature articles in the media, and to research reports written by sociologists, archeologists, and historians. In addition, business proposals often include historical profiles of their subjects.

Another time and place . . .

Discussion: Write a profile or feature article presenting information you have gathered about a particular person, place, time, or event from the past. Your writing can be based on interviews, library research, and/or personal experiences or reminiscences. The important thing to remember is that a historical profile or feature must somehow re-create (bring to life) a person, place, or event of an earlier time. Refer to the guidelines and models that follow.

Searching and Selecting

1. **Choosing** • Think of people you know who could share interesting stories about the past (neighbors, parents, grandparents, senior citizens). Think of older buildings or places in your community that you could investigate. Think of events from the past that have always interested you, or think about the history behind certain objects.
2. **Limiting** • Talk to any of your teachers about possible subjects and possible approaches. Review old newspapers in the library; talk to someone from the local historical society; dig out your family tree or photo album.

Generating the Text

3. **Preparing** • Determine how you are going to gather information related to your subject. Prepare for interviews. Put together a list of books, magazines, and newspapers that contain information related to your subject. Then begin gathering information.
4. **Collecting** • Collect as much information as possible. Tape interviews if at all possible. (Also take general notes as the interview progresses.) Write down page numbers for all quoted or summarized information you gather from texts.
5. **Assessing** • Carefully review your notes to help you identify a main idea, a story line, or a dominant impression that can serve as the focus of your writing. Also decide how you want to present your information—as a basic report of information or as something a bit more imaginative. (Review the model articles that follow for ideas.)

Writing and Revising

6. **Writing** • Write your first draft freely, working in facts and details according to your planning. As you write your rough draft, jot down any questions about your subject and writing that come to mind.
7. **Refining** • Read your essay out loud to check for gaps in thought, awkward expressions, missing transitions, and so on. Revise and refine accordingly.

Evaluating

Does the writing work? Does it re-create a sense of what it was like during this time period?

Does the writing display a sufficient amount of research?

Are sources of information cited properly?

Student Model

Some people avoid cemeteries, while others, like student writer John Nichols, seem irresistibly drawn to them. As he researched the old gravestone epitaphs in a local cemetery, he made many discoveries about the pioneers who settled in his hometown.

At the outset, the writer explains his personal interest in cemeteries.

And When I Die . . .

I've always had a feeling for cemeteries. It's hard to explain any further than that, except to say history never seems quite as real as it does when I walk between rows of old gravestones.

I know there's a cemetery in Concord, Massachusetts, where Ralph Waldo Emerson, Louisa May Alcott, and Henry David Thoreau are buried within a few feet of each other. The story behind that burying ground is pretty obvious, and no doubt quite romantic. When I first began looking into the prospects of doing an article on the Union Grove Cemetery, I was afraid I wouldn't find anything too interesting. My fears were unfounded.

I soon found that within a mile of my home was the grave of a Revolutionary War veteran and one of a man who may very well have been Abraham Lincoln's bodyguard on the night he was shot. I also found the graves of less famous but equally interesting people, many of whose gravestones are as beautiful as the artwork you might find in a museum.

Then, in the cemetery's older section, I found the graves of the Cadwell family. The Cadwells were early Union Grove area settlers. If you were to view their graves on Memorial Day (when the American Legion places flags by the graves of veterans), you'd quickly get the impression that the Cadwells believed strongly in supporting America's military efforts. Phineas Cadwell, the oldest member of the family to emigrate from New York to Wisconsin in 1850, fought in the Revolutionary War.

Phineas, who the family Bible claimed was "enticed" into the army at age 18, served under Washington and rose to the rank of corporal. By the time he reached Wisconsin, he was totally blind and seldom ventured from the family home. Still, he kept an interest in the affairs of his nation, especially the slavery situation. The inscription on his tombstone reads: "Oh my country, how sure I loved thee. In my youth I fought for, sought, and saw thy prosperity. Free all thy sons. May thy Freedom be universal and perpetual. I leave thee."

A real sense of local history emerges with the details about the Cadwell family.

Phineas' son, Ebenezer, served in the War of 1812. He was a captain in the New York Militia for four months in 1814, during the closing days of the war. Like so many veterans of the War of 1812, he received no real compensation for his service until the late 1840s when he was awarded 40 acres of land near Union Grove (in what now is the town of Paris). Ebenezer brought his father, mother, wife and children to live on that land.

Two other Cadwells, also buried in the cemetery, carried on the family tradition of service to their country. Both Erastmus and Walter fought in the Civil War. Erastmus was Union Grove's first blacksmith. He entered the Union Army in 1864 after meeting Abraham Lincoln in Racine. It seemed Erastmus was so impressed with Lincoln, he immediately joined Company A of the 22nd Wisconsin Infantry. Erastmus died in Tennessee near the end of the war, and his body was brought back to Wisconsin for burial.

The writer expands the coverage of his report by including stories about some of the other settlers in the community.

Thirty-three other Civil War veterans are buried in the cemetery. Fordyce Lincoln, veteran of the Blackhawk War, and Earl McCormick, who served in the Spanish-American War, were also laid to rest there, as was Harley Osborne, who fought in World War II as a member of the Canadian army.

More than just soldiers' graves make up the Union Grove Cemetery, though. It provides a strong tie with Union Grove's past. While John Dunnam, the village's first settler, was not buried there, many other pioneers were. Among them was Gideon Morey, the town's first store owner and postmaster. The graves of the village's presidents and local officials, its shop owners, blacksmiths, and printers are there—all with unique and wonderful names—from Miles Hulett, the only Racine County sheriff from Union Grove, to Menzo Bixby, the first Union Grove boy to die on foreign shores.

A thought about cemeteries as "living" history concludes this article.

It is in its cemetery that much of Union Grove remains alive. Beneath its grounds lies our past, and on its stones, our history, as telling as any book or article.

Student Model

In this excerpt from a much longer historical profile, Ann Cerne skillfully balances historical fact with the real-life experiences of her grandmother. You will note that the writer brings history to life in a unique and personal way.

Strangers at the Door

From six continents, seven seas, and several archipelagoes,
From points of land moved to wind and water
Out of where they used to be to where they are,
The people of the earth marched and travelled
To gather on a great plain.
—Carl Sandburg, "The People Yes"

Over 20 million men, women, and children flocked to America in search of freedom and opportunity between 1855 and 1934. Their story is one of poverty and harshness . . . and this personal tale is no exception. Grandma Martin came from a little town in Yugoslavia, and, by scraping and saving, she secured enough money to book passage on a steamship to New York. In this excerpt from an interview with her, Grandma Martin graphically outlined her past—the frightening trip across the Atlantic, the humiliating experiences on Ellis Island with the officials, and the uphill struggle to make it in the new world.

What follows is a tale of deep personal value—it provides a link between myself and the old country. In compiling this story, my grandmother and I truly gathered at a crossroad—together we captured a memory dating over fifty years.

However, this tale is also one of universal appeal. Several of my classmates, as well as members of our community, can trace their beginnings in America to immigrants similar to Grandma Martin. Her saga marks one of the most dramatic events in our nation's history—the knocking of "Strangers at the Door."

After establishing a context for this profile, the writer steps back and lets her grandmother speak.

I comm heer in ninten tventy von. I left home Janary saven an' I vent to Slatina. I den seet on train an' I ride to Italy—Trst [Trieste]. Ve vas dere for von veek, my brodder Frank an' me. Ve comm dere too soon an' ve vait eight day for sheep Vilson [Wilson]. Ve have notink to do, just vait for meal to meal.

Boat finally comm—ve vas on boat tventy von day. Dere vas a lot of pipple. Oh, dere vas a lot of pipple, datsa right! But I 'member von time it vas soo foggy you can't see close to von person. Da boat gave seegnal—our boat vas commink an' de odder boat vas commink da same vay. Dey vere goink to heet! Everybody vas frightened—an' ve vas preparink to jump in de vater. But den jinglink, da bells ver jinglink, dey say everthink is all right. My modder heer dis in Europ—dey say de Vilson sheep vas drowned: but it not true—ve vas okay.

. . . There was money in immigration—even at thirty dollars a head the steamship companies cleared a handsome profit. To drum up business, companies would distribute lavish posters describing the wonders of the New World—"The land of milk and honey." (Greenleaf 134)

Dere vas long table on boat vher ve eat. Food not really so goot. I never saw before ting like dat macaroni—look like beeg vorm. . . .

Boat vas poor—sheep vas shakink bek an' fort. Girl fromm Lika keep on sayink dat she is goink to die. I must hold her over leetle ditch in boat so she can trow up. Dere vas leetle ditch on boat just to get sick in.

The immigrants were grouped below deck in the steerage compartment. Every lunge of the ship was felt ten times worse down in steerage than in any other part of the boat. Bunks were wedged in with people sleeping shoulder to shoulder, preventing them from being spilled onto the floor. The air was foul and stifling—the tiny portholes did not provide adequate circulation. Old food, seasickness, and unwashed humanity contributed to the nauseating stench. (Novotny 7)

The writer meticulously transcribes her grandmother's grammar and rich Yugoslavian accent.

Dere vasn't much doink—ve just sat 'round an' talk, vent on boat an' look at vater. Looked at feesh jumpink in da vater.

Oh, dat vas soo lonk! I tought dat ve never comm no more.

I forget land an' I think only of vater. I tought dat ve vould never leave it.

Den ve comm to Ellis Island. But dis boy on sheep had typhus, so dey kep us for two veek—de whole sheep. Dey kep us in beeg houses. De vurst pot vas ven ve go trough de cleanink. Ve must tek off de close, de shoos, de stockinks. Ve ver naked—sterilizink, you know. Everthink goes trough machine. Dey ver women all together, men in odder room. Den dey tek a leetle mop an' vent over you body. Can you imagine? Dat vas HELL! Dey do dis tree time in our two veeks. I say if I know dis, I vould have never gone in America.

Each transcription is complemented by related factual information.

. . . Once accepted, the immigrants quickly dispersed, heading for industrial centers such as New York, Chicago, and Pittsburgh. Two immediate problems cropped up: where to sleep and how to find a job as quickly as possible. If the newcomer had relatives or friends already settled, the solutions were easy: he would be taken home, boarded in a small corner of a tiny tenement room, and introduced to a boss or foreman the next morning. (Novotny 76)

I get to de Milvaukee an' I live vit my brodder George in a boardink house. At furst I vas sick—I vas so sick dat everbody tink dat I vas goink to die. I vas seasick fromm comink over. Den I get vell. . . .

Dis neighbor lady vork in a laundry an' she ask me if I vant to vork. An' I say yeh, anyplace just for vork. So I vork in laundry pressink heavy coats. I got twenty-five cents an hour—ve vorked hard, too!

. . . Grandma Martin worked hard all her life and achieved the Great American Dream that seems to have disappeared in our society today. A penniless farm girl when she arrived, she is now the proud owner of an eight-unit apartment building in Milwaukee. Out of nothing, she created something—quite an accomplishment for an 80-year-old woman who can barely speak the English language. . . .

Professional Model

Commercial fishing was once a major industry on the Great Lakes. In the following excerpts from "There Was a Time . . . ," writer Leonard Palmer shares the story of 79-year-old Jack Myers who grew up on Simmons Island (WI), where his father ran a large commercial fishing operation. ("There Was a Time . . ." is an oral history interview with Jack Myers, compiled by Leonard Palmer. Reprinted by permission of the Kenosha County [WI] Historical Society.)

There Was a Time . . .

Letting Jack Myers tell the story (first person) adds personality to the account.

There was no real industry on the Island other than fishing. My father was, I guess, one of the largest commercial fishermen on the Great Lakes. They fished two boats out of here—the *William Engel*, which was a 78-foot steam tug; and the tug *Sport*, which was a 55-foot tug. My grandfather had skippered the *Sport* over in Michigan, and it was the first metal boat built on the Great Lakes. She was built out of iron. My father fished both of those rigs out of here—he had as many as 27 men working for him, and they were fishing, at one point, ten gangs of nets, ten boxes to a gang. It seems to me, back in those days, that a box of nets was worth a hundred dollars. They were all linen—linen nets.

Because of the ice situation that developed up in Door County, some of the Washington Island fishermen were attracted to Kenosha. The first of those were the Engelson brothers—there were Bill and Martin Engelson, they came down here with the tug *Buick* and they fished out of Kenosha. Then came the Ellefsons . . . I can't remember the name of their tug. And then there was Al Shellswig, who came down with the tug *Palmer*. Then my father had a young guy come down here and work for him by the name of Ray McDonald. Ray came down and fished for my father, and he introduced hook fishing. They'd always been net fishermen at that time, and Ray got my father into fishing hooks. They would alternate between hook fishing and net fishing. They were "set" hooks, and I remember one of the worst jobs I saw them do, [was] when they were clearing hooks because once they reeled all these in, these hooks would become all tangled in the box. They'd take the fish off, and then they had to clear these [hooks] again, so they were ready to set, and there was a little rack in each box, and they had to do this with the hooks (here Jack makes a rolling motion with both hands, as if twirling a line).

The writer adds an occasional parenthetical explanation to clarify the story.

They set the hooks with small chubs. All they caught was lake trout. Perch were never fished commercially then. It was always trout. We used to smoke chubs—my father had a smokehouse on the Island. We had a lot of customers, a lot of the butchers and so on, who sold them in their stores. My brother used to deliver smoked fish to some of these stores.

. . . The fishermen went out except during closed season. This was always a point of interest, because my father always said that it was too bad the fish couldn't read, because they'd have closed season in Wisconsin, but have open season in Illinois, Michigan, and Indiana. And the seasons varied—and very often, if the weather was fair, Michigan boats would come clear across the lake to fish in Wisconsin waters, because it was open season here. Then, as soon as the season closed here, the Wisconsin boats would go down maybe into Illinois. Now, they license only so many boats that fish chubs. I think they have only, maybe, 40 licenses for the whole lake. At one time, they had as many as 15 tugs out of this harbor alone.

Very often, when we had an east wind, in the dead of winter, heavy ice would move in and we'd sit here (his home on the Island) at night, and watch the lights of the boats coming in as they got caught in the ice. Frequently, they'd have to wait for the tug *Sport*—something about the configuration of her hull—she could back through almost anything, and she would back through the ice and make a trail for these vessels to follow in. I can remember my father, they'd leave here at four in the morning and they wouldn't return until nine at night, in the winter. A normal day, they'd maybe be back at five.

. . . I can remember my father would pull out of the lake . . . they would stop fishing if they couldn't get a thousand pounds in a lift. And it was nothing for them to catch two, three, four thousand pounds of fish in a catch. All lake trout. Occasionally a lawyer. A lawyer is in the eel family, a scale-less fish. That was one of the few fish I would eat. It was a very firm-fleshed fish with pink meat. That I would like, because it wouldn't taste as fishy. Trout, to me, was very fat. The biggest trout that I remember my father catching was 44 pounds. But my brother reminds me that he remembers a trout that went 50 pounds.

A tragic event anchors this article in a specific period of history.

. . . Directly across from us was the Hill Steamship Company. They had the *Charles McVay*, the *City of Marquette*—those were two big steamers they had. And then, post-World War I, they bought three wooden mine-sweepers—they were really seagoing tugs—and renamed them the *Sheboygan*, the *Kenosha*, and the *Waukegan*. I also remember the *Wisconsin*. As a matter of fact, our house was headquarters for the press when the *Wisconsin* went down (October 29, 1929). I think we had probably the only telephone on the Island at that time. Our telephone number was 876. The *Chicago Tribune* was here, the *Milwaukee Journal*, and so [on] and so forth, and they were calling their papers getting the reports on the *Wisconsin*. I'll always remember that night, because I was in high school at the time and I was in the Sea Scouts. We were called out of school, the Sea Scouts were, to patrol the beach looking for bodies or anything that washed up from the *Wisconsin*.

The depth of detail provided in this article indicates that Mr. Myers speaks from experience.

In those days, lake passenger shipping was a very common practice. I remember that you could set your watch by the *Christopher Columbus*, which was a whaleback passenger vessel that ran between Chicago and Milwaukee. She would pass here going north at noon and going south back to Chicago at six o'clock. Twelve and six, she would pass the Kenosha light[house], way off shore, of course. There are no big old steamers left. There used to be the *North America*, the *South America*, the *Alabama*, the *Virginia*, the *Nevada*. . . .

I can remember that my brother used to row across the harbor to go to work at the Simmons plant when he was home from the university in the summers. Then he would row back home for lunch and then back again for work in the afternoon. It wasn't like it is now. It was a different time then. ▣

"In 1990 . . . [Lori Beebe] started Beebe's Babies; some days now she auditions more than 150 of them, ranging in age from two weeks to ten years. 'Personality is everything; looks are nothing,' she says." —Cindy Pearlman

Venture Report

Magazines, Sunday editions of newspapers, job-service newsletters, and TV news programs include stories about occupations and businesses. Writers of venture reports—in-depth investigations into the world of work—get most of their information through interviews, job-site visits, and other types of direct contact. These reports help readers imagine what an occupation or a business is really like.

Nothing Ventured . . . Nothing Gained

Discussion: Do you consider yourself an entrepreneur? No? Well, consider this: Every time you start a new job or plan an extended project or plot the ultimate money-making scheme, you're doing entrepreneurial thinking. In this activity, you are going to put some of that thinking to work. First, select a venture (business, profession, project, team, etc.) that interests you. Thoroughly investigate your subject and write an in-depth report based on your findings. Photographs, illustrations, and interview quotations will add impact to your final report. (You might even consider turning your report into a video documentary.)

Searching and Selecting

1. **Selecting** • Think of occupations, professions, businesses, or organizations that you find interesting. (Focus on ventures that are practical to investigate.)
2. **Exploring** • Think about people who might be able to help you conduct your subject search and places you might visit for ideas. Also review magazines such as *Entrepreneur*, *Omni*, and *Working Woman* for potential subjects.

Generating the Text

3. **Noting** • Determine what you already know about your subject and what you would like to find out or explore. (Are there 5 to 10 key questions about the venture you would like to answer during your investigation?)
4. **Investigating** • Read about your subject, conduct in-person interviews, and gather firsthand experiences. (Don't forget that you can write or call for information as well.)
5. **Assessing** • How will you present your findings? Will you highlight information received during one or more of your interviews? Will you focus more of your attention on your firsthand experiences and observations? Or will you tie in information from a variety of resources? After determining a focus for your report, plan and organize your work accordingly.

Writing and Revising

6. **Writing** • Develop your first draft, working in facts and details according to your plan. (Include as many important details as possible.)
7. **Revising** • Review, revise, and refine your writing. Make sure that at least one or two classmates review your work as well. Any questions your classmates raise should be addressed during revising.

Evaluating

Does the profile offer an in-depth look at a specific venture?

Has proper attention been given to detail, organization, and clarity?

Will readers learn something from reading this report?

Student Model

Learning to drive a car can be a disheartening (and expensive) venture, as writer Chris Kanarick discovered. A conversational tone makes this report enjoyable as well as informative. (Reprinted with permission from *New Youth Connections: The Magazine Written By and For New York Youth*, January/February 1993.)

They're Driving Me Crazy

The writer introduces the reasons for undertaking his venture—freedom and independence.

Ever since I was little, I wanted to drive. I thought it would be so cool not having to ask anyone for a ride to the mall, or anyplace else for that matter.

Needless to say, I was quite happy when it came time to start driver education. I signed up to take it at a high school near where I live. Soon I would no longer have to thumb a ride to work with my stepfather at six o'clock on a Saturday morning. No longer would I have to greet my dates by saying, " . . .and this is my mom." I was 16 years old, and it was time to break the chains that bound me to Mommy . . . and her car.

When I went to sign up for driver's ed, I was shocked to discover that it cost $275. Driver's ed is not mandatory here in New York; but if you don't take it, you have to wait until you're 18 to get your license. If you do take it, you can get your license a year earlier. It was a lot of money, but $275 was not too high a price to pay for my freedom, right?

The first class was pretty boring. We filled our registration forms and were given our textbooks. Every Monday we met, and the teacher drew diagrams that tried to show the right way to park and turn. We learned about alcohol and driving and about different kinds of insurance policies.

NO ACTION FLICKS

Details of the driver's-ed experience add humor and interest to the report.

Overall, I already knew most of it, like not to drink and drive. They didn't even show those really cool movies like *Blood on the Highway*, the ones where you see cars ramming into people and each other, really gory stuff. Actually, the only film I remember seeing is *Mr. Smith's System of Space-Cushion Driving*. I think I fell asleep.

My first time behind the wheel I think I handled the car pretty well. I didn't hit anything, always a good sign. My major problem was turning. The hardest part was steering the car on the highway and rolling the window up at the same time. (Solution: power windows.)

The driving part was cool, though. We would always make fun of each other and crack jokes. I remember one time when my friend was driving, our teacher, Mr. Spock (we called him that because he had funny ears and showed no emotion), told her to

The writer holds the reader's interest by incorporating specific details and personal thoughts throughout the report.

This report is developed in story form, detailing the writer's experiences with driver's education as they unfolded.

make a left turn, and she quickly responded by turning on the windshield wipers. From then on, every time he wanted her to turn, we would tell her to turn on the wipers.

NOT ENOUGH HANDS-ON EXPERIENCE

We drove on Wednesday afternoon from 4:30 to 6:00. Now, that's one and a half hours for four people. That means each of us got about 20 minutes to drive. When the course ended, I still had no confidence behind the wheel, and I didn't feel ready to take the road test yet.

So I went to the Department of Motor Vehicles (DMV) to take my permit test. With a learner's permit [and if you're 17], you're allowed to practice—but only if you are accompanied by a licensed driver or, if you are 16, with a licensed driving instructor in one of those cars with a brake pedal on the passenger's side. Since I was only 16, in order to practice with Mom or Dad, we would have had to go to Long Island where it was legal.

I decided to go to a private driving school called Scott's. When I first heard the name, I imagined Scotty from *Star Trek* sitting beside me yelling, "Coptin, ya con't push it any foster than thot!" Instead, all I got was a very nice woman's voice saying, "That'll be $200 for five hour-long lessons."

But at least after that I felt confident behind the wheel. I felt like I could drive. I couldn't parallel park to save my life, but hey, not even Scott can work miracles.

A GOOD INSTRUCTOR IS HARD TO COME BY

Since I'd already passed driver's ed, I didn't have to take a written exam to get my license. I scheduled the road test, and on the morning of the big day, Nick from Scott's Driving School came to pick me up (for an extra $45). You have to use your own car for the road test, and since my parents work, this was the best way. I got in the car and handed him the papers I had with me, and he asked for the rest. Whoops.

I went back inside the house, and my mother and I searched hopelessly for the papers. I went back out and told Nick that I couldn't find them, so he said we would go to the test site. I would probably be permitted to take the test, but they wouldn't give me the results on the spot, like they usually do.

Out of the three instructors I had at Scott's Driving School, I think Nick was the best. He taught me how to parallel park using a different technique than anyone else had. Instead of lining up right next to the car you want to park behind and turning the wheel as you back up, he said to line your mirror up with the center of the other car and turn the wheel all the way to the right; then start backing up and straightening out when you're in the right position.

After I took the test, I had the feeling that I had passed. I waited for almost a week after that test to find out that the guy failed me because he said that when I started to make a broken U-turn (otherwise known as a K- or three-point turn) away from the curb, I had the car in reverse. So I had to schedule the test all over again.

The next time, John from Scott's picked me up (for $78 this time because it wasn't part of my original package deal) to take me to the test site. First we had a little practice lesson in which I screwed everything up, and John was no help at all.

STRIKE TWO

We got to the site and this time I had all the papers with me, so I could find out I failed on the spot. That's right, this time they failed me for parking. The driving inspector was a lot nicer, but apparently, if you touch the curb, it's automatic failure. Which, if you ask me, is totally unfair because if you can handle a car, and can drive well and safely, then parking should not count so much. Of course, that's only my opinion.

When you fail the road test twice on the same permit, you lose the permit, and it has to be renewed.

The report concludes by summarizing the writer's current situation: he's the owner of a car, but without a license to drive it.

So here's the present situation: I am 17 years old, I have a car that I bought from my stepsister, the car is registered with license plates and the whole bit, I am paying $1,400 a year for insurance, I know how to drive, but I don't have my license yet.

The other night, I wanted to go out to the movies with my friends, but my friend's car had just broken down. So I let him drive my car. I put gas in the car, and I haven't even driven it yet.

To tell the truth, it's really starting to get to me. Now, I have to renew my learner's permit for $10 and take the road test all over again for a third time. The whole thing just doesn't seem worth it. I tell you, it's making me car-azy.

Professional Model

In this report, writer Cindy Pearlman captures the novelty and humor of Lori Beebe's business, Beebe's Babies—a company that casts babies in television advertising. (This report originally appeared in *Chicago* magazine, January 1993. It is reprinted with permission.)

Infant Gratification

The writer's humorous approach captures an important aspect of this venture: Beebe's ability to take things in stride.

In Lori Beebe's business, success is measured in an odd way. "If I haven't been peed on once, something is wrong," she says. So it goes when you're a baby wrangler—someone who casts and directs babies in television commercials. Beebe does just that, with spots running this month for Clorox, Tyko, Osco, and Playskool. Hers is not a job for most grownups: In fact, it's full of life's little ironies. Consider that in the Clorox spot Beebe, 33, had to show a group of nine-month-old babies how to get messy. "I do whatever it takes to bring out the performer in the child," she says.

For a recent Huggies commercial, Beebe cast 25 babies, including The Biter. "He couldn't wait to sink his teeth into the other babies," she says. Sometimes she loses control—or her charges do. She was doing a diaper commercial with six naked babies. "One started peeing and suddenly they were all peeing. It was like someone flipped a switch."

Direct quotations bring interest and humor to the report, allowing the reader to learn about the business and about the entrepreneur who runs it.

When Beebe got into the business, she was a Naperville mom bored with staying home. She took her then nine-month-old son to a cattle call for a Service Merchandise ad. "On the set I was telling him what to do and finally a casting director came over and asked me if I wanted to work on her next baby job."

In 1990, she started Beebe's Babies; some days now she auditions more than 150 of them, ranging in age from two weeks to ten years. "Personality is everything; looks are nothing," she says.

Considering that she comes home with black-and-blue knees and Froot Loops in her hair, you'd think the last thing she'd want to see was kids. "I never get tired of them. I love coming home to my four boys," she says. And at least they don't bite. "They're a kick," she says, "and I don't mean that literally." ▣

Professional Model

Writer David Thome based the following venture report on interviews with his subject, the owner of a limousine business. The result is a personal, interesting, and informative account of one young woman's "ride" to success. (This article originally appeared in *Business Connections*, October 1992. It is reprinted with permission.)

Profile: Lambie's Limousines

The report immediately introduces the entrepreneur and her venture.

Many entrepreneurs continue working for someone else until a new venture gets established. But, though Shiela Lambie cut back from three jobs to one while getting Lambie's Luxury Limousines off and rolling, her new business didn't shift into full gear until she made it a full-time priority.

. . . "I get my entrepreneurial drive from my mother," Lambie says. "She's the person who pushed me into how I do things. She always told me that there's nothing you can't do if you put your heart into it, and that whatever you do, do it to the best of your ability."

. . . The day after graduating from high school, Lambie went to work in the business department of the Kenosha Public Library, where she did general secretarial work and some bookkeeping. She says she liked the job, but she wasn't sure where she wanted her career path to lead. So, she took classes at Gateway Technical Institute (now Gateway Technical College) to fill the core requirements for a degree.

She never received a degree, but instead took a job in the service department of Vigansky's TV and Appliance, where she did secretarial work and served as a dispatcher.

She stayed with Vigansky's for four years, working up to manager of the parts department.

Background information establishes the starting point for the venture.

"I left after the birth of my first child, thinking I'd never work again," she says. "I had this idea of being a wonderful, perfect mother who stayed home all the time. Within two weeks, I was back at Vigansky's."

The store had already filled Lambie's old position, but the owners needed someone to sell microwave ovens—a new, unfamiliar item at the time. After taking cooking courses offered by a few major manufacturers, Lambie gave cooking demonstrations at the store. About the same time, she started teaching cooking classes at Gateway and worked independently as a home decorator.

She kept on working all three jobs to support herself and her two children after a divorce in the early '80s. A few years later she became engaged to Al Lambie, an over-the-road trucker who was growing tired of making the long hauls. Vigansky's, hurt by the recession and the closing of Kenosha's AMC plant, began to cut back Lambie's hours. At the same time Lambie's sister, Sherri, and her husband, John, bought a limousine so they could make extra money chauffeuring wedding parties on weekends, but with John's job as a sheriff's deputy, the couple found it increasingly difficult to continue moonlighting.

Lambie recognized an opportunity in this confluence of events. "It was incredibly good timing," Lambie says. "Sherri and John wanted to get rid of the limo, and Al and I thought a limo service could be a good business if you did things a certain way."

Shiela and Al bought a house and used the equity to buy the limo for $9,000. At first, they too limited the limo service to weekends, while Al kept his job and Shiela quit Vigansky's to open a kiosk for Total Furniture in the Kenosha Factory Outlet Centre. They soon found that with the cost of gas, repairs, insurance, phone calls, advertising and hiring an answering service, the limousine service did little to enhance their income.

Direct quotations add authenticity, insight, and human interest to the report.

"In fact, we were losing money," Lambie says. "I was taking my entire paycheck and putting it into the limo business. We weren't getting the results we wanted, so we decided we had to make a commitment."

Lambie quit her job in 1985 to devote her energies to the limo service. Business doubled the first month and tripled again in the second.

At first, most of Lambie's business came from weddings. "Our biggest competition was funeral homes," she recalls. "Of course, they all had black cars, so rather than go head-to-head with them, I had only white cars."

To expand her business, Lambie placed ads in the Yellow Pages and *Happenings* magazine. She did some prospecting. And, by approaching businesses about driving executives and clients to and from airports, she hit upon a rich vein that had been largely untapped in this locality.

The growth of the venture is described step-by-step.

By 1989, Lambie's had moved into a former boat builder's shop. . . . The company grew to 11 cars that year—still mostly white. Clientele included steady corporate customers, as well as one-time patrons who wanted to ride to the prom in style.

. . . Today, transporting corporate executives and guests has supplanted weddings, dances, and funerals as Lambie's bread and butter. And she's not shy about telling people that taking a limo can be as good for one's business as it is for one's ego.

"Often, we're driving people who are on their way to important business conferences, and they can relax or get a lot of work done if they take a limo," she says. "And on the way home, they can take care of their expense accounts and finish any other paperwork in the car, so that when they get home, they can watch TV or play with their kids."

The way of the future is offering more service, and more services, she asserts.

. . . Lambie sums up the importance of service with this story: "One of our drivers took a man to Chicago for a morning meeting. He was supposed to return at 11 a.m., but the meeting kept getting delayed. The chauffeur went out and got the man some lunch so it was waiting for him when he finally got back into the car at 2 p.m. The guy was overjoyed. He said, 'You don't know how many lunches I miss because of meetings that get delayed.' Little things make a difference. We like to spoil our clients."

Spoiling clients, of course, begins with the car. Since none of the major automakers builds limos anymore, all new limos have to be custom-built by cutting stock models in half and extending them in the middle. Add posh interiors, compact disc juke boxes, cellular phones, color TVs, and wet bars, and the price can run up to well over $60,000.

. . . Lambie said that in spite of the rising cost of cars, insurance, repairs, and gas, she expects her business to grow over the next few years. She should know: Lambie's has already grown from $5,000 in sales in 1985 to nearly $500,000 in 1991.

The report ends with the subject's business philosophy: a statement that summarizes her entrepreneurial spirit.

She has two simple secrets for success: work hard, and keep in touch.

"You work three times as hard when you work for yourself as you do working for someone else," she says. "An employee can punch a clock and go home. When you work for yourself you can't do that. The business becomes part of your life. . . ."

" 'You can imagine how these people felt,' says Shaw. 'They had nothing when they got here. They were just full of hope.' The immigrants could not speak the American language, they did not know American customs, but they knew they wanted to be American." —Sylvia Chan

Personal Research Report

In a personal research report, you investigate a subject that interests you (a new technology, unique place, current fad) and report what you find. People in the workplace also do research and write reports, usually on subjects closely related to their jobs.

"I was just wondering . . ."

Discussion: Investigate a subject of personal interest and compile a report based on your discoveries. Your subject may be related to a profession, a place, a lifestyle, an upcoming purchase (the best computer for the money), a curiosity (how do you tear down a building?), and so on. Base your investigation as much as possible on interviews, firsthand experiences, and observations. Then share the results of your work in one of two ways—as a personalized story recalling the details of your research as it unfolded or as a more traditional, factual report. Refer to the guidelines below and the models that follow for help.

Searching and Selecting

1. **Searching** • To begin your search for a subject, think of the different categories listed in the opening discussion (professions, places, etc.). What would you like to be when you grow up? Is there a particular place or building that you would like to explore?
2. **Reviewing** • If you are still not sure what to write about, review the local newspaper or the yellow pages for ideas, or brainstorm for subjects with your classmates. (Try to select a subject that comes from a genuine interest and is practical to research.)

Generating the Text

3. **Planning** • Determine what you already know about your subject, what you hope to find out, and how you plan to conduct your research. Remember: Your first and primary source of information should be people.
4. **Exploring** • Make contacts. Conduct interviews and record observations. Also refer to magazines and books that have been recommended to you.
5. **Assessing** • Decide how you are going to compile the results of your research. A personalized account of your work should address four basic areas: *what I already knew, what I hoped to find out, what happened as I conducted my investigation*, and *what I learned*. If you are going to compile a more traditional report, decide on a focus for your work and plan accordingly.

Writing and Revising

6. **Writing** • Develop your first draft according to your planning and organizing.
7. **Revising** • Carefully review, revise, and refine your writing. Make sure that your writing accurately reflects the results of your investigation, and double-check to make sure that you quote your sources correctly.

Evaluating

?...?

Is the report informative, entertaining, and based on sincere investigative efforts?

Has proper attention been given to accuracy and detail?

Will readers appreciate the treatment of this subject?

Student Model

Memorable childhood experiences often influence a person's decision to investigate a particular profession or occupation. In the following research report, the lingering memory of his grandmother's funeral motivates writer Ben Meyer to investigate the mortuary business. Notice that this model is compiled as a *personalized* story recalling the details of an interview and a visit.

The Dead Business

This essay grabs the reader's attention by beginning with a question—and a rather shocking answer.

"You're going to tour a what?"

"A funeral home."

My friends were shocked. They giggled as they described scenes from *Night of the Living Dead* and *The Shining*.

Their ghoulish stories didn't frighten me; I was scared of something else.

When I was ten years old, my grandmother died. When my family arrived at the funeral home to view the body, I noticed the funeral director standing in the corner looking like a too-eager-to-please salesman who'd made a deal he didn't deserve . . . a sort of twentieth-century grim reaper in a business suit. The guy's plastic, thin-lipped smile seemed unnatural—almost glib—in the presence of a death that unnaturally stopped my grandmother's beating heart midway through the doxology that cold January night in Calvary Christian Reformed Church. Death shattered her relationship with me. No more cookies, no more coloring books, no more Rook games, no more laughing, no more.

I chose to investigate a funeral home to cure myself of the grim-reaper syndrome. But I was still scared. I drove to the VanderPloeg Furniture Store/Funeral Home with visions of the thin-lipped smile I had seen when I was ten.

When I walked inside, I half expected to meet a well-dressed ghoul standing by his cash register, sharpening his sickle. Suddenly, a man from behind his desk hopped out of his chair.

"Hi!"

The writer's account of first entering the funeral home reflects his negative feelings toward morticians.

I looked at the tall, smiling man, paused a moment, and glanced back at the door. His skinny partner had stepped in front of the exit while scribbling on tags that dangled from Lazy Boy rockers. I realized this interview was something painful I had to do . . . like getting a tetanus shot.

Howard Biernink led me into a jungle of furniture until he found a soft, purple couch. We sat down, and he narrated the tale of the furniture store/funeral home.

In 1892, a pioneer community established the town of Sioux Center, Iowa. Winter storms and disease pummeled the tiny community, and soon someone was needed to bury the dead. A funeral director wasn't available; a furniture craftsman was. He was the only person who had the tools, the hardwood,

The interview with Mr. Biernink and the tour of the embalming room provide the writer with all he needs to know for his report.

Honest expressions like "I was baffled" and specific details like "Howard pulled out another bottle . . ." add a personal touch to the report.

and the knowledge to make coffins. As a result, VanderPloeg Furniture Store/Funeral Home was born.

Today, a funeral home director must complete two years of college and one year of embalming school to become a qualified embalmer. After he or she graduates, the person must perform as an apprentice for one year. Every subsequent year the embalmer must pass a state exam in order to retain certification for his work.

"But why a funeral home director?" I was baffled. Why would anyone want to embalm dead bodies for a living?

"Because it's a family business." Howard smiled as if he expected my question. "VanderPloegs and Bierninks have run this place for generations. Today it's difficult to start a funeral home because there are so many of them with long histories and good reputations."

After he buried the rest of my questions, Howard asked if I wanted to see the embalming room.

"Ok," I said, still a little scared.

He led me through doors, hallways, staircases, and a well-lighted display room containing several coffins. Finally, we entered a small, cold room that contained a row of cupboards, a large ceramic table, and a small machine that resembled a bottled water cooler.

"We like to keep the room cold when we're not using it."

"What is all this stuff?"

Howard described the process of embalming.

The purpose of embalming a corpse is to extend the period for viewing the body. Embalming consists of draining the body fluids and replacing them with embalming fluid.

Howard opened a cupboard and pulled out a bottle of fluid.

"Here . . . smell."

"It sorta smells like Pepto-Bismal."

After he embalms the body, Howard applies makeup so the body appears "more natural." His cosmetics consist of powders and tints sold by the local Avon lady.

"But sometimes we also have to use this." Howard pulled out another bottle from the cupboard.

"Tissue builder?" I asked, squinting at the label.

"It's sort of like silicon implants. We inject it into the cheeks if they're sunk in, like the cheeks of a cancer victim."

When the body is ready for burial, the funeral director must show a price list to the family of the deceased. The Funeral Rule, adopted in 1984 by the Federal Trade Commission, requires that a price list be shown to the family before they see caskets, cement boxes, and vaults. The purpose of the Funeral Rule is to prevent unethical funeral directors from manipulating the customer with

The writer closes by explaining what he has learned from his investigation.

comments like, "But that's a pauper's casket, you wouldn't want to bury your mother in that. Bury her in this beauty over here." Unfortunately, only a third of the country's 22,000 funeral homes abide by the Funeral Rule.

"After I show them where the casket is, I step away from the customers and let them talk among themselves," said Howard. "It's unethical to bother the family at this difficult time."

When they bury the body, Howard and his partner place the casket in either a cement box or a vault. A cement box is a container that is neither sealed or waterproofed; a vault is both sealed and waterproofed.

"Years ago, cemeteries began to sink and cave in on spots. That's why state authorities demanded containers. It makes the cemetery look nicer."

After the tour I asked Howard, "What impact has this job made on your life?"

He smiled, glanced at the ceiling and said, "It's very fulfilling. My partner and I try to comfort families during a very upsetting and emotional time, and it strengthens our bond with them."

As I walked back to my car, I thought about Howard's comment. He was right. His job isn't to remind me of broken relationships; he helps create new ones. He comforts families and encourages them to move on in their lives.

I started up my car and decided I wasn't afraid of the grim reaper anymore. I'm still scared of death. I'm still scared of the pain of losing someone I love. But am I scared of the grim reaper? No. The grim reaper has been replaced by the compassionate funeral director. He is as necessary in a community as the man in the local supermarket, providing food and services to the community. ▣

Student Model

It is the history of an "incredible place" that prompts this detailed research report by Sylvia Chan. Notice that this report is more objective than the other models. (Reprinted from *East Bay Teen Voices* [July 19, 1991], which is published by the Center for Integration and Improvement of Journalism at San Francisco State University.)

Angel Island Reveals Poignant History

On this day of the eclipse, the sun continues to beat down on Angel Island.

People in this state park on the 11th of July are asking others if they have seen the overlapping of the moon and sun. Many say no, they did not see it, they did not even notice it. Not surprising though, because most likely, their attentions have been focused on the incredible history of this place.

The writer puts Angel Island in historical perspective by providing background information about this setting.

Between 1910 and 1940, Angel Island served as an immigration station for the West Coast. Immigrants had to pass through this station to either obtain entrance to the United States or be sentenced to deportation back to where they had come from. Ninety-five percent of these immigrants were Chinese, while the other five percent were Japanese mail-order brides, Europeans, and Africans.

Due to the Chinese Exclusion Law of 1882, it was very difficult for a Chinese person to obtain citizenship in the U.S. The immigrant had to have a relation that was a citizen, or arrive in the U.S. as a student. It was also much easier for wealthy families to obtain citizenship. Many were honest about their backgrounds, but many Chinese obtained false papers claiming they were somebody else. All had to endure a grueling interrogation process to test the truth of their stories. The film *Carved in Silence* by filmmaker Felicia Lowe gives examples of the questions asked by the Angel Island administration. "How many windows do you have in your house?" "Do you have a dog?" "How many feet apart is your house from your neighbors?" The same interrogation questions could be asked of the same person repeatedly for confirmation purposes.

A good deal of the important information for this report is gained through an interview with a park official.

Since the questioning was exhaustive and extremely detailed, a series of questioning sessions would usually have to be conducted for each immigrant. According to park docent John Shaw, the shortest stay at the island was three days, while the longest was 22 months.

"You can imagine how these people felt," says Shaw. "They had nothing when they got here. They were just full of hope." The immigrants could not speak the American language, they did not know American customs, but they knew they wanted to be American. The stories of "gum san," or "Gold Mountain," meaning California, were those of a beautiful, prosperous land, one where all people could succeed and make a better life for themselves.

The green foliage of Angel Island fits the image of the Gold Mountain. The air is clean, the trees rustle gently in the wind, and the view of the San Francisco Bay is magnificent. But most likely, the detainees

Ms. Chan's close observations help readers see Angel Island in their mind's eye.

Note how smoothly the writer is able to incorporate the comments of the interviewee, her own observations, and other facts and details gained through reading.

Ms. Chan closes her report on an emotional note.

at the immigration camp never got a chance to see these things without the glare of a guard nearby. Shaw explains that guards followed the immigrants everywhere they went. No one was ever left alone.

In seeing how cramped the living quarters were, one sees that these people could never be alone on their stay here. . . . There was less than half a foot of space between the three-tiered steel bunk-bed structures. The beds themselves were about two feet wide. Sometimes a mother and her child would have to share one of these beds. Families were always separated, not even allowed to speak to each other. The rooms were dirty and loud, says Shaw. Many resorted to carving poetry on the wooden walls to vent frustrations about their situation. One of the poems, supposedly written by a woman, speaks of leaving the station:

From now on I am departing from this building
All of my fellow villagers are rejoicing with me
Don't say that everything within is Western styled
Even if it is built of jade, it has turned into a cage
Detained in this wooden house for several tens of days
It is all because of the Mexican exclusion law which implicates me
It's a pity heroes have no way of exercising their prowess
I can only await the word so that I can sway Zu's whip.

Though poetry on the walls could expose one's soul, it was much easier for the Chinese to expose their souls than their bodies. The toilets and bathing facilities in the living quarters were completely open, with no doors or covers of any sort. "The Chinese are very modest; they don't like to expose their bodies," says Shaw. In entering the washroom called the "New Women's Toilets," one can almost feel the embarrassment of the women at the station. Also felt by many is the presence of spirits in this room. Undocumented reports by witnesses on the island tell a story that explains this presence.

At times, the U.S. government would sentence immigrants to be deported because they could not pass the interrogations or could not prove their rights to American citizenship. For the immigrant, returning to China was an admittance of failure. Their families had sent them to the United States to become a success. The only time they could return to China was when they had succeeded in the U.S., not before. Success was defined as making enough money to support the rest of the family. Rather than return, some chose to commit suicide. The sounds of their self-inflicted deaths were muddled by the running water of the showers.

The air in the washroom does hang heavy, and if not with spirits, then with memories. The toilets lie rusting, the tiled walls are covered with mildew, the sinks are dry with brown dust, and the smell of age lingers in the air. Many have forgotten about this little immigration station in the San Francisco Bay. But among the wooden walls of a building on this island, immigrants once lived. And carved on a part of the wall in the men's living quarters is this poem:

There are tens of thousands of poems on these walls
They are all cries of suffering and sadness
The day I am rid of this prison and become successful
I must remember that this chapter once existed. ▣

Professional Model

Curiosity plays an important role in personal research. In the following model, columnist Jan Brunvand investigates the origin of an urban legend—and, while the exact source is never identified, the writer discovers some interesting information along the way. (Reprinted from *Curses! Broiled Again!* by Jan Harold Brunvand, with the permission of W. W. Norton & Company, Inc. Copyright © 1989 by Jan Harold Brunvand.)

"The Body on the Car"

The reason for the writer's investigation is immediately identified.

The question is: Was Ann Landers taken in by a horrifying urban legend? Many of her readers—at least, those who are also *my* readers—seem to think she was, and they wrote to ask my opinion.

People from coast to coast, plus a few from abroad, sent me Ann's column dated September 24, 1986. In it, a reader relates a tragic story of drunken driving.

It seems that a woman's husband came home from work at 2:00 A.M., cockeyed drunk. He managed to get up for work in time, though, and began pulling his car out of the garage, into the driveway. His wife realized that he had forgotten to take his lunch and began running out to give it to him. She got "as far as the porch and fainted." The husband got out of the car to see what was the matter. There, embedded in the grill of his car, was the lifeless body of an eight-year-old girl.

The letter was signed, "Still Horrified in Portland."

Ann Landers replied, "What a grisly story! Bone-chilling, to say the least. I hope it makes an impact on drivers who chance 'a few' and don't think it will make any difference."

I also hope it has an impact, but not because I think it's true. Until someone can offer conclusive proof that this cautionary tale really happened, I'll have to say that that's just what it is: a mini-morality play that got started up and gained currency because it demonstrates our rising concern with the dangers of drunken driving.

The writer analyzes a letter to Ann Landers and then contacts MADD to get their feelings about the authenticity of the letter.

There are a number of questionable elements here. For one thing, there are no corroborating details of time or place. The letter writer simply begins, "I would like to tell you about another woman who had a nervous breakdown because of the same problem"—i.e., her husband's drunken driving, discussed in a previous Ann Landers column.

I called Mothers Against Drunk Driving (MADD) in Houston, Texas, which keeps track of alcohol-related accidents. They told me that they assumed the story to be true—but even they could provide no further details.

Yet, in April 1987—seven months after the Ann Landers column—I received a letter from a Covina, California, reader who had heard a variation of "The Body on the Car" told at a Students Against Drunk Driving (SADD) presentation. In this version, the wife goes out for the morning newspaper and discovers the "embedded" body, while her husband, still passed out from the night before, is lying on the living-room couch. Either other versions of the story had been circulating, or the one in the Ann Landers column was acquiring variations from repetitions.

Most of the evidence and information for this report are provided by individuals who read Mr. Brunvand's newspaper column.

Another letter sent in the spring of '87 reported "The Body on the Car" told in Carbondale, Illinois. One slight variation here: she was a seven-year-old girl.

The notion implied in all versions that a young child was out on the streets at 2:00 A.M. seems farfetched. We're asked to believe that the girl became integrated with the car's grillwork (like the VW Bug in the preceding legend) instead of being hurled through the air, which is what normally happens in a head-on collision with a pedestrian. We're also supposed to accept the idea that the driver was so drunk, he didn't notice that he'd just hit a young child—nor did anyone else on the road—as he drove around town with her riding on his car like a hood ornament. Yet, this semiconscious man was still alert enough to park his car in the garage without incident.

The fainting woman is another familiar touch of urban-legend fantasy, as is the unlikely detail that the driver was up bright and early for work the day after his adventurous night.

One reader sending me the clip added the footnote, "Please, Ann, tell us it's just a story." Several others sent me copies of their own letters to Ann Landers, tipping her off that it smelled like a legend to them. But as far as I know, there has been no disclaimer for this one in any subsequent Ann Landers column. . . .

The day after most of the above discussion appeared in my column (in late March 1987), Professor Malcolm K. Shuman of the Museum of Geoscience at Louisiana State University in Baton Rouge wrote. He remembers reading a story very similar to the legend while browsing through the comic-book collection of a younger cousin some thirty years ago ("ca. 1953, give or take a couple of years").

As Professor Shuman recalls the horror-comic episode, a man driving on a highway (fast, but not under the influence) is well aware that he has struck a pedestrian but decides to ignore the accident and drive on. But in the next town, an angry crowd stops him when they see the dead pedestrian caught between bumper and grill. So the hit-and-run element of the story seems to have existed much earlier than the 1980s, although the ultimate source of all details in "The Body on the Car" is still obscure.

The writer closes by explaining what he has learned from this mini-investigation.

Considering all these references to "The Body on the Car"—yes, folks, I do believe that Ann Landers fell for a legend, although her motives were only the best. After all, the reason so many grisly urban legends like this one continue to circulate is that they teach us worthwhile lessons in highly dramatic ways. The warning contained in "The Body on the Car" story should certainly be heeded, but that does not mean that the incident is true.

Moral(s): Don't drink and drive. But don't believe all the scare stories you hear, either. ▣

Academic Writing

"Overcrowding can also contribute to the dropout rate. Students feel neglected and may want to leave school and not return. The EPP report found that schools with the greatest number of students at risk of dropping out are also the most overcrowded." —Monica Bermudez

Problem/Solution Essay

A problem/solution essay states a problem clearly, analyzes it carefully, and presents a possible solution. Students use these thinking and writing skills for essays, research papers, and essay tests. Workplace writers use the same skills for complaint, bad-news, and sales letters; for troubleshooting, research, and sales proposals; as well as for crisis plans and position papers.

"A problem well stated is a problem half solved."

Discussion: Write an essay in which you analyze a problem and present one or more solutions. Choose a problem in your own life, and explore it thoroughly, proposing possible solutions (or reporting an actual solution). Or take a problem in the world around you, and analyze it completely before suggesting possible solutions or recording what is already being done.

Searching and Selecting

1. **Searching** • Think about the things students complain most about: crowded classrooms, jobs, grades, nothing to do, etc. Could you discover a solution for any of these problems? What about a problem that developed around your neighborhood, at your school, or in your personal life? What about environmental issues, politics, or other areas that affect your world? What is being done to address these problems? Do you have suggestions, solutions?
2. **Selecting** • As a class, list ten top problems or concerns for today's students. Could you analyze and propose a solution for one of these problems? Do you know someone who solved a difficult problem in a unique way? Have you resolved a problem in your own life or been part of the solution to a problem?

Generating the Text

3. **Forming** • After you've selected a problem, write it out in the form of a clear statement. Then analyze it thoroughly, exploring the problem's parts, history, and causes. Weigh possible solutions. Try listing reasons why solutions might work, or why they might not. (Use the "Mapping the Problem" organizer on the next page.)
4. **Assessing** • Are you dealing with a manageable problem for your essay? If not, could you address just one aspect of the larger problem? Have you got enough background material? Do you need facts and statistics to clearly establish the problem? Do you have illustrations of the problem? Anecdotes? Powerful and convincing examples?

Writing and Revising

5. **Writing** • Once you have analyzed the problem, write your first draft. Organize your information so it will be clear to any readers unfamiliar with the problem.
6. **Refining** • What anecdote, statistic, or quotation could you develop into an exciting lead? For readers to care about your solution, they must first care about the problem. What details could make your problem/solution engaging for readers?

Evaluating

Is a real solution offered for a real problem?

Is the writing interesting? The lead engaging? The conclusion logical?

Will readers understand and appreciate the essay?

Mapping the Problem

A. **The Problem:**
- Write the specific **Problem** in the center of the map.
- List as many **Causes of the Problem** as you can.
- List the **Parts of the Problem**: its history, different aspects of problem, etc.

B. **The Solution:**
- List as many **Possible Solutions** as you can.

C. **The Future:**
- Consider the **Future Implications** of each solution.

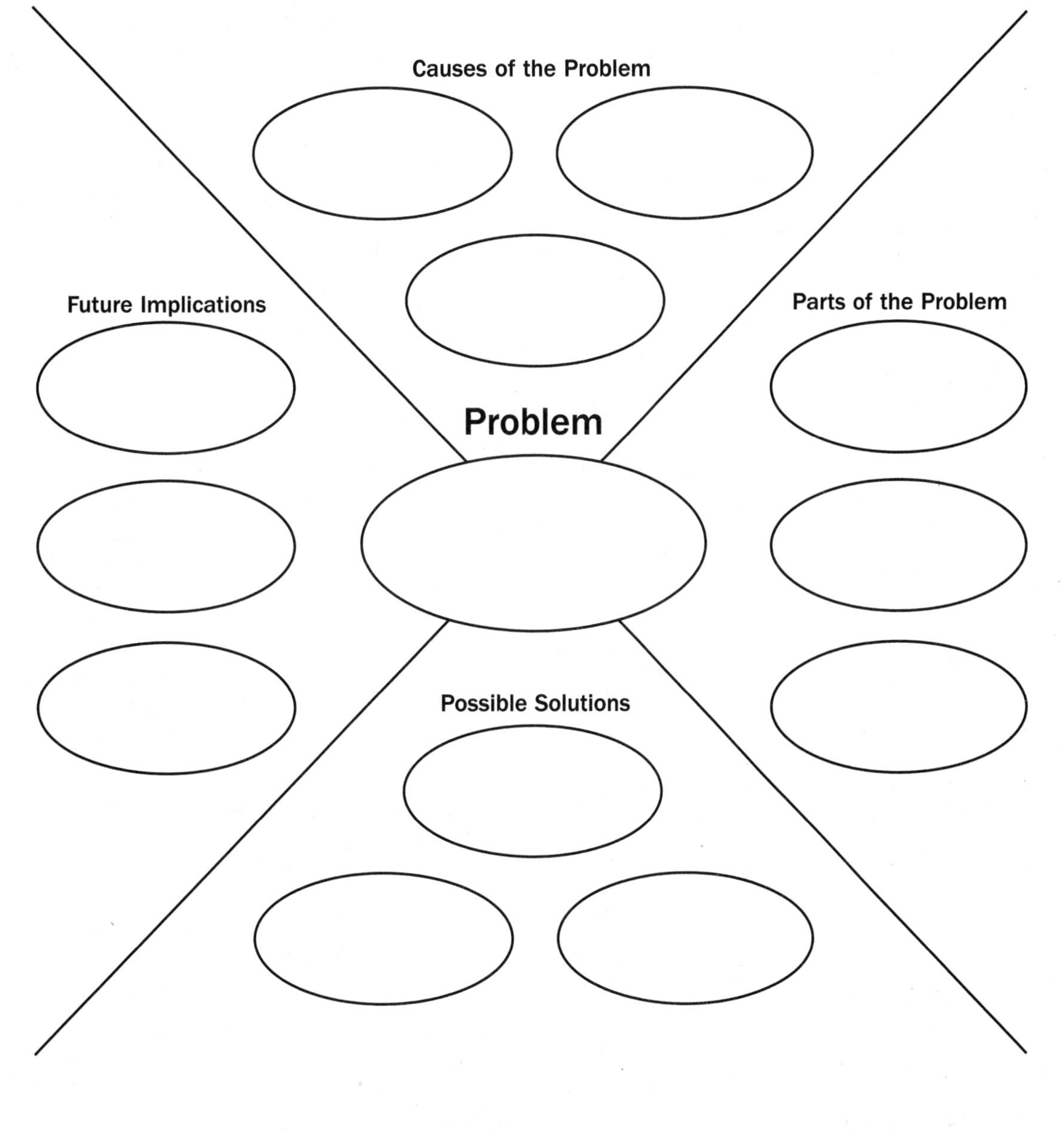

Student Model

In this essay Monica Bermudez discusses the problem of overcrowded classrooms. Some people believe that schools alone hold the key to solving this problem, but as this writer suggests, everyone needs to become involved. (This article is reprinted with permission from *New Youth Connections: The Magazine Written By and For New York Youth*, December 1991.)

The writer describes the scene in overcrowded classrooms (the problem) and suggests two main causes.

Overcrowded Classrooms: Do You Ever Feel Like a Teen Sardine?

You know the scene, the first week of school and your classes are packed. You walk in a little late only to find that all the seats have been taken, so you have to stand. Usually they manage to find a seat for you by the second week (even if they have to take it from another overcrowded class).

Sometimes it's because the program office has screwed up and [has] accidentally given you a class you took last term or a class you didn't ask for. But most of the time there are just too many students and not enough teachers or classrooms. Immigration is one big factor in why schools are so jammed. But the main reason is that there is no money.

At Humanities HS, for instance, Jan Zubiarr, 15, has 38 people in his math class, four over the limit set by the teachers' union contract.

"Lots of people don't have seats," he said. "It's not fair."

The school has room for 1702 students but last year 1860 registered. This means that the school was at what the board of education calls "109% utilization." (If 1702 had registered it would have been 100% utilized—full to capacity.)

No Place to Sit Down

Effects of overcrowding are discussed.

Students from several high schools all had the same complaint: with so many kids in one room, the time for learning is being taken up just getting the class together. "We deserve 41 minutes [of education]," said Nancy Alfaro, 16, of Grover Cleveland HS, "and not to spend half of it finding out where people sit."

Students also complained that there aren't enough supplies to go around. Amy Herget, 16, also from Cleveland, says in her classes not only are people always standing, there aren't enough books either. (Cleveland is 111% utilized.)

Another problem is that with so many people in one class, the teacher just doesn't have time for all of them.

Claudia Ramos, a senior at Richmond Hill HS (129% utilized), is planning to pursue a career in the fashion industry. With 40 people in her fashion design class, she says it's hard to get the teacher to look at her work. "It bothers me. I feel I'm getting less attention . . . a lot of kids are getting short-changed on their education."

Overcrowding Causes Tension and Violence

Noreen Connell, executive director of the Educational Priorities Panel (EPP), an organization working to improve public education in New York City, says, "Overcrowding also affects morale."

A 1989 EPP report on overcrowding said that "the school's atmosphere can become tense and, in some cases, violent."

Overcrowding can also contribute to the dropout rate. Students feel neglected and may want to leave school and not return. The EPP report found that schools with the greatest number of students at risk of dropping out are also the most overcrowded. And schools which are predominately Black and Latino are consistently more crowded than those with a large white population.

The writer shows that the impact of overcrowding affects everyone.

Many schools have tried to adapt by creating "double sessions." At Bushwick HS, which is 170% utilized—serving almost twice as many students as it should be—this means that the 11th and 12th grades start their day at 7:50 and end at 2:00. The 9th and 10th grades start at 9:15 and finish at 3:30. But this often prevents students from participating in after-school activities.

Temporary Solutions

Rose T. Diamond, director of strategic planning at the New York City Board of Education's division of School Facilities, said some schools are moving administrative offices out of their buildings to make more space for students. During our interview, Diamond got a phone call about two school districts fighting over classroom space. Her solution was to use another place such as the auditorium or gym. This has been the common remedy around the city, and not a great one, many teens say.

Present solutions offer little relief. Successful solutions will involve the students themselves.

The EPP report goes on to say that the schools that aren't overcrowded should try to create special programs to draw students away from those that are. It also suggested that schools that were closed be reopened and other alternative spaces be found in office buildings for example.

Meanwhile, the board of education has a five-year plan to build new schools and add and lease new space. By the year 1995, they say they will need to make room for almost 50,000 more students. In Queens they will be building West Queens HS which will accommodate 2500 students. Townsend Harris (also Queens) will house 1000 students. In Port Richmond HS, on Staten Island, there will be room for 800 more.

"Solving this problem," Ms. Diamond says, "is the chancellor's top priority." In the mean time, she says we should "try to be patient and understand."

But Connell doesn't think so. She says that teens are a great "political force" and they should write letters to their legislators and invite them to "observe overcrowding firsthand." She recommends that teens "tell as many people as possible how bad things really are."

Student Model

Student writer Zeba A. Khann tackles a big problem—air pollution in New York—by focusing specifically on two organizations that promote solutions. (This essay is reprinted with permission from *New Youth Connections: The Magazine Written By and For New York Youth*, September/October 1991.)

Transportation Alternatives:

Take a Hike, Ride a Bike . . . Clear the Air

Every time you decide to walk, ride a bike, or take public transportation instead of driving, you're doing something positive for the environment.

Currently, New York City has the second worst air pollution in the country, after Los Angeles. According to Joseph Rappaport, Coordinator of the Straphangers' Campaign of the New York Public Interest Research Group (NYPIRG), "People in L.A. live and die by the car . . . we don't, and it should stay that way."

A dramatic quotation highlights New York's pollution problem.

Automobile exhaust is one of the main causes of air pollution. Not only is air pollution a leading cause of asthma, it also reduces lung capacity, aggravates heart problems, and can even cause cancer.

The Straphangers' Campaign promotes mass transportation as an alternative to cars. They believe that mass transit means cleaner air. To help make public transportation more attractive to riders, the Straphangers' Campaign fights for better, more reliable subway and bus service. It tries to get the state to pay for new subway cars, track work, and programs to make the subway safer. After successfully fighting state budget cuts last spring, the campaign is now doing everything it can to stop the 35-cent fare hike the Transit Authority has proposed for next year.

Transportation Alternatives is another group working to decrease people's dependence on cars in order to reduce air pollution. But Transportation Alternatives puts a greater emphasis on bicycling and walking than on mass transit. It fought for better bike lanes on the Brooklyn and George Washington bridges as well as on many other roadways. With easier access, the group expects more people to bike instead of drive.

The writer addresses this problem from a position of authority, citing names, providing direct quotations, and offering relevant statistics.

People who walk, bike, or take mass transit generally find commuting more enjoyable than people who drive, says John Orcutt, Executive Director of Transportation Alternatives. They don't spend long hours stuck in traffic. They get exercise, read, or talk to other people. The end result is also less air pollution.

Still, the number of drivers has doubled since the early 1970's. Meanwhile, the number of subway riders has been declining. In 1948, the subway system carried two billion people per year. Now, just a little over a billion people ride the subways each year.

NYPIRG has 17 chapters located at colleges and universities in New York, and a student board headed by a student chairperson. Transportation Alternatives' Auto-Free Committee has 1,500 members, many of the most active ones being teenagers. In fact, teens play an active role in both organization, as volunteers and as interns.

Student Model

In this essay, Tristan Ching addresses a rather universal problem: there just aren't enough hours in the day. This writer finds a unique solution to this problem without compromising her love of ballet or learning.

Backseat Driver

I've spent half my high school life buckled up in the backseat of a car. Nestled comfortably on those gray leather seats, I eat dinner, do my homework, and sleep. The car isn't just a means of transportation anymore; it has become a home away from home.

The primary methods of development in this writing are personal narrative and analysis.

I haven't always spent so much time in the car. I began the three-hour commute to Santa Monica for ballet classes four years ago. When I chugged along the Pacific Coast Highway that first time, I had no idea what I was getting myself into. The Westside Ballet School, with its world famous teachers and talented students, opened the door to technical skill and artistry. Ironically, it also opened the door to the unpleasant realities of ballet. Although I was expressive and musical, I didn't have the ideal body for ballet. While I accepted the fact that I was too short and too dark to blend in with a *corps de ballet*, I also reached another conclusion. If I couldn't blend in, then I would work until I was good enough to stand out as a soloist in a company.

While other people entertain friends in their living rooms, I have had some of my most memorable discussions in the car. I have carpooled with several dancers, but Kirsten has been the most influential of the group. She showed me the degree of sacrifice, determination, and devotion needed to succeed, not just in ballet, but in life. I began to study video tapes of ballets to see what made dancers like Gelsey Kirkland and Makarova truly outstanding. I read books, magazines, and anything remotely related to ballet. I was addicted.

Kirsten helped me develop a love for ballet. Unwittingly, she also helped me appreciate school. She had dropped out of high school and did independent study instead. She insisted that independent study was just as good as a traditional education, but I wasn't convinced. How could in-class discussions about *The Scarlet Letter* or *The Great Gatsby* be replaced with a textbook? By defending the importance of school, I discovered that I really did believe that education should be an essential part of everyone's life. When I refused to skip school to go to an extra rehearsal, Kirsten said, "Tristan, you have to make the choice between ballet and school." I didn't agree; I was going to do my best in both.

"Doing my best in both" was similar to juggling. At first, I dropped a lot of balls. Finally, I learned that if I ate dinner and did homework in the car, I could maintain a balance between school and ballet. Looking back, I understand Kirsten's point of view better. Devoting herself entirely to ballet was all right for her because all she ever wanted to do was dance. For me, just dancing isn't enough. I want more than performing someone else's work, I want to create something of my own.

The writer points out that what works for one person does not necessarily work for another.

Professional Model

In this model, writer Beth Brophy describes an exciting program in Washington, D.C., designed "to do more than throw money at the homeless problem." (This article first appeared in *U.S. News & World Report*, April 19, 1993. It is reprinted by permission of *U.S. News & World Report*.)

Feeding Those Who Are Hungry

A description of one day in the D.C. Central Kitchen naturally draws readers into the essay.

WASHINGTON, D.C.—The D.C. Central Kitchen looks like any professional kitchen—clean, well-lighted, with plenty of pantry and counter space. One recent day, Mary Richter, the energetic, redheaded chef of the trendy local restaurant Cities, demonstrated cooking techniques to six aspiring chefs. Hands washed, in clean white aprons, they listened to Richter explain how to tell leafy from woody herbs as they made pesto.

But the students of D.C. Central Kitchen are unusual: They're homeless people who live in a shelter in the same building. Since 1990, 70 people have graduated from the 12-week job-training program, which is partially funded by the hunger-relief organization Share Our Strength. Six hours a day, five days a week, trainees learn the ins and outs of professional kitchens and, perhaps more important, tips for keeping a job, such as showing up on time.

The writer incorporates many important facts about Central Kitchen into her essay.

The program, which costs about $18,000 a year for 32 students, aims to do more than throw money at the homeless problem. According to the Bureau of Labor Statistics, the number of food-service jobs in the United States will jump 35 percent over the next 15 years. "Not jobs flipping hamburgers," notes Robert Egger, D.C. Central Kitchen's executive director, "but skilled work that pays $6.50 to $8.50 an hour at first and then gets more lucrative."

The second paycheck. Egger has a not-so-hidden agenda. His guest lecturers are local chefs who learn a lesson themselves: Homeless people are worth employing. Once the trainees graduate, Central Kitchen taps an extensive network of restaurant and food-service contacts for jobs. Of the program's 70 graduates, 40 remain employed, 16 of whom live and work on their own.

As noted here, solutions often create new problems.

But some have further problems. Richter, for example, has seen mixed results; the first graduate she hired disappeared after one paycheck, the second found the job too stressful and the third did well and then left for a bakery job. "Going through our program and getting a job is the easy part," explains Egger. "Maintaining the job, and making it past the second paycheck, is the hard part."

In the wake of the most recent defection, Egger plans to revamp the program by June to exclude those who haven't completed drug and alcohol rehabilitation programs and aren't living in halfway houses. Yet despite the frustrations, Egger hopes to replicate D.C. Central Kitchen's program in 15 other cities such as Minneapolis, Kansas City and San Francisco. The kitchen, says Richter, is where she can do her best work to improve the world: "Cooking is nurturing. Feeding people, whether they make $100,000 a year or $1,000, involves taking hungry people and making them not hungry." ▣

"For as long as I can remember, I have always wished I could become Laura Ingalls. I have longed to go running through golden wheat fields wearing a calico dress and sunbonnet."

—Lisa Cochrum

Essay of Evaluation

In an essay of evaluation, you think about a subject (like a personal experience, current trend, or new product), and answer this question: "How has the subject affected my life and the lives of others?" People in the workplace answer similar questions when writing project evaluations; field-trip, inspection, and incident reports; as well as special feature reports for the media.

"I'm almost glad it happened."

Discussion: Judge the worth of a particular event, incident, project, class, idea, person, or enterprise (business) in an essay of evaluation. The manner in which you develop your writing depends on your subject. An evaluation of a personal incident or performance will quite naturally be very personal in nature—a self-evaluation, if you will. An evaluation of a class, a group activity, or an enterprise will be more public in nature and speak to a wider audience. An evaluation of a product may result in a very objective report. Think in terms of your subject's value, impact, and significance, of its strengths and weaknesses. Provided below are basic guidelines to help you develop your writing.

Searching and Selecting

1. **Listing** • If you have trouble thinking of a subject to evaluate, write *people*, *places*, *events*, and *ideas* on a piece of paper turned lengthwise. Then freely list ideas under each heading. Somewhere along the way, you should hit upon a subject or two.
2. **Selecting** • You may also try one or more of the selecting activities listed in the handbook to help you find a subject. (Refer to "Selecting a subject" in the index for this information.) If needed, enlist the help of friends and family members. (Here's a point to consider: To evaluate a subject, you must know it well.)

Generating the Text

3. **Recording** • Once you have an idea in mind, write freely about your subject for at least 8 minutes, recording as many thoughts, feelings, and ideas as possible.
4. **Assessing** • Carefully review your exploratory writing—noting the important points you've made, deciding what more needs to be said, and so on. (Remember that you are trying to put your subject into perspective, to rate it, to measure it.)
5. **Focusing** • State a focus for your work—a sentence (or two) expressing a feeling or dominant impression you want to express in your writing. Then make some preliminary decisions about the arrangement of ideas in your writing.

Writing and Revising

6. **Writing** • Write your first draft freely, working in facts and details as they naturally come to mind or according to your planning and organizing.
7. **Revising** • Review, revise, and refine your writing until it says what you want it to say—and it's ready to share with your readers. (Refer to the Proofreader's Guide in the handbook when you are ready to proofread your work.)

Evaluating

Is the writing complete and meaningful?

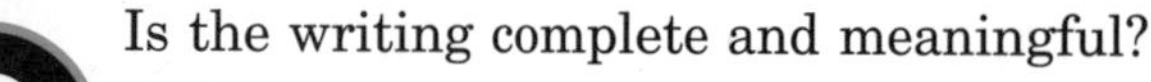

Is some form of evaluation or assessment taking place in the essay?

Will readers appreciate the treatment of the subject?

Student Model

In this essay of evaluation by Gail Scott, we learn about the importance of a brief but unforgettable moment in her life. The writer re-creates her memory with clarity and intensity, making it seem very real. (Reprinted with permission from *New Youth Connections: The Magazine Written By and For New York Youth*, November 1991.)

Readers are naturally drawn into the essay in the first paragraph.

I Thought I Was White

When I was a little girl, I thought that all Blacks were dark-skinned and anyone lighter than that was White. It wasn't until I was about 5 or 6 years old that I learned otherwise. I didn't mean to start any trouble, but I said something that got the whole family ready to bite my head off.

We were all at my grandparents' house—my parents, my grandparents, my sister Lorene, Cousin Alice, Uncle David, and his girlfriend Billie. It must have been some sort of holiday since we were all together like that. The big dinner table was set up and everyone was milling around the living room, waiting for dinner to be served. For some reason Lorene and I began discussing our difference in skin color. Although we share similarities in our appearance, she is darker than me. I announced to her that we didn't really look alike at all because I was White and she was Black.

My Grandmother Yelled at Me

The intensity of the moment is effectively re-created through the grandmother's words and actions.

Before Lorene had a chance to agree or disagree with me, my grandmother, who had overheard, shouted, "Don't you ever say that!"

All action came to a halt. Everyone, including me, turned around to look at her. Her eyes, which were blazing with fury, stared into my big, brown, innocent eyes. "You are Black," she told me. "Maybe you're not that dark, but you're still Black. Your mother is light and she's Black, just like you."

Whispers of "What happened, what did she say?" filled the room. Grandma repeated my words and I received confused looks from the other adults. I remember someone telling my grandmother, "Calm down, she didn't mean any harm." I still had no idea why Grandma was so angry.

The description of the moment after the grandmother's outburst adds drama to the essay.

I looked to my mother and my sister for help, hoping they would save me from another humiliating lecture. Lorene glanced at me for a moment, then she focused her eyes on the floor. My mother just looked at me and then at my grandmother as though she didn't know what to say, and that's just what happened—my mother didn't say a word, either to scold me or defend me.

I Felt Terrible

I remember having this terrible feeling, like I had said a swear word or knocked over and broken an expensive plate. I felt all alone and for a 5-year-old, that's an awful feeling. I didn't understand what was going on or why they were making me feel this way. All I knew was that I had made the mistake of opening my mouth in the first place.

My memory of that day ends with the entire room looking at me as though I had murdered someone. I never mentioned the incident after it happened for fear of the angry memories it would spark.

The writer's thoughtful evaluation of the experience helps her see her grandmother's actions as necessary and important.

Now that I am older, I can understand why my grandmother was so upset. She didn't want me growing up with a false image of myself. I feel that being Black means being proud of where you come from. My saying that I was White made it seem as though I was denying my heritage. Grandma was only pointing that out and setting me straight.

Of course, Grandma didn't have to yell at me, but I guess if she hadn't, then the moment would not have been as powerful. I might even have forgotten about it. Instead, I have always kept that day in the back of my mind to keep me from losing sight of who I am. I'm almost glad that it happened because that was my first step in learning about myself as a Black person.

Student Model

In this essay, Lisa Cochrum assesses her feelings about a favorite childhood TV character—Laura Ingalls Wilder—from an older and wiser perspective. Note how clearly the writer makes her assessment, moving smoothly from one main point to the next. Also note how effectively she supports her main thoughts with references from an Ingall's biography.

The focus, or thesis, stated at the end of the second paragraph sets the tone and direction for the essay.

What follows is the writer's perceptive evaluation of the made-for-TV Laura Ingalls Wilder as compared to the real person.

Oh to Have a Sunbonnet

Throughout my childhood, Monday nights were always an event in my household. All work and play stopped and we would plop ourselves in front of the TV, gluing ourselves to the screen for the next hour. The object of our most fixed attention was *Little House on the Prairie*. Centered around the small-town activities of Walnut Grove, Minnesota, it depicted the life of the prairie settlers in the 1800's. . . .

For as long as I can remember, I have always wished I could become Laura Ingalls. I have longed to go running through golden wheat fields wearing a calico dress and sunbonnet. How rich her life seemed, filled with nature, a sense of community and the utmost respect for other people and her God. Yet, as I have gotten older and have read about the life of the real Laura Ingalls Wilder, many of my idealistic images have been altered.

The true Laura Ingalls Wilder was born Feb. 7, 1867, in Wisconsin. Her early childhood was spent in Pepin, Wisconsin, in a little house at the edge of a big woods. In the years that followed, her family made several moves by means of a covered wagon. First to Independence, Kansas; then Plum Creek, Minnesota; Burr Oak, Iowa; Walnut Grove, Minnesota; and finally DeSmet, South Dakota. Throughout these years, Laura kept a personal diary in yellow school notebooks. It is upon these accounts of her life and how she wrote about them in her Little House on the Prairie that the television series was based. Most of the main characters and large events of her life were not altered in the depiction on TV, but the overall picture was. As I said earlier, most of the problems that came Laura's way could usually be solved in the hour show, yet in the diary of the real Laura Ingalls, she told of the many hardships that couldn't ever be solved. In her biography, the author, Donald Zochert, recounted the many blizzards, plagues, droughts, fires, and severe illnesses that threatened her family's financial and physical existence.

While in Plum Creek, Minnesota, the Ingalls family faced one of their most tragic trials, a seasonal occurrence of grasshopper plagues. Laura later describes it in the following way:

> *With the coming of summer, Pa's little patch of wheat was washed with a faint green. The wheat sprouts were coming up. But at the same time, the grasshoppers hatched. The ground squirmed with grasshoppers, as they marched and ate and tried their wings. They ate everything. Pa watched them sadly, but he didn't fight them. He knew what was going to happen and he was helpless to stop it. The first hot winds off the prairies to*

> *the west brought more grasshoppers, drifted across Dakota and Minnesota. The air filled with the sound of angry buzzing and Pa knew that his days on Plum Creek were over. With the small wheat crop devoured even before it had grown, there would be nothing to live on. In the prairie evenings Pa sat with Ma on the doorstep of the little house. In silence they watched the sun move slowly toward the dark edge of the western prairie. That was where Pa's heart was—west with the setting sun and the wide spaces and the high silences. But now to the west were grasshoppers, devouring dreams and lives as well as crops.*

With their livelihood gone, the family was forced to move to Burr Oak, Iowa, and begin a new life managing a hotel there. Yet, they all longed to return to the country and eventually moved back to Minnesota, but this time to Walnut Grove. The television series used this town as the basis for their show. Upon reading Wilder's biography, I found many of the same people and places that had become so dear to me on *Little House on the Prairie*. But again, the biography revealed that there were many hardships associated with life in that time. The blinding blizzards that would overtake the area were a constant threat to the people that lived there. Donald Zochert described one account that Laura wrote about in her diary.

Excerpts from Wilder's biography effectively support and authenticate the writer's main points and make for very interesting reading.

> *Winter storms sometimes kept Laura and Mary and Carrie home from school. Blizzards struck quickly and without warning, and the girls knew that the safest thing to do was to stay in one place. Not everyone followed this sensible rule, however. One day after a blizzard had blown itself out, word spread around town that some children were missing from their house, three miles out in the country. . . . Pa was one of the men who helped search for them. The children were finally found buried in a snowdrift; they had left the safety of the house and wandered into the fury of the storm. Three of them, two boys and a girl, were frozen to death. The oldest child, a girl Laura's age, was badly frozen but still alive. She had kept the baby of the family inside her coat all the time they were out in the storm and the heat of her own body kept the baby alive. But one of the girl's own legs was frozen so badly the doctor had to cut it off. Pa told Laura about this, and no doubt used it as a lesson on what not to do in a blizzard.*

One of the things *Little House on the Prairie* depicted correctly was Laura's marriage to a local farm boy named Almanzo Wilder. What they didn't show was that their first year of marriage was very difficult. Laura would later refer to her married life as the years of "sunshine and shadow." Laura and Almanzo were living in DeSmet, South Dakota, trying to establish their first farm. They were desolate times and when Laura wrote about them, anguish echoed in her words:

> *They were dry years in the Dakotas when we were beginning our life together. How heart breaking it was to watch the grain we had sown with such high hopes wither and yellow in the hot winds! And it was back breaking as well as heart breaking to carry water from the well to my garden and see it dry up despite all my efforts.*

In the years that followed they lost several crops, their house and barn burned down, and their second child died only twelve days after she was born. In fact, Laura and Almanzo would only have one child in their sixty-four years of marriage, a daughter, Rose, born during their first year together. They were also struck by ill health. Two years into their marriage, Almanzo and Laura contracted diphtheria. They lay sick in bed for several weeks, fighting an illness that was near-fatal for both of them. Almanzo had always been a fighter, and unfortunately he fought too hard this time. He forced himself up from his bed and suffered a stroke that left him paralyzed. Though he was able to regain most of his lost movement, he never fully recovered. He was only thirty years old, and he couldn't do a whole day's work. For the rest of his long life he shuffled as he walked.

In closing, the writer reaffirms her position . . . but not without feeling a little bit of the magic of her childhood dream.

Although *Little House on the Prairie* depicted some of the sorrows that touched Laura's life, like her sister's blindness that resulted from a fever, and the death of the only son that her parents bore, it painted a very rosy picture of Laura's life on the prairie. Upon reading her biography, I began to see the true life of a woman on the plains. Laura was strong, persevering, and flexible; she had to be because her environment was physically draining and emotionally trying. The true story of her life made me realize what the human spirit can do when it is pushed to the limit, but it also made me see that my dream of becoming Laura Ingalls Wilder was one based on fantasy. But there is still a part of me that longs to go running through golden wheat fields wearing a calico dress and sunbonnet.

Professional Model

Jill Robinson, the speaker in this excerpt from "Fantasia," evaluates the effects of growing up in Hollywood as a member of a family closely tied to the movie industry. (From *American Dreams* by Studs Terkel. Copyright © 1980 by Studs Terkel. Reprinted by permission of Pantheon Books, a division of Random House, Inc.)

Note that this model is part of a transcription (written version) of an interview.

"Fantasia"

. . . Out of the corner of my eye, I knew there were people watching who seemed smarter than we were. These would be the writers, who were cynical. They didn't believe it was all gonna work out all right. They didn't believe all movies were wonderful. I sensed this coming. I think the snake in the Garden of Eden was my growing awareness. The reality was always there. I chose not to see it. The thing that terrified me most was my own intelligence and power of observation. The more I saw, the more I tried not to see.

Couldn't bear it, the reality. Couldn't bear to feel my father was wrong. Couldn't bear the idea that it was not the best of all possible worlds. Couldn't bear the idea that there was a living to be made. That punishment does not always come to those that deserve it. That good people die in the end.

The triumph of the small man was another wonderful Hollywood myth, very popular in the mid forties. Once that dream went, once that illusion went, we all began to suspect what was really going on. Once we became conscious, that was the snake. It was the awareness of the power, awareness that war was not a parade, awareness of reality. This is what killed the old movies. It was the consciousness of the extras, and I became one of the extras.

The speaker talks pessimistically and forcefully about the American myth.

I think we're all skidding away, we're destroying. California is just a little bit of it. The more bleak I become, the more—I live in Connecticut, okay? I read somewhere Connecticut has the highest incidence of intestinal cancer in the world. I think that's because we eat ourselves alive there. We're filled with despair, and it just rots us away. Where I live looks exactly like the MGM back-lot idea of a small New England town. There's no pressure in Connecticut, it's all okay. Nobody is working much, there aren't many jobs, a lot of businesses are failing. But it looks so sweet. It looks endearing. During the blizzard, you would have thought that Currier and Ives came in there. That several people I know lost everything they own in that endearing blizzard, nobody really thinks about that. It looks like the American Dream.

Okay, we found Connecticut, and it doesn't work either. They go out to retirement homes in California, and they still get sick. And they worry about earthquakes. We always knew there'd be an earthquake. I loved the people who were trying to make it happen in the sixties. They were down there, on the Andreas Fault, with chisels and hammers, a whole group of fanatics, trying to saw it off. They needed the ending to make the earthquake happen. They predicted it and, fearful that it would not come true, they actually went up there. They really believed that God needed help. I say He's never needed help with that. Even my God is a movie god. He really runs the studio. Into the ground, as my grandmother would have said.

The speaker's evaluation extends from one coast to the other, from California to Connecticut.

The Hollywood dream has driven us crazy, but no more than any other mythology. Religious orders that govern whole states and decide what they should believe. Greek and Roman gods and goddesses. Catholicism. Hollywood is just another draft, a more polished version.

What else are we gonna live by if not dreams? We need to believe in something. What would really drive us crazy is to believe this reality we run into every day is all there is. If I don't believe there's that happy ending out there—that will-you-marry-me in the sky—I can't keep working today. That's true, I think, for all of us. ▣

Persuasive Writing

"When Congress passed the Gun Control Act, it didn't anticipate that Americans would desire to own civilian semiautomatic versions of military automatic weapons. Thus, the law allows the Russian-designed AK-47 to be categorized as a 'rifle' even though the weapon can easily be altered for automatic firing."

—Michael Pollock

Position Paper

In a position paper, you examine the issues related to an important question, test alternative ideas, and explain your own view. While many forms of workplace writing test alternative ideas and then support one choice, the recommendation report and the company-position paper most closely resemble the essays in this section.

Heavy on My Mind

Discussion: Present your personal stand or position on a significant issue of local, national, or global importance. Develop your paper so readers can clearly follow your train of thought—from your opening claim(s) to any background information you offer, from your analysis of the issue to the facts and details supporting your position. Provided below are basic guidelines to help you develop your paper. Also note the model papers following these guidelines.

Searching and Selecting

1. **Selecting** • Think of current developments in the news (decisions, trends, laws, advancements, or controversial issues) that will be of interest to you and your readers. Also study newspapers, magazines, journal entries, class notes, etc., for ideas.
2. **Reviewing** • If need be, review a current issue of the *Readers' Guide to Periodical Literature* for subjects as well as other guides or indexes in the library. Think about possible ideas as you read for pleasure or for a particular class, as you observe the day-to-day events in your community, or as you overhear conversations in the cafeteria line.

Generating the Text

3. **Noting** • Determine what you already know about your subject and your initial feelings or position on it—perhaps by doing a free writing. Also state what you hope to find out during your investigation of the issue.
4. **Investigating** • Collect as many facts and details as you can to help you develop your work. While reading may be your most important source of information, also consider conducting interviews, writing letters, gaining firsthand experiences, and so on.
5. **Assessing** • State your position on your subject now that you have thoroughly researched it, and then determine how you can most effectively present and support it. Plan accordingly. (Think of a position paper as a form of argumentation offering the reasons for your initial claim, entertaining one or two alternative points of view, supporting your position, and so on.)

Writing and Revising

6. **Writing** • Write your first draft freely, working in facts and details as they come naturally to you—or according to your planning and organizing.
7. **Revising** • Carefully review your writing; have at least two of your classmates read and react to your work as well. Revise and refine your writing accordingly. (Refer to the Proofreader's Guide when you are ready to proofread your work.)

Evaluating

Does the paper present an in-depth discussion of a timely issue?
Has a position been effectively presented and supported?
Will readers appreciate the treatment of the subject?

Student Model

The following essay presents student writer Cristina Lehman's position on the issue of religion in public schools. The essay unfolds clearly and logically, and avoids the common mistake of basing one's position on emotion rather than on fact.

The opening scenario presents the writer's position and introduces the basis of her argument.

The writer concedes a point to the opposition and then explains why this concession does not alter her position.

Examples establish the writer's "authority" and further clarify her argument.

Continued Debate on Religion in Public Schools

Picture this—after a long day in public school, the students learn that a guest speaker is coming tomorrow. Excited, they find out it is not the local weatherman, but a priest from the nearby Catholic church. Then, in the few remaining minutes of class, the students pick up their Bibles and read a few passages. As one might have already guessed, all of this would be strange indeed. Thankfully, this kind of education is not allowed in public school systems. One of the reasons can be inferred from Eunice Edgar's statement: "A religious program will make people in minority religions or without affiliation feel uncomfortable" (Dodge 2). This brings one to think that if one religion were allowed in public schools, the result would be resentment of other religions, or conformity under pressure. Therefore, religion should be kept out of public schools.

It is true that Americans have the right to practice whatever religion they want. But the issue of whether it should be permissible in public schools touches sensitive ground. To begin with, religion in public schools goes against the Constitution of the United States. Debate on this issue is based on the Constitution's amendments. The First Amendment clearly states its desire to leave religion out of public schooling. The establishment clause says there can be no official religion (Arbetman, ART. 95). The free-exercise clause relates how one can practice whatever religion one chooses (95). If religious education were to be mandated in public schools, both of these rights would be violated. In addition, the First Amendment is interpreted to prevent government agencies from giving support to religion in public schools (Peach, ART. 81). The First Amendment, however, is not the only one which deals with this issue. The Fourteenth Amendment contains an equal protection clause which states the separation of church and state (Arbetman, ART. 95). The Supreme Court has also voiced its opinion that having religion affiliated with public schooling is unconstitutional (95). Also, the American Civil Liberties Union feels that the wishes of the majority are not as important as constitutional law (Dodge 2). All in all, one can see how religion in public schools directly goes against the Constitution of the United States.

Granted, having religion in public schools might lead students down a more religious path of life. But it might also lead to chaos, disbelief, and confusion. The United States courts already feel this chaos. Many have used the courts to fight for their rights concerning this issue, but have failed. The public support to have religion in public schools has been as high as 81 percent, consisting primarily of Catholics (Thompson 1-2).

The "Students for Voluntary Prayer" is a specific example of failure. This group tried to have prayer meetings in public classrooms on the school campus. Yet, after much time and effort in dealing with the courts, the case was dismissed (Arbetman, ART. 95). In another example, President Reagan went as far as to propose a constitutional amendment that would permit voluntary group prayer in schools (Thompson 1). His proposal would allow the government to dictate certain religious exercises and let the students participate voluntarily (2). Fortunately, Reagan's plan was rejected. People ranging from young students to the president have persistently fought to affiliate religion with the public schools, but to no avail.

The final section offers compromises and alternatives to practicing religion in the public schools.

Instead of continuing the fight against the courts and the Constitution, protestors should start to accept the compromises and alternatives that governments and schools have made. First of all, an "equal access" policy allows the state to create an open forum on campus (Arbetman, ART. 95). In addition, some schools permit prayers, invocations, or benedictions during graduation ceremonies. Many schools, such as Pulaski High School in Wisconsin, allow prayers which do not promote a particular religion. Also, some schools permit a moment of silence to respect all religious views. This also avoids legal fights (Dodge 2). Another compromise is allowing education "about" religion. This includes classes such as Biblical Literature, in which the teacher teaches in an objective, historical, and non-devotional manner. The courts also allow "release time" for students to attend classes of religious instruction (Peach, ART. 81). These alternatives allow some leeway, yet also avoid confusion.

Religion should be kept out of public schools. It is such a personal issue that people should not have to feel pressured to practice their faith the way others wish them to. . . . So, to allow children their freedom of religion and to obey the law, the guest speaker from the nearby Catholic church will not be coming in tomorrow or anytime in the near future. ◼

Works Cited

Arbetman, Lee. "Religion in the Public Schools: The Debate Goes On." Street Law News Fall 1983: 4-7. Rpt. in School, Vol. 2. Ed. Eleanor C. Goldstein, Boca Raton, FL: Social Issues Resources Series, 1984. ART. 95.

Dodge, Gary. "Many Area Graduations Still Will Open With Prayer." Green Bay Press-Gazette 1 June 1990: 1-2.

Peach, Lucinda J. "Why Do I Have to Go to School?" Update on Law-Related Education Winter 1988: 23+. Rpt. in School, Vol. 3. Ed. Eleanor C. Goldstein. Boca Raton, FL: Social Issues Resources Series, Inc., 1989. ART. 81.

Thompson, Roger. "School Prayer." News Brief. Editorial Research Reports 16 Sept. 1983: 1-2.

Student Model

Student writer Michael Pollock presents his position on gun control in this forceful paper. Throughout the writing, Mr. Pollock employs anecdotes, facts, specific details, and analysis to state his position. (This essay originally appeared in the October/November 1990 issue of *Merlyn's Pen: The National Magazine of Student Writing*. All of the quotations appeared first in "The Right to Bear and Die by Arms," a story by Fred Bruning in the June 19, 1989, issue of *Maclean's* magazine. It is reprinted by permission of *Merlyn's Pen*.)

Peace on Earth

The opening scenario immediately catches the reader's attention and serves as a lead-in to the writer's position on gun control.

The door to the bank shatters as a Volkswagen van sails through and comes to a halt inside the lobby. The man dressed in black and wearing a pig mask jumps out of the van holding an AK-47 semiautomatic rifle. He immediately opens fire, spraying bullets all over the room. Customers are being shot and falling to the floor as what feel like magicians' swords tear at their organs. With screams and cries, they crumple to the floor like jelly, holding their chests.

This is one event that can happen to anyone if action is not taken to decrease the number of semiautomatic weapons being bought and used in America today.

We started our history with an armed revolt, and the West, North, South, and even East were won by black powder and well-placed slugs. Our Constitution speaks to the bearing of arms, although it is quite certain that the leaders of yesteryear did not anticipate that centuries later their descendants would exhibit a zeal for guns that verges on the psychopathic. How could Jefferson and Franklin have known that, in 1990, schools would install metal detectors to ferret out students carrying pistols, or that ordinary citizens could drop by their local gun shop and walk away with enough firepower to restage the Revolution? Little did the politicians of old know that in 1990 something called the National Rifle Association would function almost as a fourth branch of government. In the past, the NRA has been able to outshoot gun control advocates and coerce members of Congress, but lately the organization looks as if it is losing ground and becoming less formidable.

Details recalling a specific experience support the writer's position.

Trouble began early in 1989 when a gunman killed five children and wounded twenty-nine others and one adult in Stockton, California. The weapon of choice was a Chinese-made AK-47 assault rifle, which is able to fire nearly 100 shots without reloading. Almost immediately, it occurred to citizens of California and elsewhere that the AK-47 should not be as easy to buy as a loaf of bread. Predictably, the NRA disagreed. "Outlaw the assault rifle," said the organization, "and you tamper with America's soul."

George Bush, an NRA member himself, hesitated at first, but when fury over the Stockton incident grew like a raging inferno, the president banned imported assault rifles and called for prohibitions on high-capacity ammunition magazines manufactured in the U.S. and overseas.

The NRA was livid. The NRA got more bad news when Colt Industries suspended commercial sales of the AR-15 semiautomatic rifle. Another setback came to the NRA when the California legislature voted to ban manufacture and marketing of all semiautomatic assault weapons. Setbacks like these are unusual for the NRA and may signal that gun control activists are making progress.

The writer concedes that assault weaponry has a specific purpose and use.

There are certain situations in which extreme forms of weaponry, such as submachine guns, are useful. But these situations rarely involve ordinary citizens. Sawed-off shotguns were purchased by the U.S. government and used in World War I as "trench guns" and later in World War II and the Vietnam War. In 1939 the Supreme Court, in *U.S. vs Miller*, sustained the National Firearms Act of 1934, which required their registration.

The writer's analysis of the Gun Control Act adds further support to his argument.

When Congress passed the Gun Control Act, it didn't anticipate that Americans would desire to own civilian semiautomatic versions of military automatic weapons. Thus, the law allows the Russian-designed AK-47 to be categorized as a "rifle" even though the weapon can easily be altered for automatic firing. Typically, such weapons, which are often used by gangs and drug dealers, can fire 300 to 1,200 rounds a minute. Their bullets penetrate cars, walls, police officers' vests, and maybe even your body. Law enforcement officials have sought for a long time to outlaw assault rifles. The NRA insists tenaciously that the AK-47 and other assault rifles are used for "hunting" by thousands of "sportsmen." I've yet to meet a hunter who would rather have a shredded elk rack from an assault rifle than a whole rack from an elk shot with a single-shot rifle. The "sportsmen" the NRA is talking about are gang members and drug dealers who are "hunting" police officers and other people.

In closing, the writer's position is clearly reaffirmed—and a call to action is made.

It's time America made a choice. Either we follow the letter of the Constitution and let anyone have possession of a mass murdering tool, or we pass laws to regulate and decrease the sale of semiautomatic "hunting rifles." If enough young people learn of this life or death dispute, they can put pressure on the politicians, and action will be taken. I hope my descendants will hunt only wild animals—with a rifle that shoots only one deadly piece of lead at a time. ▣

Professional Model

In the following "memo," writer Stephen Budiansky offers his views on recent attempts to limit immigration to the United States. He urges readers to consider the following scenario: What if the first Americans had behaved like our government has and told the new arrivals to go home? (Reprinted from the June 7, 1992, issue of *U.S. News & World Report* with permission. Copyright 1992, *U.S. News & World Report*.)

1620 to 1992: Long Ago but Not So Far Away

TO: Massasoit, Chief, Wampanoag tribe
FROM: Squanto
RE: Immigration interview report, 26 DEC 1620

The writer puts himself in the shoes of a Native American reporting on the recent influx of Europeans.

One hundred so-called boat people filing claims for political asylum were interviewed. The vast majority of these claims are nonsensical. None could show a justifiable, immediate fear for their lives if they returned to Holland and/or that they had held a sensitive position in a persecuted political or religious organization. In fact, several admitted that they had only several years earlier voluntarily relocated to Holland specifically because it was an open society that would tolerate their sect ("the Separatists"). The obvious contradictions in their stories suggest that these are not bona fide political refugees but rather economic refugees, merely out to better their lives.

By referring to the arrivals as "boat people," he establishes a link between early European immigrants and contemporary refugees.

Their claim to permanent residency status based on special skills or professional training is likewise unsubstantiated. Most lack even the most basic job skills, as the earlier wave of boat people who were admitted to Jamestown has unfortunately demonstrated. Most of those immigrants were listed on the ship's manifest as "Gentleman," which they themselves define as "whosoever can live without manual labor." They are lazy, prone to acts of violence and unable or unwilling to become productive members of society. Established residents of the area complain of a rash of petty thefts and of being accosted by immigrants begging for food. Even when faced with outright starvation—and more than two thirds already have starved to death—they are unwilling to find gainful employment. In one well-documented incident, the immigrants chopped down their own houses for firewood. It is perhaps relevant that several prominent authorities in England have explicitly encouraged emigration to America as a way to rid their country of "idle and worthless" persons.

Reasons for denying the Europeans access to America are presented in the final portion of the memo.

The conditions aboard these boats are horrendous. Interviewees report that five persons in fact died in transit. Smallpox, scurvy and typhus are rampant aboard these crowded ships, which allot a space of only 7 feet by 2-1/2 feet, below decks, for each passenger. More than 150 boat people died of disease on one ship that arrived in Virginia two years ago. The ships are also in poor physical condition. Interviewees reported that a second boat, the *Speedwell*, was forced to turn back twice because of leaks and eventually abandoned the voyage. Firm action now can effectively discourage other Englishmen from taking to unseaworthy vessels, which will only lead to a further unnecessary and tragic loss of life. . . .

Recommendation on applications for asylum: DENY.

"Mike discovered he had the disease last June. After breaking out in a rash, he underwent a series of tests, including one for HIV. The HIV test came back positive, and his near-perfect life was changed forever. 'It has affected every area of my life,' Mike says about the virus which inhabits his body." —Amy Taylor

Essay of Speculation

Writing an essay of speculation involves thought: you (1) think about what happened in the past, (2) consider how this affects what's happening today, and (3) develop a logical prediction about what may happen in the future. Workplace writers use these thinking and writing skills in troubleshooting reports; sales projections; purchase proposals; as well as in crisis, long-range, and product-development plans.

What if . . .

Discussion: Write about the "future," something that hasn't happened. See what futuristic thoughts come to mind when you ask the question, "What if . . . ?" In writing an essay of speculation you must think carefully about something in the present and make an educated guess about its future. You could write about global issues, or make projections (of science fiction proportion) about a specific arena of life. Examine a current trend or present-day technology and consider what effect it might have in the future. Read the models on the following pages to see how other writers handled essays of speculation. Then consult the guidelines below to help you develop your essay.

Searching and Selecting

1. **Searching** • What if we suddenly ran out of . . . ? What if cars . . . ? What if . . . ? Consider all the possibilities; then select a topic you really do have an interest in. Speculation requires a personal investment of both time and thought. Notice that the model essay writers all speak with personal conviction.
2. **Selecting** • If no subjects come readily to mind, try reading publications such as *Prevention Magazine*, *Men's Health*, *National Geographic*, *Discovery*, and *Omni* for possible ideas.

Generating the Text

3. **Collecting** • Have you got all the facts you need? (In the models notice the environmental facts, AIDS statistics, and the Huck quotations and dates, all supporting the authors' points.)
4. **Focusing** • Have you narrowed your topic? If you have a large issue, do you have a plan to tie everything together? Have you thought about the possible domino effect of your "what if . . ."? One change often causes another change. Will you make your point through a story or an interview (AIDS), by building a case almost like an attorney (Huck), or by using a voice of humor or satire (environment)?

Writing and Revising

5. **Writing** • After finding a topic you know and care about, begin writing. You can expect new ideas to evolve as you write.
6. **Refining** • Hold mock trials to test the logic of your speculation. In a small group, you (the defense attorney) read your essay to your peers (the prosecuting attorneys). They will question *only* your logic, using statements like, "If you say that, how can this be . . . ?"

Evaluating

?...?

Are sufficient background and factual information established?

Does the speculation (the projected effect) follow logically from its cause?

Is the "What if . . .?" clearly stated?

Is "So what?" adequately addressed?

Student Model

In this essay, student writer Amy Taylor speculates on the devastating consequences of the question, What if young people do not receive, or choose to ignore, information about AIDS? (This essay first appeared in the March 20, 1992, issue of *MHS Today*, the Milton [WI] High School student newspaper.)

The essay focuses on the story of an AIDS victim and his wife; the writer provides background information and explanations as needed.

AIDS Can Happen Here!

"The difference between good people and bad people is good people learn from their mistakes. You shouldn't have to pay for your mistakes with your life."

Unfortunately, Mike Johnson of Milton, Wisconsin, will pay for his mistake with his life.

At first glance, Mike, 29, appears to be a typical up-and-coming businessman. He is well dressed, highly intelligent, articulate, and healthy in appearance. However, he is not your typical businessman. Mike Johnson has AIDS.

He was infected at least six years ago by a former girlfriend. Unaware that he had been exposed to the HIV virus, Mike married. His wife, Sherie, has also tested positive for HIV.

Mike discovered he had the disease last June. After breaking out in a rash, he underwent a series of tests, including one for HIV. The HIV test came back positive, and his near-perfect life was changed forever.

"It has affected every area of my life," Mike says about the virus which inhabits his body.

But Mike is a positive person.

"There's always a reason to be depressed," Mike says. "I choose not to be. I am faced with my eminent demise; therefore, life becomes a very precious thing. Self-pity is not a very productive state of emotion, so why do it?"

Mike and Sherie were living in Dallas, Texas, when they tested positive for HIV. They moved back to Milton to be near their families and friends.

Since moving back to Milton, Mike and Sherie have been speaking at schools throughout the state, believing the only way to overcome the epidemic is for people to fight against AIDS.

Since teenagers are currently the highest risk group, the Johnsons are especially concerned with educating teens.

"We have been trying to let people know that HIV is a behavior-oriented disease, and you can absolutely eliminate the risk of HIV by modifying the way you behave," Mike says.

They also encourage members of the communities they visit to give teens all the facts.

"People who are afraid to be pro-active in the fight against HIV are going to have to answer to the parents two years from now who say, 'Why didn't you do something when you had the chance? Now my child is dying!' " Mike added.

Mike and Sherie are doing their best to give teens all the facts and encourage them to practice abstinence.

"We have 5,000 kids sitting there, and you can hear a pin drop. We make them laugh, we make them cry, and we tell them the truth," Mike says.

One-third of the world's population destroyed? That statistic is speculation, based on current projections of the spread of AIDS.

The truths that they share are scary. If a cure is not found for AIDS, overpopulation will not be a problem in the future because more than one-third of the population will die of it.

"AIDS is everybody's problem," Mike explains. "Even if you're not sexually active, someone you know or care about is."

Except for taking AZT, a drug which slows the HIV virus, and Bactrim, an anti-pneumonia drug, Mike does not take many precautions to protect his health. He's too busy trying to reach as many people as possible while there is still time.

"This disease will probably kill me," Mike says. "Ironically, I have the potential to do more good than I ever would have had before."

Student Model

In this model, writer Andrew Chrisomalis questions everyone's concern about the environment. "Why the big fuss?" he says. However, once you read this essay, it's easy to see that Mr. Chrisomalis is playing with mirrors. The environment is a big deal to him; he's simply making his point through indirection (and sarcasm)—stating the opposite of what he really believes. (This model first appeared in the December/January 1991 issue of *Merlyn's Pen: The National Magazine of Student Writing*. It is reprinted with permission.)

The Environment Can Take Care of Itself

The maintenance and the survival of our environment have become sensitive and disputable issues. Various groups make different claims, from the possible near end of life as we know it, to assertions that the environment is still safe and stable. Well, I know that the environment is safe and stable.

The writer's use of indirection and understatement creates awareness of perhaps the biggest environmental problem—the attitude that there is no problem.

Why the big fuss about oil in our water? It mixes in eventually; anyone with common sense knows that. And there is plenty of water on this earth, so why get into such a stew about it? Someone is bound to invent something to solve the problem . . . it always works out in the end.

And all that ocean pollution everybody is getting so uptight about, especially in the summer: I'm more worried about the sand! Messy stuff, it just gets stuck in my hair spray and caught in my bologna sandwich when I'm trying to enjoy a relaxing beach picnic. My solution? Build more swimming pools. Such a big hullabaloo about 11 million gallons of oil that blanketed Prince William Sound. Personally, I don't relate to all those fish and ocean creatures: what did they ever do for me? Should I care that it took 22 minutes for the crew to report that they had run aground? Who's counting? They eventually did call in. People keep criticizing Exxon for having inadequate cleanup gear, just enough for a 1,000-2,000-barrel spill. Hey, at least they had something! Exxon actually did a very good job of cleaning up. I wouldn't have wasted my time recovering 2.5 million gallons of oil from the water, much less 11 million. The Exxon crews recovered almost 23 percent before they decided to call it quits. To tell you the truth, I feel sorry for Exxon. They're the poor fish that lost 200,000 barrels of oil.

The writer jumps from issue to issue, quickly dispatching each one regardless of its magnitude.

And speaking of problem solving in the good old H_2O, what about those whales? Everybody loved the book *Moby Dick*, and awesome old Ahab hunted a whale for heaven's sake! A big white one, grandfather of them all! Nowadays, these "Greenpeace" characters get all bent out of shape when people hunt those clumsy sea monsters. They call them an "endangered species" and breathe heavily at the thought of losing them. But what about us? Human beings will be an endangered species, too, if we can't

The devil-may-care final remark brings this essay to an effective conclusion.

eat or do anything else natural to us . . . like killing animals. Nobody criticized Daniel Boone or Davy Crockett when they hunted animals for their fur—they were our frontier heroes! Nowadays we treat furriers like Chapter 11 people. Mustn't "mistreat animals" or cause them any itsy-bitsy pain! Isn't it just as cruel for my aunt to be left shivering on a cold day?

Another one of my gripes is this recycling. Who has time to separate the green glass from the clear glass from the newspapers from the aluminum cans? My grandfather's generation didn't have to take all that trouble, so why should I? Realists like me can leave that to the "environmentalists." Or let the next generation worry about it.

And one other thing: this ozone layer business. I mean, what's it to me, as long as my Big Mac is hot? I'd breathe a lot easier if all those environmental hotheads just cooled off.

Well, it's time for my daily run. After all, I have to maintain my body so I can enjoy life on this planet in all its beauty and diversity!

Professional Model

The writer reveals the groundbreaking research that led Twain scholar Shelley Fisher Fishkin to suggest that the source of Huckleberry Finn's voice was a young black servant named Jimmy. Because this suggestion cannot be proven, it remains scholarly speculation. This essay appeared in the *Milwaukee Journal* (July 7, 1992) as a news service release. (Copyright © 1992 by the New York Times Company. Reprinted by permission.)

Twain's 'Huck' May Have Been Based on Black Youth's Voice

Opening lines imitating Huckleberry Finn's voice attract the reader's curiosity and interest.

You don't know about this without you have read a book by the name of *The Adventures of Huckleberry Finn*; but that ain't no matter. Mr. Mark Twain wrote it and he got considerable praise for using a boy's voice to tell a tangled story about race and about America, and nobody kin say for sure where that voice come from.

Now a Twain scholar has linked Huck's voice to a 10-year-old black servant Twain met just before starting work on the book. Twain described the boy in an almost-forgotten article in the *New York Times* in 1874 as "the most artless, sociable and exhaustless talker I ever came across."

Shelley Fisher Fishkin, an associate professor of American studies at the University of Texas, shows that the speech patterns of the black boy, whom Twain calls Jimmy, and of Huck Finn are similar and in some ways identical.

But more important, given that the entire book is told by Huck, she shows how both voices mixed sassiness with satire, a point of view that helped make Twain's book one of the most important American novels. Fishkin lays out the theory in a book to be published in 1993 by Oxford University Press called *Was Huck Black? Mark Twain and African-American Voices*.

"For Professor Fishkin to come up with this," said T. Walter Herbert, a professor of English at Southwestern University in Georgetown, Texas, and an expert on 19th-century authors, "does not refute Hemingway's line that 'All modern American literature comes from one book by Mark Twain called *Huckleberry Finn*.' It simply complicates and enriches that claim."

A New Perspective

The main part of the essay provides valuable background information and expert analysis.

Uncovering the roots of Twain's art could lead to a reconsideration of the author and his most important work, which has been banned in some places because of its attitudes and language.

Twain's defenders always have argued that Huck's language was satiric and meant to expose his late 19th-century audience to its own hypocrisy and intolerance.

Tracing Huck's voice to a black source also could change the way the book is taught.

"This shows a real black root in a white consciousness," said David Sloane, a professor of English at the University of New Haven and president of the Mark Twain Circle of America.

Fishkin said she was not arguing that Twain envisioned Huck as a black child, but that "his voice in key ways was modeled on black speakers."

The heart of Fiskin's argument rests with "Sociable Jimmy," which appeared on page 7 of a 12-page issue of the *New York Times* on Sunday, Nov. 29, 1874. The page on which it ran also included obituaries, advertisements and brief news items.

In his introduction to the article, which was Twain's first published work dominated by the voice of a child, he said he had been enthralled by Jimmy's unpretentious performance.

"He did not tell me a single remarkable thing, or one that was worth remembering," Twain wrote, "and yet he was himself so interested in his small marvels, and they flowed so naturally and comfortably from his lips that his talk got the upper hand of my interest, too, and I listened as one who receives a revelation."

After coming across it in her research for another book on Twain, Fishkin was struck by Jimmy's voice. She reread *Huckleberry Finn* 20 times and reread "Sociable Jimmy" more often, as well as examining much of Twain's writing for similar clues. She found passages in both the article and *Huckleberry Finn* that shared the same linguistic roots.

The writer summarizes Fishkin's argument and offers a Twain quote to support the speculation.

Fishkin found that Huck and Jimmy constantly repeat the same words, make frequent use of present participles, and often make the same mistakes. The two boys often use the same adjectives in place of adverbs. Jimmy says "He's powerful sick." Huck says "I was most most powerful thirsty."

The boys are alike in other ways, too, she says.

The only real family each has is "Pa," and both fathers drink too much. The boys are entranced by a particular clock, both consider themselves judges of good taste, and they are comfortable around dead animals, especially dead cats.

While they disagree about how much of Huck derives from Jimmy, all the scholars who have read the manuscript said it demonstrates—for the first time—strong black roots in Huck's speech.

Writing in the Workplace

Letter Writing

Letter-Writing Basics

You've been writing letters all your life—thank-you letters to Grandma, letters from camp to Mom and Dad, letters to friends. Business letters are more formal. You don't need to use five-dollar words and long sentences to sound business-like, but there are some basic guidelines you should follow.

REVIEW: Answer the following questions by remembering what you already know about business writing and by using your own common sense. (If you need help, look at sections 181-193 and 215 in your handbook.)

1. Why write a letter or memo instead of just using the phone? List several reasons.

2. Why should the signature in a letter be both written and typed?

3. Name the three categories of letters and give one example of each.

4. What's an inside address?

5. What salutation should you use if you can't get the reader's name?

6. What is the three-part organization of most business correspondence?

7. Summarize the USPS guidelines for addressing envelopes.

8. What's a subject line in a memo? Why is it important?

9. How are memos distributed?

10. List the parts of a memo heading.

Correspondence Basics: Letters and Memos

Letters, memos—same thing, right? Well, okay . . . if you think that watermelons and grapes are the same because they're both fruit. Letters and memos are in the same category (they're both correspondence), but in the business world they have different uses.

CHECK IT OUT: If you're going to earn your living in business, you'd better know the difference between letters and memos. Read "Writing the Business Letter" (186-193) and "Writing Memos" (215). Then list characteristics of letters and memos below:

	Letters	**Memos**
readers: (Who are they?)		
purpose of documents:		
form parts (heading, date, etc.):		
organization of message:		
method of sending (use your own judgment):		

Correspondence Samples: Collecting and Analyzing

READ & RESPOND: Collect business letters from your home, your parents, and businesses in your neighborhood. Read through the correspondence you've gathered and sections 183-184 and 215 in your handbook. Then respond to the following:

1. List three main purposes of workplace writing.

2. What are the three positive characteristics of form and voice in workplace letters and memos?

3. List three qualities of effective memos.

follow-up

If you were Calamity Jane and wanted to send your friend Wild Bill Hickock a birthday card, you'd have three slow choices: train, stagecoach, or pony express. But today you have options that are much faster.

With two classmates, research your options for sending (1) a letter, and (2) a 10-pound package the size of a basketball.

- Check out the United States Postal Service. What delivery services (first class, third class, etc.) does it offer? What are the differences in service and price? Compare and contrast the USPS with another delivery service like United Parcel Service (UPS) or Federal Express. (Hint: Check the phone book for phone numbers and addresses and call or write for information.) Report the results of your research to the class.
- Is paper the only way to go for sending letters and memos? What are your other choices? (See 336, "Using Technology . . .," in your handbook.)

The Write Attitude

Correspondence is more than information: it's information that's been tailored to a reader. Good-news messages call for a simple approach. But bad-news and persuasive messages require special attention to tone. In letters, an effective tone is polite, positive, and tactful. How does this actually work?

- Choose a model letter from your handbook, read it carefully, and describe the tone.
- On your own paper, jot down words and phrases that create that tone.
- Examine a model letter or memo you've gathered. Check it for problems with tone. Circle words and phrases that create the problem.

THINKING ABOUT YOU: Reader-friendly messages—ones with a positive tone—use personal pronouns like "you" carefully. The pronoun "you" helps keep the focus on the reader's situation, perspective, and needs. (For information on personal pronouns, see 714 and 716 in your handbook.)

READ & RESPOND to the message to Mr. Coyote below. What's the tone, and how is the tone related to the personal pronouns?

We at ACME Corporation are pleased to announce the invention of the latest and best in laser technology: our ACME Roadrunner Beam—guaranteed to nail the fastest roadrunners in your life. Without a doubt, our laser leaves our competition in the dust. Our laser is lighter, more compact, and more accurate than theirs. In fact, it's probably twice as effective as the piece of junk you own now. We are absolutely confident that you will be enthralled with our ACME Roadrunner Beam. After all, we made it and we're the best in the business. You should know that by now.

1. With a pencil, circle all the personal pronouns. What do these pronouns tell you about the focus of the message?

2. How does the passage make you feel about the writer? How would you feel as Mr. Coyote, the reader?

READ & RESPOND to this revised passage. How does the change in the use of personal pronouns change the overall tone of this message?

Is your present laser beam catching all the roadrunners you need, Mr. Coyote? Or is it leaving you flattened and in a bad mood? ACME Corporation can help you.

Our new ACME Roadrunner Beam is light and compact. You can move it quickly and easily to avoid having it crush you at the bottom of a cliff. Moreover, the ACME Beam is accurate up to 10 miles so that you can reach your meal from a safe distance. Finally, the ACME Beam comes equipped with dual parachutes—one for the machine, and one for the operator—in case you are standing on an over-hanging cliff that you accidentally cut off.

If the Acme Roadrunner Beam sounds like a step forward in your search for the ultimate weapon, call one of our friendly operators at 1-800-GOTTCHA.

1. Circle all the personal pronouns. How has the message's focus shifted?

2. What does the message make you think or feel about the writer? How do you feel as the reader?

INSIDE

Here are guidelines for using personal pronouns:

Use "you" in positive or neutral situations. Avoid "you" if it aggressively accuses the reader, puts the reader down, or assumes how the reader will feel. Too much of "you" starts to sound like a hyperactive sales pitch. Too little of "you" makes the reader disappear between the lines of the letter. Avoid "I, we, us, our" if they draw unnecessary attention to you or your organization. Use moderation.

Choose (1) a letter or memo in your handbook and (2) one of the models you've gathered. In each, identify the pronouns and judge their effectiveness.

The Letter of Complaint

When you pay for someone else's work—whether a product or service—do you expect quality? If you don't get what you expect, what do you do? A well-worded complaint letter just might solve the problem.

READ & REACT: When you write a complaint letter, you have to build a persuasive argument in order to get satisfaction and resolve your problem. Read "The Letter of Complaint," 197-198 in your handbook. Then work through the following:

1. Based on what you have read, explain what a letter of complaint must do.

2. Why would you choose to write a letter of complaint rather than speak to a person?

3. A complaint letter focuses on (1) a problem and (2) a solution. If that's the case, what is your purpose for writing? What can you do to make your letter successful?

4. If you worked at the Shoe Company, how would you respond to Mark Hammons' letter (198)? Why?

INSIDE info

Complaint messages seek to solve problems when something goes wrong. When things go well, however, you may want to respond with a thank-you message. (See 200-201 in your handbook.)

DRAFT & SHARE: Are the aisles in the grocery store too narrow? Do people in your neighborhood ignore recycling rules? Think about home, school, work, and public situations. Pick something that bugs you and write a complaint letter to someone in authority. But don't whine!

When you're done, exchange your letter for a classmate's. How convincing are the arguments?

READ, REACT, & REVISE: With two classmates, read the text of the letter below and answer the questions that follow. Then revise the message on your own paper.

Mr. Reynolds!

I am upset and I demand that you act, now! I've just returned from your store, yet again, having brought your incompetent repair staff my CD player for the same problem.

Would you put up with a CD player that doesn't work well? I bought it on good faith and resent now finding out that you care only about making the stupid sale, not about taking care of the customer afterward.

The first time I came in I was told there was nothing wrong with it and the problem must be my CD's. The second time, one of your sales staff tried to get me to buy a more expensive player. Mr. Reynolds, I am a student and can't afford a more expensive CD player. And now, the icing on the cake: I brought it in today for yet again the same problem and was told that my warranty had expired last week, and I'd have to pay for further repairs.

What are you going to do about it?

Sincerely,

Cicely Sandora

Cicely Sandora

1. Describe the tone of this letter. Circle words and phrases that communicate that tone. How do you think the reader of this letter would feel?

2. How much information does Cicely give about the problem? What facts and details support her complaint? What is her solution?

Writing Successful Complaints

Don't try to complain until you have all the facts and figures in front of you. Your success in getting what you want depends on your ability to build a strong, persuasive case.

ANALYZE: Use the following questions to make sure you have everything you need to write an effective letter of complaint.

1. **When** is it reasonable to write a complaint letter? Brainstorm a list of examples for each category below:

   Consumer products:

   Services:

   Situations within a company:

   Situations related to a house or an apartment:

2. **Whom** do you write to with your complaint?

3. **How** should you support your claim?

4. **What** should you ask for?

INSIDE

If you don't get a satisfactory response, send a second letter to the company and a copy to the Better Business Bureau, the Chamber of Commerce, a consumer advocacy group, or a consumer-action columnist for a local newspaper. This lets the company know that you are serious!

WRITE a complaint letter for one of the following situations. Before you write, list the information you need: the **transaction**, the **product** or **service**, the **problem**, any **attempted solutions**, the **solution** you want. Use the sample complaint letter form below to help you cover all the bases.

OPTION #1: You recently bought a product that turned out to be defective.

OPTION #2: You weren't satisfied with a repair or maintenance job done on some item you own (car, camera, dry cleaning, etc.).

OPTION #3: You have been poorly treated in a service situation (restaurant, store, bus, vacation resort, etc.).

OPTION #4: You have discovered a financial error on your bank or credit-card statement or on your paycheck.

Your address and the date
(3 lines)

Company name and address
(3 lines)

Attention: Customer Service Department

I am writing about (describe product, service, or event using specific dates and places).

The problem is (describe your problem briefly and any solutions you have tried). Enclosed you will find copies of (bills, receipts, canceled checks, warranties. etc.).

I would like (explain exactly what you would like to have happen). I look forward to hearing from you (add deadline, such as "in 30 days," or just say "soon").

Sincerely,

Signature

The Bad-News Letter

Break it to him gently. Walk a mile in her shoes. Bad-news messages can be hard on readers—creating frustration, anger, and disappointment. A poor message could have long-term side effects—hard feelings, lost business, a tarnished company reputation.

How do you soften the blow? Think about the bad news from the reader's point of view. Then give the FACTS, but do it with TACT.

DEFINE: Read the "Essay of Definition," 165-166 in your handbook, where Martina Lowry defines "tact." Then answer these questions:

1. What is tact?

2. What is at stake in matters of tact?

REACT: Read the bad-news message that follows. Circle words or sentences that lack tact.

BEETLES & BAILEY PUBLISHERS
55 HORNER AVE
NEW YORK, NY 10001

ACCOUNT # - 18845 | OUR ORDER # - 752869
FEBRUARY 2, 1996 | SALESPERSON 112

ATTENTION - DAVID BENTLEY

HAUNTED: TALES OF THE GROTESQUE 94 OATES ISBN 0-525-93655-6 IS OUT OF STOCK INDEFINITELY. YOUR ORDER FOR ONE COPY HAS BEEN CANCELED. NEXT TIME CHECK *BOOKS IN PRINT* BEFORE ORDERING. YOU WILL SAVE US TIME AND TROUBLE.

The Indirect Approach

Writing a good bad-news message involves more than a tactful tone. It involves using an indirect approach. In addition to the guidelines in your handbook (199), consider the following:

Buffer: When writing a buffer, communicate something you can agree on, an appreciation of the reader, or a statement of fact.

Reason: This section of the letter presents the logic behind the bad news. When writing the explanation, use clear and detailed business reasoning (don't get personal!) and simple explanations (avoid "it's our policy" statements).

Bad News: When writing the bad news, make sure it follows naturally from the explanation. Be tactful, but don't bury your refusal in double-talk. If possible, talk about what you can do rather than what you can't do.

Friendly Close: When writing a friendly close, avoid apologies and conclude with a statement of appreciation and the possibility of future business.

REACT: Read the bad-news messages below and on the next page. Label the buffer, reason, bad news, and friendly close in each.

BULLETIN

Date: 22 February 1996

To: Jefferson High Students

From: Jefferson High Student Council

Subject: Hours of School Dances

Your support of the monthly dances has shown fantastic school spirit. At its meeting last Wednesday, the council considered your suggestion to keep the dances open until 12:30 a.m.

The $3.00 admission you now pay covers the cost of the DJ and the maintenance staff. If dances were extended from 11:30 p.m. to 12:30 a.m., those costs would increase. Rather than make the dances too expensive for many students, the council decided to keep the cost low by keeping the current hours. Ending at 11:30 also gives you time to go out and eat after the dance and still be home by the 1:00 a.m. curfew time.

The next dance on April 24 will feature the DJ Rockin' Roadster. See you there!

Renae's Beauty Salon

TO: Stylists
FROM: Renae Alnot
DATE: April 1, 1996
SUBJECT: Professionalism

Thanks for your good work this quarter! I'm proud of how our clients look when they step out of our salon. You all have a great deal of hairdressing skill, and I'm impressed.

Of course, professionalism is more than just technical skill; it also includes a hairdresser's behavior and speech. Your training taught you that personality is 85 percent of this business, and, as you know, it's personality that attracts clients and keeps them.

Recently I noticed a client who arrived early for his appointment. His stylist flew in from the back room, whipped a brush through her own hair, and gave a big sigh. I could see that the client was somewhat uncomfortable with this behavior.

Our behavior, like our language, should always be professional. Remember that gray hair is *silver*. Hair is never frizzy but is sometimes *flyaway*. We don't pluck eyebrows (like farmers pluck chickens); we *tweeze* them.

During the coming busy months (Mother's Day, prom, graduation, and June weddings), let's do our best to demonstrate professionalism that will inspire our clients' respect.

ROLE-PLAY: Get some practice at being the bearer of bad news. Imagine that you are in a situation where you have to share some bad news with a friend or family member. With a group of classmates, role-play the situation and ask for feedback. Discuss whether or not it is easier to share bad news in person or in a letter.

WRITE: Now's the time to bite the bad-news bullet. Choose one of the options below and draft a bad-news message that both gives the bad news and keeps the reader's goodwill.

OPTION #1: You are a varsity basketball coach, and the janitorial staff has complained for the second time about the mess in the locker room after games. Address the problem in a bulletin written to the players and posted in the locker room.

OPTION #2: You are in charge of a large project for your company (landscaping, construction, office remodeling, new computer system installation). You are having problems getting the project finished successfully and/or finishing it on time. Write a letter to the client or a memo to your boss.

OPTION #3: You work in a sales division of a specific company. (Choose one you know.) You have the job of informing specific customers of a big change in one of your products or services (e.g., a 15 percent price increase or no more Saturday deliveries).

OPTION #4: You are the principal at your school. You have to let staff and students know that part of the school's program must be canceled because of budget cuts.

OPTION #5: You are an athlete, a musician, or an actor. (Choose someone you admire.) A nonprofit organization has written a very moving request for your participation in a fund-raising activity. Unfortunately, you can't accept. (You create the reason.)

OPTION #6: You are a loan officer in a bank. Amanda Powers has been late on every car payment and missed the last two entirely. Write a letter in which you tell her that she must change her ways and get and stay current with her loan, or her new car will be repossessed.

follow-up Have a classmate review your bad-news message to make sure it includes a buffer, an explanation, a bad-news statement, and a positive close. Ask this person if your letter seems both factual and tactful.

The Sales Letter

If your mailbox is like most people's, it usually has "junk mail" in it—sales letters and other ads trying to convince you to buy products or services. Some sales letters are "junk" because they present misleading or false information.

Tired of using a do-nothing shampoo? Get VIBRA-SCALP—the deep-penetrating gel that will make your bald spots grow thick hair in just two days!

Other sales letters promote good products, but the writers sound harsh, pushy, or manipulative.

Like a Rock Life Insurance is offering you an economical, whole-life policy that your family can't afford to live without! In fact, if you love your spouse or care about your children, you won't go to sleep tonight before calling and making an appointment.

However, a good sales letter—whether directed to a mass market or to one important customer—is neither tricky nor pushy. It promotes a product or service honestly by giving the reader enough information to make an informed choice.

Sales Letter

Think about your sales letter as a contract between you and the reader. Then write the "contract" so that it . . .

- offers true information—no exaggeration or misleading details
- presents well-organized information—allowing for a well-informed decision
- respects the reader—no slick tricks or emotional manipulation
- promises only what can be delivered
- states clearly how the reader may purchase the product or service
- informs the reader of the benefit he or she will receive
- tells the reader what action to take ("Call today" or "Send for . . .")

RESEARCH: Rescue some of your family's junk mail from the garbage and find three examples of sales letters. Bring the letters to class and rank them on the basis of the guidelines on the next page. Which of your letters is most effective? Why?

Sales-Letter Guidelines

Writing sales letters that people will read and respond to isn't easy. It requires the gentle art of persuasion. See "Persuasive Writing" (170-180) in your handbook. Read through the following guidelines.

Preparation: Before you begin to write a sales letter, you need to think about the general audience, the specific purpose of the letter, the facts about the product, and the needs of the reader.

- ☐ **1. Audience:** Who are you trying to reach?
- ☐ **2. Purpose:** What information do you need to communicate? What, if anything, does the reader already know about your product, and what does she or he need to know? What should be emphasized in this sales letter?
- ☐ **3. Facts:** What's it made of, and how is it made? How does it work? What is its impact on the environment? What are its features, its warranty, its maintenance requirements? How is it marketed, and what is its price? Who is the competition?
- ☐ **4. Need:** Why does the reader need your product or service? State how the reader may buy your product or service. Anticipate possible reader questions. Consider ways to make the reader's response as easy as possible. (To better understand needs, turn to "Human Needs and Communication," 401 in your handbook.)

Organization: Most sales letters follow an indirect method of organization. Many follow the AIDA pattern—Attention, Interest, Desire, Action.

- ☐ **1. Attention:** Get your reader's attention immediately. Use an imaginative first sentence. Ask a question. Present a fact. Make a startling statement. Tell a little story. Make readers an offer they can't refuse. Keep the opening short and relevant to your main selling point.
- ☐ **2. Interest and Desire:** Build up the reader's interest and desire. Describe the product or service in concrete details. Help the reader understand and appreciate the benefits. Support your claims with expert opinions, facts, statistics, and examples.
- ☐ **3. Action:** Encourage reader action. Clearly state what she or he must do to gain more information and purchase the product.

Style: Your writing style should reflect your product or service in the most positive light.

- ☐ **1. KISS (Keep It Short and Simple):** To create a friendly tone, use short sentences, bullets, short paragraphs, and words that you know your reader will understand.
- ☐ **2. Language:** Choose strong verbs. Avoid using too many adjectives and adverbs.
- ☐ **3. Visuals:** Select appropriate desktop-publishing options like boldface, typeface, print size, colors, arrows, photos, and other visuals. Avoid overpowering messages with special effects.

READ: Imagine that Valentine's Day is approaching, and you have received the following letter. Read it carefully. Would you buy this product?

Greensleeves Floral Expressions

401 Blooming Way
Portland, OR 97201-9978
1-800-546-LEAF

February 2, 1996

Dear Waterston College Student:

Did your biology professor ever tell you that plants can speak? Flowers can say at least a thousand words.

Sometimes it's hard for people to say how much they love, admire, or appreciate someone special. With Valentine's Day less than two weeks away, are you already at a loss for words?

This year, let flowers from Greensleeves speak for you. Roses, one or a dozen, speak the language of love in traditional red. An English garden bouquet in a glass vase expresses affection in cultured tones. Or choose a special Valentine arrangement in a porcelain keepsake vase.

Make Valentine's Day special for someone you love. Send flowers from Greensleeves. Enclosed you will find a full-color floral selection guide. Just phone in your order to 1-800-546-LEAF by February 13, and we guarantee fresh flowers delivered on Valentine's Day. Order by February 10, and you'll receive a 10 percent discount.

Let flowers help you start a conversation that could last a lifetime.

Yours sincerely,

Jeri Greensleeves

Jeri Greensleeves
Owner

P.S. As part of the telefloral network, we can deliver flowers anywhere in the world within 24 hours.

Writing Sales Letters

ANALYZE: Evaluate the letter of the previous page by answering the questions that follow.

1. **Preparation:** Review the four steps in preparing to write a sales letter. Does Jeri demonstrate that she has worked through these steps. How?

2. **Organization:** Is the letter effectively organized? Label the letter's parts, using AIDA.

3. **Style:** Is the style positive, professional, and effective? Why or why not?

WRITE: Use the sales-letter guidelines to write a sales message—one that helps the reader make an informed decision—for one of the following situations. Make up necessary details.

OPTION #1: Imagine that you, a student, are running your own small business (lawn care, tutoring, etc.). Write a sales letter to potential customers.

OPTION #2: Research a specific consumer product using product catalogs, visits to stores, or a magazine such as *Consumer Reports*. Based on your research, draft a sales letter to a well-defined group of potential customers.

OPTION #3: Write a sales letter using one of the following handbook models as the context.

- You are a public-relations writer for the Utah Jazz. (See 194.) Write a letter to high-school basketball coaches in Utah promoting a new "team-trip package" that the Jazz is offering to state high schools.
- You are Sam of Sam's Slickprint in the "Model Proposal" (226) written by Donna Kao. Write a T-shirt sales letter to be sent to several organizations whose employees or volunteers are frequently in the public eye.
- You are Sandi Walker in Eric Rowe's "Model Short Report" (228-229). With the help of Hobart's police, you've put together a rollerblading and bike safety class for kids. Write a letter to your town's parents encouraging enrollment in the course.

The Special-Request Letter

Like an inquiry letter, the special-request letter asks the reader for something. But the inquiry asks for something simple (like information on travel packages to Tahiti), whereas the special request makes bigger demands on the reader's resources (like a contribution to a fund-raising campaign or a request to be a guest speaker).

Like a sales letter, the special request must be persuasive. But the sales letter tries to sell a product or service, whereas the special request promotes a cause. The writer must appeal to something other than the reader's need for a product or service.

ORGANIZE: Like most correspondence, the special request follows a three-part structure—situation, explanation, action.

1. **Situation:** Capture the reader's attention and interest in a short paragraph that connects your cause with the reader.

2. **Explanation:** In the body of the letter, construct your argument. Make the case for your request using appeals (logical and emotional) that will touch your reader. Deal with obstacles that your reader would raise. Help him or her make an informed decision.

3. **Action:** Make your request in specific terms—clear, reasonable, as easy to fulfill as possible.

READ & WRITE: Read the special-request letter on the next page. Label the three parts mentioned above—situation, explanation, and action. Then choose one of the situations below and draft your own special request letter. But first think carefully about the following:

- **Who** is my reader?
- **What** do I want her or him to do?
- **What** motivates her or him?
- **Why** may she or he not want to support my cause?

OPTION #1: Think of a club or activity that you participate in. Who would be a knock-your-socks-off speaker for this organization?

OPTION #2: You need a free, safe site for an all-night after-prom party. Write to the director of the recreation center of a local college asking for permission to use the center for this worthy cause.

OPTION #3: You are on a school committee in charge of raising funds for a charity adopted by the school. Invite local people to a charity event (dance, basketball tournament, wacky olympics, etc.).

City Water Department
368 Main Street
Dustbowl, Nevada 89403-4365

April 25, 1996

Dear Homeowner:

Did you know that one-third of the water we use in Dustbowl during the summer goes to water lawns and other plants? That's a lot of water just to keep things green!

Summertime watering puts tremendous stress on the city's water supply. All of us need to conserve water so that costs stay low and the water-system work continues efficiently. Here are some ways you can help:

1. Aerate your lawn every year or two. Aeration loosens soil and reduces compaction so that more water can reach plant roots.
2. Mulch your lawn or use a mulching lawn mower. Mulch keeps moisture in the soil, protects plants during the winter, and reduces moisture loss during the summer.
3. Replace part of your lawn with a different ground cover, such as rosemary, lavender, periwinkle, or ivy. These attractive plants spread naturally along the ground and require less moisture.
4. Water early in the morning, the coolest part of the day, to reduce evaporation.
5. Water efficiently. Use a sprinkler that sends large drops of water close to the ground. Those that send small drops high in the air waste a lot of water through evaporation.

If everyone follows this commonsense advice, Dustbowl will remain an attractive town while we conserve water.

Sincerely,

Priscilla Precipitant

Priscilla Precipitant
Water Department Manager

Writing to Get a Job

Applying for a Job

Unless you are independently wealthy and can lead a life of leisure, you'll need to spend time and energy searching for a satisfying job. Sooner or later you will be looking for a part-time job while you attend a technical school or college. Or perhaps you'll be looking for your first full-time job. In either case, you'll need to gather information efficiently, fill out forms correctly, and compose convincing letters and résumés.

READ & REACT: Read "Filling Out Forms" (204) in the handbook and answer the questions below.

1. Why should you fill in all designated blanks on an application form, even if it's with an N/A (for "not applicable")?

2. What should you do with areas labeled "For Office Use Only"?

3. What ink colors are acceptable for an application form?

READ & REACT: Turn to "The Résumé" (206-207) in your handbook. Answer the following questions.

1. What are the six parts of a résumé?

2. What is the purpose of a résumé?

3. What should you include under "work experience" in your résumé?

4. What sorts of information should you include under "achievements"?

5. What is the purpose of the job objective in your résumé?

6. What is the correct time order to use when organizing work experiences and education in your résumé?

READ & REACT: Check out "The Letter of Application" (208-209) in your handbook. Then answer the following questions.

1. What is the purpose of a letter of application?

2. Name one way that you can focus on the employer's needs in your application letter.

3. What should you do in the conclusion to an application letter?

INSIDE

How important are neat, error-free résumés and letters? Very! Employers receive piles of letters and résumés, and a messy or error-filled paper is likely to end up in the wastebasket. That's why proofreading is so important. Ask someone who is a good proofreader to double-check your work. Often a second pair of eyes will see what your eyes missed.

Preparing to Apply for a Job

RESEARCH: Choose two of the following activities, research them thoroughly, and draft your answers on a separate sheet of paper. Share your answers with the rest of the class.

1. Visit local businesses and collect at least five different application forms. Review the forms. Make a list of the types of information employers request.

2. Talk with teachers or other individuals (coaches, clergy, employers) who have acted as references for students. Ask them what information they need in order to write a good reference.

3. Gather résumés from friends, family members, and library books that contain model résumés. Topic number 206 in your handbook says that a résumé is a "vivid word picture." What word picture is created in each résumé?

4. Collect job ads from newspapers or journals. Choose six ads and analyze them carefully. List one quality from each ad that these employers are looking for.

5. Interview someone who has been on a successful job hunt in the last year or two. Ask him or her for advice and tips on the application process. Then write a summary of the best advice.

6. Interview a job recruiter, personnel manager, or business owner about what she or he looks for on application forms as well as in résumés and application letters.

7. With a group of your classmates, brainstorm and jot down a list of possible employers in your area.

8. Often the best way to get a job is through networking—letting as many people as possible know that you are job hunting. List several working people that you could contact about employment possibilities. Remember, while these people may not have opportunities in their own companies or businesses, they may refer you to others who do.

follow-up In small groups, share your plans (even if you're not completely sure yet) following graduation. What will be your first step? Will you find a summer job or look for a full-time, permanent job? Have you made plans for job training, an apprenticeship, technical or training school, or college? What steps have you taken and what steps do you need to take? Sometimes talking out loud to someone helps to jump-start your thinking and planning.

Analyzing Your Strengths and Skills

Before you decide what you want to do on the job front, it's a good idea to take an inventory of your personal traits.

RESPOND: You may not realize how many positive qualities and strengths you already have. Look at the list of words that follows and mark each one on a scale of 1-5, according to how often, in appropriate circumstances, you demonstrate a particular quality.

1. = never
2. = occasionally
3. = sometimes
4. = often
5. = usually

_____ Creative
_____ Quick thinking
_____ Adaptable
_____ Clever
_____ Practical
_____ Realistic
_____ Strong
_____ Grace under pressure
_____ Team player
_____ Problem solver
_____ Fast working
_____ Friendly
_____ Diplomatic (Tactful)
_____ Honest
_____ Gracious
_____ Hard working
_____ Independent

_____ Curious
_____ Self-starting
_____ Deep thinker
_____ Careful
_____ Patient
_____ Objective
_____ Balanced
_____ Good with numbers
_____ Good with tools
_____ Good with machines
_____ Good with people
_____ Good with words
_____ Healthy
_____ Active
_____ Energetic
_____ Resourceful
_____ Motivated

_____ Punctual
_____ Innovative
_____ Steady
_____ Secure
_____ Detail oriented
_____ Sense of humor
_____ Risk-taker
_____ Cheerful
_____ Kind
_____ Reliable
_____ Loyal
_____ Tolerant
_____ Polite
_____ Ambitious
_____ Efficient
_____ Flexible
_____ Organized

Assessing Your Skills and Career Goals

Think about who you are and what you'd like to do with your life. A job should use as many parts of you as possible—your personality strengths, your skills and interests, as well as your education and experience.

REFLECT: Choose five of your "5's" from the previous page and list some of the ways you have demonstrated these qualities in school, in extracurricular activities and sports, doing volunteer work, working, participating in clubs and community organizations (including religious organizations), and in your family and neighborhood.

1.

2.

3.

4.

5.

WRITE: Describe your ideal next job. Be realistic, but don't be afraid to stretch your expectations. Think about the following:

- who you are, what you enjoy, and how you relate to others
- skills you have learned, are learning, and want to learn
- special knowledge you've gained in school, internships, jobs, extracurricular activities, sports, and volunteer work
- the workplace types you would enjoy—structured or informal, individual or teamwork, indoor or outdoor setting, physical work or office work, small business, large corporation, etc.
- your immediate needs and goals and your long-term goals

Writing Résumés

READ & REACT: Review "The Résumé," 206-207 in your handbook. Then read Justin Lark's résumé below and answer the questions that follow.

JUSTIN LARK

21 Larkspur Lane NW, Salem, Oreg. 362-3601
internet address available

JOB OBJECTIVE: internship in a BIG company with lots of opportunities for me to do different stuff.

EXPERIENCE:
Sept. 94-now. Computer Service Assistant, Simpson Tech. Collage. Do alot of repair and installation.

Summer of 93. Student agricultural technician, Ridgetown Collage. Farm work.

Feb-August 92. Diesel Injector Mechanic, Portland Fuel Injection, Portland. Worked with fuel injectors and pumps.

EDUCATION:
Simpson Tech. Collage, 1993-95. I'm into computers and I've got a good gpa overall but I'm doing better in my major. I've taken alot of courses like Programming, Database, information Systems, and Computer Technology courses and I reaally enjoy it. Some business courses. I know alot of language. I graduated from h.s. 2 years ago.

PERSONAL INFO:
Simpson Tech Collage Computer Club member, windsurfing; born 9/20/75. I haven't got any health problems, but I'd rather not work too early in the morning.

REACT: Answer the following questions and support your ideas by citing examples in Justin's résumé.

1. What does Justin Lark's résumé communicate to an employer?

2. Describe Justin's skills and knowledge according to the résumé.

3. Based solely on the résumé, what kind of worker do you think Justin would be?

4. Evaluate the résumé in terms of organization and content.

5. How good a job has Justin done in communicating specific information that would be helpful to a potential employer? Explain.

6. How would you describe the level of language or tone that Justin uses? Why is this not an appropriate tone?

7. How could Justin improve the form of his résumé?

8. Has Justin's résumé been carefully proofread? Give specific examples.

REVISE: Once you have checked Justin's résumé, revise it with a partner. Create and add any details you think are necessary.

Organizing Your Résumé

How do you organize information about yourself on a résumé so that it shows your abilities? You have three choices—chronological, functional, or a combination of the two.

- A **chronological résumé** lists work experience and education from most recent to earliest—now to then. (See 207 in your handbook for an example.) Chronological organization works best when your work history is strong—when you've worked at good companies, progressed well, and stuck to a single career path. For someone who is starting out, a chronological résumé may not be best.
- A **functional résumé** places skills and achievements in categories, regardless of where or when you picked up those skills. (See pages 125-126.) Functional organization is most effective when work experience for a specific career is not your greatest selling point:
  - when you are entering a career or have been out of the job market for a while
  - when you've had jobs that aren't closely related to each other
  - when you want to stress skills you haven't used in a recent job
- A **combination résumé** mixes features of both chronological and functional résumés. It usually presents work experience in chronological order but spotlights skills as a functional résumé does.

READ & REACT: Look at the lists of basic competencies in the handbook, 450. Evaluate yourself according to skills you have and skills you'd like to develop. Use a 1 to 5 scale with "1" being "little skill or interest" and "5" being "highly skilled or interested in."

	Present	Future
• **technical skills** (needed for a particular job)	_____	_____
• **communication skills** (writing, speaking)	_____	_____
• **computer skills** (languages, programming, systems)	_____	_____
• **persuasive skills** (sales, public relations)	_____	_____
• **interpersonal skills** (working with or helping people)	_____	_____
• **organizational skills** (time, materials, people)	_____	_____
• **management skills** (leading and managing people, money, other resources)	_____	_____
• **problem-solving skills** (people, machines, systems, procedures)	_____	_____

REACT: Read the examples of résumés on the next two pages. Imagine that you are a potential employer. What would be your dominant impression of these two candidates on the basis of their résumés?

Arnetta Washington

Campus Address (until 6/1/96):
215 Tech Drive
Huntsville, AL 35801-3553
(205) 468-8890

Home Address:
14 King St.
Montgomery, AL 36101-9942
(334) 298-2449

Job Objective: To work as a surgical technician for a mid-sized hospital in the Southeast

Education: Vocational Diploma for Surgical Technician expected in June 1996 from Northern Alabama Technical College, Huntsville, Alabama.

Taking and have completed courses in Medical Terminology, Human Body Structure and Functions, Functional Microbiology, Operating Room Procedures and Functions, Social Behavior. g.p.a. 3.2

Surgical Technician Skills:
- Take patient history
- Perform blood pressure and weight maintenance
- Perform room set-up and cleaning
- Write requisitions for laboratory and surgical specimens

Organizational Skills:
- Schedule patient appointments
- File patient history and insurance
- Organize office laboratory for efficiency
- Pay attention to details and follow procedures accurately
- Work with computers and documentation

Communication Skills:
- Handle telephone calls with courtesy and efficiency
- Work well on a team
- Write clear and concise letters and memos

Achievements and Activities:
- CPR certification — July 1995
- Boys and Girls Club volunteer from 1993 to present

Work History:

1992 to present	Office manager to Dr. Karen Johnson, Family Practice, Huntsville, Alabama
1990 - 1992	Finisher Packer, Continental Can Corporation, Montgomery, Alabama. Visually inspected bottles and packed for shipping.

References available upon request.

Thomas Sprague

Campus Address (until 6/1/96):
Box 239
Central Technical College
Bangor, ME 04401-0245
(207) 567-4321

Home Address:
1145 4500 St.
Belfast, ME 04915-6675
(207) 732-6125

Job Target:

To work as a production-line welder for a modern manufacturer in the Northeast.

Education:

Welding and Maintenance Fabrication Diploma expected June 1996 from Central Technical College, Bangor, Maine. Current g.p.a. 3.8

Welding Skills:

Perform Gas, Mig, Tig, and Stick Ark welding
Perform a variety of machine operations

Communication Skills:

Work well on teams; encourage others to give their points of view
Compose clear, problem-solving reports and proposals

Leadership, Quality, and Training Achievements:

Assisted management with work-safety program
Completed total quality control program
Served as team leader for company problem-solving groups
Served as team leader for total-loss control group
Completed cost-analysis data for company projects
Completed time-saving techniques class
Completed CPR training

Community Outreach:

Two years on Belfast Volunteer Fire Department 1993-95
Red Cross volunteer since 1992

Work History:

Finisher/Packer Utility. East Coast Cannery, Belfast, Maine	9/93 - 8/95
Machine Operator. HiLiter Graphics, Belfast, Maine	5/90 - 9/93
AB Dick 360 offset press and ITEK 430 camera	

References available upon request.

Planning Your Résumé

Using what you've learned about types of résumés and your skills, it's time to draft or update your own résumé.

PLAN: Work through the following steps to pull together all the information you need. Be sure to jot down dates and places for all jobs and education.

1. **Job Objective:** A "Job Objective" is not an absolutely necessary part of a résumé, but it can help you focus your search. One way to write a simple job objective is to personalize the following model.

   Example: To work as a (job title) for a (type of company) in the (area of the country)

   Your turn: To work as a ______________________________ for a ______________________ in the ______________________

2. **Skills:** Include technical skills as well as communication, leadership, and organizational skills. Emphasize business, computer, and industrial-arts skills.

3. **Work History:** List the work experience you have, starting with your most recent job.

4. **Achievements:** Include volunteer and community work (including all positions of responsibility), awards, and certification programs.

5. **References:** Even though you'll probably want to write, "References available upon request" on your résumé, and not list names, you should have in mind two or three people who might be willing to write a reference or answer a telephone call from someone requesting information about you. List names of references you might ask.

DRAFT, REVISE, & SHARE: There's no great mystery to résumé writing. The next two pages contain formats for types of résumés. Use one or the other of these worksheets (feel free to modify), write in the information you've gathered on this page, and "play" with the page until it looks good. Proofread carefully and exchange papers within a small group of your classmates for feedback on content and appearance. Prepare a final draft.

Chronological Résumé Worksheet

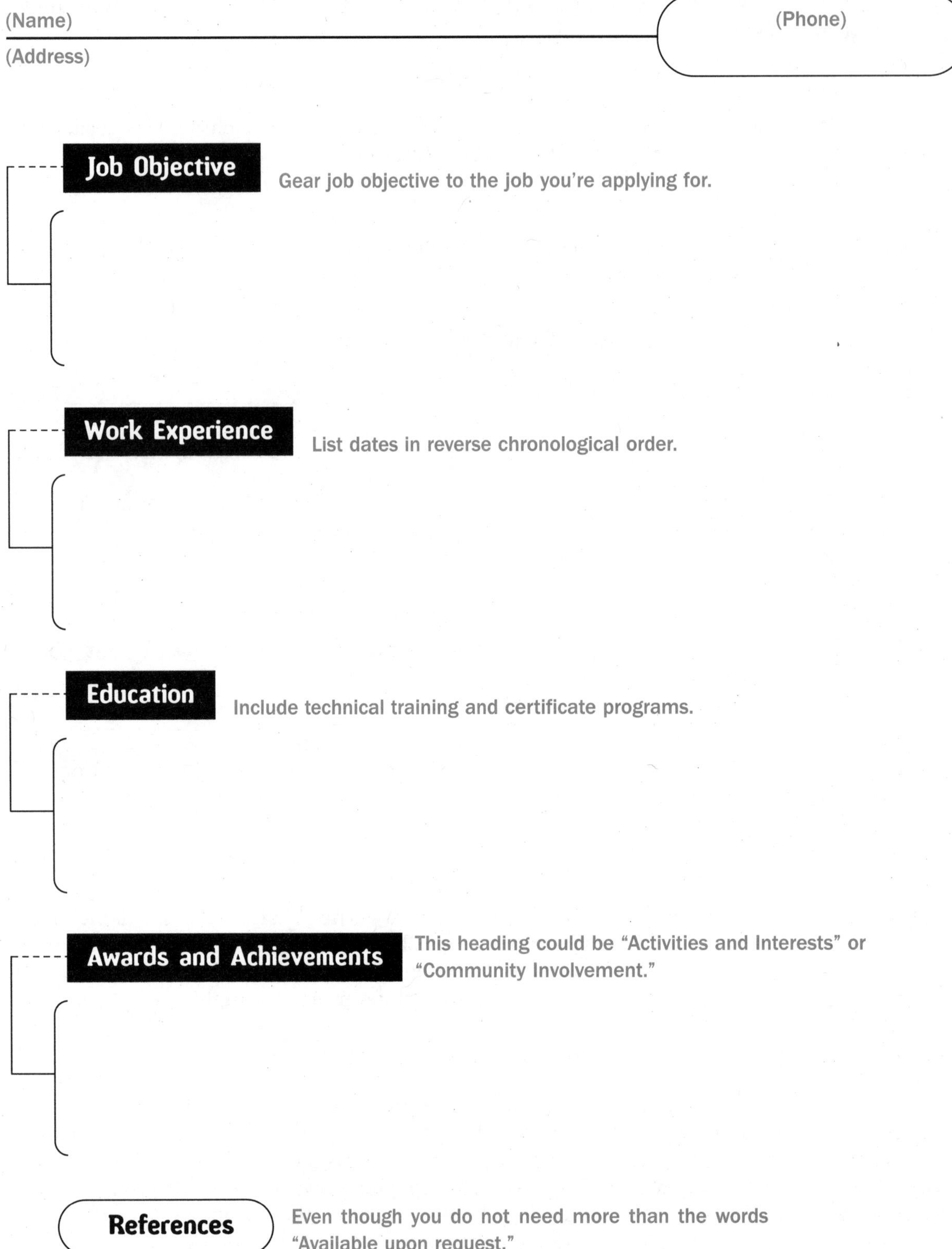

Functional Résumé Worksheet

(Permanent Address)

(Name & *Phone Number)

(Temporary Address)

*Very Important

Objective

Keep it short and simple.

Education

These two headings can be reversed if your skills are particularly strong.

Skills

Highlight special skills no matter where you learned them.

Achievements

Mention anything that relates to your career goals.

Work Experience

Use parallel structure in this and the three previous sections.

***References**

You do not need the names here, just the three words "Available upon request."

***Although you do not need to list the names here, have some ready.**

Writing Letters of Application

A good application letter builds a bridge between you and an employer—a bridge that helps you get an interview. An application (or cover) letter is written in response to an actual job opening. An inquiry letter is written "cold" to a company or employer. Whichever option you choose, remember that the letter's purpose is to sell yourself.

1. **Application Letter or Cover Letter:** This letter is written in response to an ad or a lead about a job opening. In it, you give a summary of your qualifications. An application letter may or may not include a résumé. (If it includes a résumé, the letter is often shorter and is usually called a cover letter.)

2. **Inquiry Letter:** In this letter, you write to a company, ask about possible openings, and perhaps submit your résumé. In this case, you are initiating the contact, not responding to an ad in the paper.

3. **Money Matters:** Some jobs ads will ask for your "salary history" or "salary requirements." Beware! Experienced job seekers say that you should never divulge salary history or requirements in an application letter. Simply saying "salary is negotiable" is sufficient.

DRAFT: Review "The Letter of Application" (208-209) in your handbook. Then imagine that you are either Arnetta Washington or Thomas Sprague in the résumés on pages 125 and 126 in your SourceBook. You want to apply for one of the jobs in the ads below. On a separate piece of paper, draft an application letter based on the information in the résumé and the ad.

Surgical Technicians

Montgomery Regional Medical Center, a 500-bed community hospital, is seeking full-time and part-time surgical technicians. Our surgical services consist of general, open heart, and several specialties. Candidates must have a degree and certification from a surgical technologist program, knowledge of standard operating room practices, and good communication skills. Duties include assisting operating room team by preparing surgical supplies and equipment, passing proper supplies and equipment to surgeon, maintaining sterile field, post-surgery clean-up. Competitive wages and benefits. Send résumé to:

Human Resources Department
Montgomery Regional
Medical Center
333 Healthway Dr.
Montgomery, AL 36101-3367

FABRICATION WELDER WANTED

Leading food processing and packaging equipment manufacturer is seeking full-time fabrication welder. FoodTech develops, fabricates, and installs equipment for the food industry, specializing in fish processing plants. You will set up and weld a variety of stainless steel and aluminum parts to close tolerances. Candidate must have technical school training and be able to read blueprints, set-up/operate machines, perform MIG/TIG, build specialized equipment from the ground up. We offer a competitive salary with comprehensive benefits. Mail résumé to:

FoodTech, Box 552,
Roe Industrial Park,
Bangor, ME 04915-2911

WRITE: Refer to your own résumé and draft an application, cover, or inquiry letter on your own paper for one of the following situations:

1. Find an ad for a part-time or summer job and write an application letter for the position. For help, see #1 on the previous page or 209 in your handbook.

2. Find an ad for an entry-level job (connected with your career field, if possible) and write a cover letter to go along with your résumé.

3. Think of a local business you could work for and write an inquiry letter concerning job or internship opportunities.

SHARE: Bring both the ads and letters to class. Learn as much as you can about each from the comments of your classmates.

INSIDE

The standard opening in an application letter states the job title and the source of knowledge (newspaper, journal, name of individual) about the opening. For an introduction with more punch, research the company and refer to it (its products, services, philosophy, reputation, etc.) in the first paragraph.

Requesting References or Recommendations

When you apply for a job, you usually need references or recommendations to back you up. A courteous and clear request letter will help you get the backup support you need.

READ & BRAINSTORM: Review "The Request Letter" (205) in your handbook. Note the organization and tone of this letter, as well as the information it includes. Then brainstorm a list of three people who could act as references for you. (Remember that the best references are teachers and employers, not friends or family.) Why would these people make good references? Jot down a few reasons why each person would be a good reference for you.

1.

2.

3.

DRAFT: Using your list of possible references, draft three request letters. The references or recommendation letters that you request may be for a job, college application, or internship.

INSIDE

Here are two tips to make your request easier:

1. Don't be afraid to ask a teacher for a reference. Most teachers consider it an important part of their jobs.
2. Make the recommendation writer's job easier by giving him or her a copy of your résumé, your career plan (if you have one) or a few sentences about your goals, and a copy of the job ad or program description.

Interviewing for a Job

Though there is no way to know exactly what an interviewer might ask you, there are some frequently asked questions. Practicing your answers to these questions will help you prepare for the interview.

ROLE-PLAY: In teams or small groups, take turns answering and giving feedback to each other, using the following commonly asked interview questions:

1. Can you tell me something about yourself?
2. Why are you leaving your present job (or why did you leave your last job)?
3. What have you accomplished that gives you the greatest satisfaction?
4. Why should I hire you?
5. What are your strengths? Your weaknesses?
6. What subjects in school did you like best? Why?
7. Why do you want this job?
8. How do you feel about overtime work?
9. Are you willing to spend at least six months as a trainee?
10. What are your long-term goals?
11. What kind of work environment makes you most comfortable?
12. How do you work under pressure?
13. How would you define success?
14. What do you know about this organization?
15. How would you describe yourself to another person?
16. What motivates you to do your best?
17. What are your salary/wage requirements?
18. What computer software are you familiar with?

Writing Follow-Up Letters

In a job interview (210 in your handbook) you get a good shot at convincing an employer that you match the job. So why write a follow-up letter? A letter can do the following:

- show the employer that you're interested in the job
- remind the interviewer who you are
- show professional courtesy

ANALYZE: How do you write a good follow-up letter? Give yourself a chance after the interview to follow these steps.

1. Soon after an interview, review and record what happened.
    - What questions did the interviewer ask you, and how did you answer?
    - What did you ask, and what answers were you given?
    - What did you learn about the position, the interviewer, and the company?

2. Based on your review of the interview, think about details that could go into your letter.
    - Should you emphasize anything that you communicated earlier?
    - Should you communicate any new information?
    - What details could be the focus of your message?

3. Draft the letter so that it fits your interview. Avoid writing a form letter.
    - Show that the interview reinforced your interest in the position (if it did!).
    - Show that you were attentive during the interview.
    - Avoid referring to what you thought was a problem in the interview.
    - Focus on the contribution you could make to this company in this position—demonstrate a "team" attitude.

DRAFT: With a classmate, work through the activities below to draft a follow-up letter:

1. What is an activity that you excel at or could excel at? Could you be the official class clown, someone's best friend, the dissection expert in biology class? Do you want to star in the class play or be the treasurer of the Investing for Fun and Profit Club? Pick something.

2. Now get your partner to interview you for this "position." (Check out "Conducting Interviews," 341-344 in your handbook.)

3. Based on the interview, write a follow-up letter to your interviewing partner.

Writing Job Acceptance Letters

Being offered a job you want feels great. A good acceptance letter is not only a professional way to begin your new position, but it also puts into writing the terms of your employment as you understand them. This can be helpful if a misunderstanding arises later.

READ & RESPOND: Turn to "Accepting a Job Offer," 212 in your handbook. Read the guidelines and model letter. Then respond to the following:

1. What message does a good acceptance letter send to the employer?

2. What is the main point of Jack Delaney's acceptance letter?

3. List five details that Jack includes in the body of the letter.

4. What does Jack's attention to detail say to the reader?

DRAFT: In the follow-up letter activity on the previous page, a partner interviewed you for a "position." Imagine you've been offered that position. Draft an enthusiastic acceptance letter.

Writing Job Refusal Letters

For some reason or another, you may be offered a job that you can't accept—because you get another, more attractive offer, or because you realize that the job wouldn't work for you or the employer. What do you do? Blow it off and turn your attention to more interesting offers?

Never burn your bridges behind you! Write a job refusal letter. A good refusal letter, like all bad-news letters (199 in your handbook), tells the truth tactfully. By doing so, you do the following:

- behave professionally and politely
- demonstrate that your interest in the job was sincere
- keep the employer's goodwill (which just might come in handy in the future)

A good refusal letter contains the following:

1. a neutral but relevant opening statement, such as a thank you
2. a clear, exact, polite explanation of why you are turning down the job offer
3. a final statement of appreciation and goodwill

READ & RESPOND: Read Jack Delaney's refusal letter on the next page and respond to the following:

1. Locate the actual bad-news refusal statement. How does Jack state the refusal politely?

2. How does the letter build up to the refusal?

3. What follows the refusal?

806 E. Seventh St.
Del Rio, TX 78003-3667
23 February 1995

Ms. Ruby Villanueva
Director of Personnel
Del Rio Community Clinic and Hospital
400 Valley Rd.
Del Rio, TX 78003-7829

Dear Ms. Villanueva:

Thank you for offering me the position of registered nurse in the obstetrics unit at Del Rio. I appreciate your confidence in me.

Two of the factors that I weighed in my decision were the institution's size and the public it serves. For these reasons I've decided not to accept your attractive offer. Instead, I've accepted a position at a small, inner-city clinic in Houston where the nursing needs are more pressing.

I enjoyed the opportunity to meet you and become familiar with Del Rio. Best wishes in your search to fill the position.

Yours sincerely,

Jack Delaney

Jack Delaney

follow-up Imagine again that you were offered the job you accepted on page 135 but this time draft a refusal letter.

Writing on the Job

Writing Instructions and Procedures

Well-written instructions always pass the CCO test—they're Clear, Complete, and Organized. When instructions pass that test, you and I find it easier to

- program a watch,
- learn a computer program,
- find a destination,
- set an electronic flash for a camera,
- log on to a library computer terminal,
- make a deposit with an automated bank teller,
- program a VCR,
- install a smoke detector,
- assemble a new modular desk, and
- do hundreds of other things at school, home, and work.

REVIEW: Parallel structure helps make instructions and procedures clear (see 101 in your handbook). All parts of a sentence that have parallel meanings should be parallel in structure. Rewrite the following instructions so that all the lettered items are parallel. (Some items are OK as written.)

1. Major steps to take in applying for a job seen in the newspaper:

a. write or phone the potential employer
b. setting up an appointment
c. update of your résumé

2. To assemble this table, take these steps:

a. attach top to legs
b. installing privacy panels
c. you should attach the shelves
d. adjust floor levelers

3. Before our next meeting, please do the following:

a. meet with your committee
b. a summary of your recommendations
c. complete the enclosed survey
d. mailing it back to me so I can make lunch reservations

4. To prevent your bike from being stolen, do these things:

a. a record of its serial number
b. you should register your bike with the local police
c. buying a lock that can't be cut by bolt cutters and saws
d. use your lock

follow-up Find a written set of instructions at home and bring it to class. Evaluate the instructions on the basis of the CCO (clear, complete, and organized) guidelines and the use of parallel structure. With a classmate, exchange instructions and compare the results of your evaluation.

READ the instructions that follow for opening the Sheeres County Library.

Procedure for Opening Sheeres County Library

Open the library by following the steps below. You will need six keys:

- your personal key for the front doors
- Allen key (in the key cupboard behind the circulation desk)
- workroom key (labeled and in the key cupboard)
- copy-machine key (labeled and in the key cupboard)
- cash-drawer key (labeled and in the workroom cabinet, second drawer from the left)
- book-drop key (labeled and in the key cupboard)

Materials needed are listed up front.

1. Unlock the front doors using your personal key and fasten the door latches open using the Allen key.
2. Unlock the workroom using the workroom key.
3. Shut off porch lights (switch is in the electrical panel behind the workroom door).
4. Turn on lights in the following areas:
   - main areas on the first and second floors (switches in the electrical panel)
   - reference room (switch on the east end of the south wall)
   - N-PT room (switch on the south end of the east wall)
   - Q-Z room (switch in the middle of the east wall)
5. Turn on the four copy machines using the copy-machine key. Open the door in front of each machine, turn the machine on, close and lock the door.
6. Unlock the cash drawer using the cash-drawer key.
7. Change dates on the two book stamps:
   - OUT—set two weeks ahead of current date
   - IN—set for the current date
8. Turn on PC's, printers, and terminals in the main area of the second floor.
9. Turn on the computer on the public-service desk and log in.
10. Open the book drop (using the book-drop key) and check in items.
11. Get daily newspapers from the book drop and place them on rods in the newspaper rack.
12. Return all keys to their proper places.

Numbers 1-12 give the steps in the process.

Small bullets highlight additional information when needed.

Using the instructions above as a model, write instructions on some process with which you're familiar: opening a workplace; operating a small hand tool; making pancakes, pies, or tacos; planting a tree; or changing a tire. Use parallel structure.

Writing Instructions

You know the old saying, "A picture is worth a thousand words." Look through the sections on diagrams in your handbook (512-515). Many instructions include diagrams that show as well as tell how something should be done. Picture diagrams and line diagrams can help you show how something is made or how it works. Another type of graphic that's often used with instructions is the flowchart. This kind of chart shows how the procedure should "flow" through time.

In business flowcharts, an oval usually stands for stop or start, a diamond stands for a decision, and a rectangle for an action.

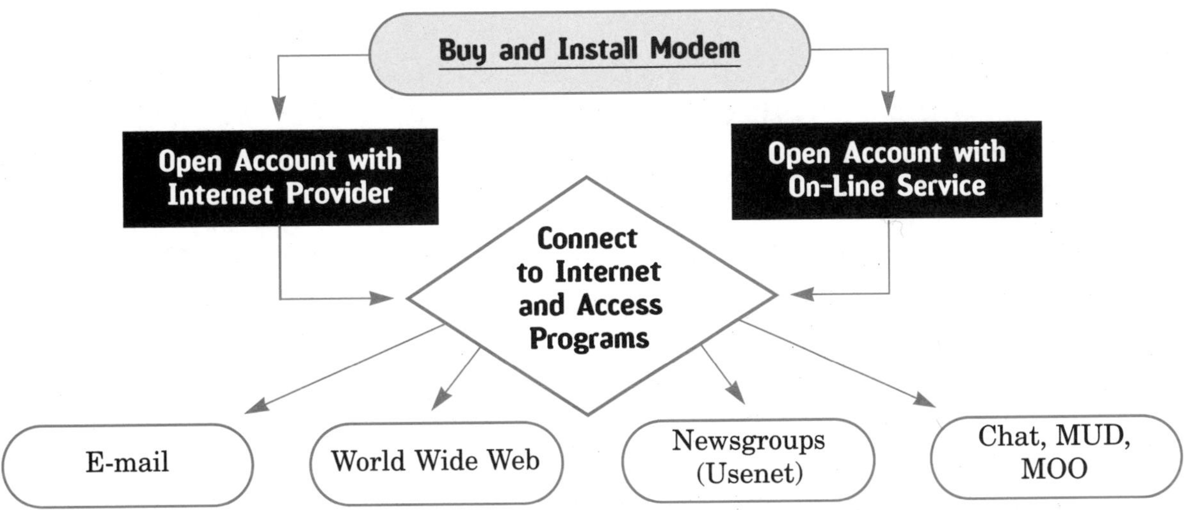

ILLUSTRATE a set of instructions. If you completed the challenge activity on the previous page, add a diagram or flowchart to your instructions. Or choose a different process that you know about and would like to teach to a classmate. Include diagrams or a flowchart that clearly lays out the process. If you can't think of a topic, consider the following:

Things that you've mastered

- how to "clip and paste" using your word-processing program
- how to get a ketchup stain out of a white shirt
- how to parallel park in one smooth sequence of actions

Things that you're trying to master

- how to ace a history (or physics or Spanish or electronics) test
- how to find an available and worthwhile internship
- how to find a job ad in the *New York Times* using the World Wide Web

Things in your own world that only you know how to do

- how to train your dog to pick up your dirty socks—and put them under the bed
- how to make a great late-night sandwich
- how to decorate your room so you're the only one who feels at home

Writing Summaries

Have you ever listened to a friend's five-minute description of a three-hour party, seen a 30-second TV ad about an upcoming program, read Cliffs Notes, or skimmed the book jacket of a novel? Then you know something about summaries. For more information, read "Writing Summaries" (220) in your handbook.

REFLECT: What kind of summary would you find in each of the following places, and what purpose does it serve?

1. Front page of a newspaper

- kind of summary

- purpose

2. TV magazine or guide

- kind of summary

- purpose

3. Opening pages in a textbook

- kind of summary

- purpose

4. A business meeting (*Hint:* See handbook topic 416 and note the first duty listed under "Secretary.")

- kind of summary

- purpose

5. A librarian's monthly newsletter describing new books

- kind of summary

- purpose

CHOOSE: Writing a good summary involves choosing the most important information in the original document and restating the information briefly. See "Summarizing a Document" (221) in your handbook. Summaries help readers get an overview, or the main points, without having to experience the whole. The first list below shows what to include, and the second shows what not to include in a summary.

Summarize	Do Not Summarize
purpose statement	opinions
main points	specific details
recommendations	explanations
outcomes	background information
conclusion	examples
	jargon

READ & REACT: Review the article "Suiting Up for Success" (223 in your handbook). Study what the writer includes and doesn't include and answer the following questions.

1. What is the purpose statement in this article?

2. What are the main points?

3. What is the conclusion?

A Closer Look

Park officials point sightseers toward their main attractions by using signs like "Holy Cow Hill—2 miles ahead" or "Turn right to Lotta-Water Falls." In a similar way, writers use "signs" (like the ones in the left column below) to point readers toward the main ideas in their writing. Learning to follow the signs will help you find the information that should be included in a summary.

CHOOSE: Match the letters on the right with the items on the left that help readers understand summaries.

1. .... opening paragraph
2. .... topic sentence (108 in your handbook)
3. .... graph or illustration
4. .... concluding paragraph
5. .... *similar to, on the other hand, furthermore*
6. .... *first, second, third*
7. .... *because, as a result, therefore*
8. .... *major, basic, crucial, significant*
9. .... *in conclusion, to summarize*

a. tells the subject of a paragraph and what the writer plans to say about it (Remember: Not all paragraphs have topic sentences.)

b. introduces a subject

c. words that show cause and effect

d. words that indicate an order of importance or chronological order

e. sums up the subject

f. words that compare, contrast, or link

g. words that introduce the ending

h. words that stress importance

i. visually shows what the words say

SUMMARIZE: Review the steps for writing a summary listed in your handbook (221) and note that the third step is "List the main ideas." Read Lisa Tebben's research paper (311-318) in your handbook. Use the "word signs" above to locate her main ideas. Highlight (on a photocopy) or list these main points, and then write a summary of her paper on a separate piece of paper. Compare your summary with your classmates'.

Find articles in newspapers or magazines related to dressing for job interviews. Write a summary of the best article you find. Collect summaries from your classmates and create a booklet for your class or school library called "Looking the Part: How to Create a Lasting First Impression."

Minutes Are Summaries, Too!

Have you or someone you know ever been in a meeting of an organization when some members started arguing about what had or had not been decided in a previous meeting? What happened? Most likely, the minutes from the previous meeting were pulled out and read. Minutes of a meeting summarize the main points of a meeting. They answer the who? what? when? where? why? and how? questions about that meeting.

- Where and when did the meeting take place?
- Who attended the meeting?
- What happened and in what order?
- How did the group decide, and how did it plan to implement the decisions?
- Why did the group make the decisions it made—what were its reasons?
- When does the group plan to implement the decisions it made?
- Where will the group's planned activities take place?
- Where and when is the next meeting?

READ: Check out the "Order of Business for a Meeting," 417 in your handbook, and look at item #3. Why do you think minutes have to be approved by the whole group, and why would they become an "official—and legal—record of the meeting"?

RESPOND: Read the minutes of the Horace Mann High School Student Council Meeting, 224 in your handbook. Then list ways that secretary Brian McCarthy answered the following questions:

Who attended the meeting (first names only), who contributed, and how?

When and **where** did the meeting take place?

What was planned, and **when** will it take place?

RESEARCH: With two or three classmates, attend a meeting of some business or nonprofit group in your community: the Lion's Club, city council, school board, a religious youth group, Amnesty International, farmers' co-op, Big Brother or Big Sister, neighborhood watch committee, recreation department, union meeting, or another choice. Do the following:

- Choose a group that interests you and your partners.
- Call the organization, explain why you would like to attend their meeting, and ask permission to do so.
- Talk with an officer of the group and discuss the organization:
  - What is the group's purpose?
  - How often does the group meet?
  - What kinds of things does it discuss, and how does it make its decisions?
  - Does the group keep minutes of its meetings? Why?
  - Has the accuracy of the minutes ever been challenged by a group member or by someone outside the group? What happened?
  - Have the minutes ever been used to settle a financial or legal dispute?
  - Request an agenda for the meeting.
  - Request that a copy of the secretary's minutes be sent to you after the meeting.
- Sit in on the meeting and take notes so you can write the minutes later.
- Prepare a set of minutes and compare it with those written by your partners.
- Compare your minutes with the set written by the group's secretary. What differences do you notice in the style and content? Which set is more accurate? Which is more complete? Why?
- Join other members of your group and report on your experience to the class. Show copies of each set of minutes as part of your report.

Writing Reports

Good short reports present accurate information carefully organized for specific readers. But what is information? And what's the best way to organize it?

ORGANIZE: Below is a list of five methods for organizing information and an example of each. Add one additional example to each item.

category—grouping things according to similarities and differences

example: newspaper—organized into sections such as national news, local news, business, sports, entertainment

your example:

time—arranging events in a time sequence, or chronologically

example: *TV Guide*—organizes TV schedule into time blocks

your example:

location—arranging according to spatial placement

example: a map—organizes geographic information on a grid

your example:

continuum—placing information in order of increasing or decreasing importance

example: credits at the end of a film

your example:

alphabet—ordering information by placing it in alphabetical order

example: a telephone book

your example:

REFLECT: Read Michelle's report on the next page. Which of the above methods of organization did she use in her report?

READ & REACT: Read "Defining Information" (319-320) in your handbook. What's the difference between information and data? Why is information more important than data to a report reader?

NORTHWEST PIPELINE CORPORATION
one of the WILLIAMS COMPANIES

DATE: 14 August 1996
To: Charlie Cameron, PASCO DOS department head
From: Michelle Angelo, PASCO CREW
Subject: Problems with Painting Equipment
Copy To: Ben Canvas

I'm writing this incident report to inform you of problems Ben and I have been having with our painting equipment. In the last month, the regulator on the large canister paint sprayer has failed three times while we worked on painting meter stations: July 16 at the Gordon Center station, August 4 at the Oka station, and August 13 at the Yakima station.

When the regulator fails, two things happen. First, the paint is pushed through the gun at a higher rate. Second, the force of the paint either creates a poorly painted surface or strips the nozzle off the gun. When the nozzle comes off, the paint sprays much farther and covers a wider area. During the last regulator failure, Ben was covered with paint before I could release the trigger and turn off the air compressor. Fortunately, he didn't get any paint in his eyes, nose, ears, or mouth.

The regulator failures have created the following problems:

- We are behind schedule by four days.
- The paint jobs at two of the meter stations need to be re-done.
- The Yakima station needs a cleanup project. Almost five gallons of paint escaped onto the gravel there.
- The cost of repeatedly fixing the regulator continues to build: each repair is about $25.00 in parts and labor.
- The safety code needs to be changed. Right now, we don't need to wear a respirator or goggles when not personally operating the sprayer. As the last incident shows, faulty equipment makes this unsafe.

In conclusion, repairing the regulator doesn't seem to be working. As a result, the sprayer is dangerous and wasteful to operate. I suggest that we check into purchasing a new sprayer or regulator. The cost would be made up quickly through savings on repairs, cleanup, and work hours.

If you have questions, need more information, or would like me to investigate the new equipment, please call me in truck number 1603, radio number 24538.

Understanding Reports

If a company is like a body, reports are the circulatory system. They carry food (information or messages) to the body parts that use it to do the body's work.

REFLECT: Reports provide people with information on a specific topic—information they want or need for a specific purpose. Who gives reports? We all do. Listed below are examples of some of the places where reports are made. After each example, list (a) one possible purpose of the report and (b) the types of information that might be included.

1. family members around the dinner table

- purpose
- information

2. TV evening news

- purpose
- information

3. utility company newsletter

- purpose
- information

The Short Report

READ: Review "Writing Short Reports" (227-229) in your handbook. With the guidelines and model in mind, read the model report on the previous page. Does Michelle's report demonstrate the five points under "Preparing the Report" (227)? Explore this question on your own paper. Also decide how Michelle's report answers the following "day-to-day" questions. If a question does not apply, write N/A.

1. How's it going?

2. What's finished?

3. What's left to be done?

4. What's the problem?

5. What's the solution?

Types of Business Reports

In business, short reports come in many types and serve many functions within a company. The major types are defined below.

incident: informs about and examines an accident; legal offense; danger; or problem with machines, delays, costs, production

investigative: researches an issue through experimentation, testing, inspections, interviews, reading, or other methods

periodic: provides information at regular time intervals so that products, services, and work can be tracked, planned, and adjusted

progress: reviews what has been done, what is currently being done, and what is left to do on a project

recommendation or proposal: presents, analyzes, and evaluates the variety of options available in a given situation, suggesting one option as the best

sales: provides a numerical record of products and services sold, company costs, profits, and losses

trip: informs about activities away from the company—field research, conventions, visits to customers and clients

Writing Your Own Short Business Report

IDENTIFY: Which of the above types of reports does each of the following situations call for? Write your answer in the space provided.

1. Keep a log of the work you do for one week during an internship, at school, or in a part-time job. At the end of the week, write a weekly work report on your activities.
   Type of Report:
2. Write a report on your house or apartment that tells how you are coming along with decorating, repairs, or improvements.
   Type of Report:
3. Write a report that suggests a possible site for holding the senior prom.
   Type of Report:
4. Write a report for your supervisor similar to Michelle Angelo's paint-sprayer report.
   Type of Report:
5. Report on the outcome of a fund-raising event in which you participated.
   Type of Report:

follow-up Choose one of the options and write a short report. Refer to "Writing Short Reports," (227-229) in your handbook.

Adding Headings and Other Organizers to Reports

Look at how headings, boldface, frequent paragraphs, and numbered steps are used in the model short report (228) in your handbook. Using these organizers will help make your report clear. Listed below are some common headings (there are many others you could use) that are used in business reports. The point to remember is that headings help you organize your report and help your reader understand it.

- **Introduction**
- **Overview**
- **Background Information**
- **Recommendations**
- **Statement of Purpose**
- **Advantages of ____________**
- **Disadvantages of ____________**
- **Action Requested**

Adding Graphics

Reports often include tables, graphs, charts, pictures, drawings, and diagrams. Review "Reading Charts and Graphs," 502-518 in your handbook. In addition to quickly explaining something in a chart, graph, or diagram that might take pages of words to explain (and might be harder to understand with words only), graphics add visual interest to your report. Look at the pages below for some possible ways to use graphics in a report.

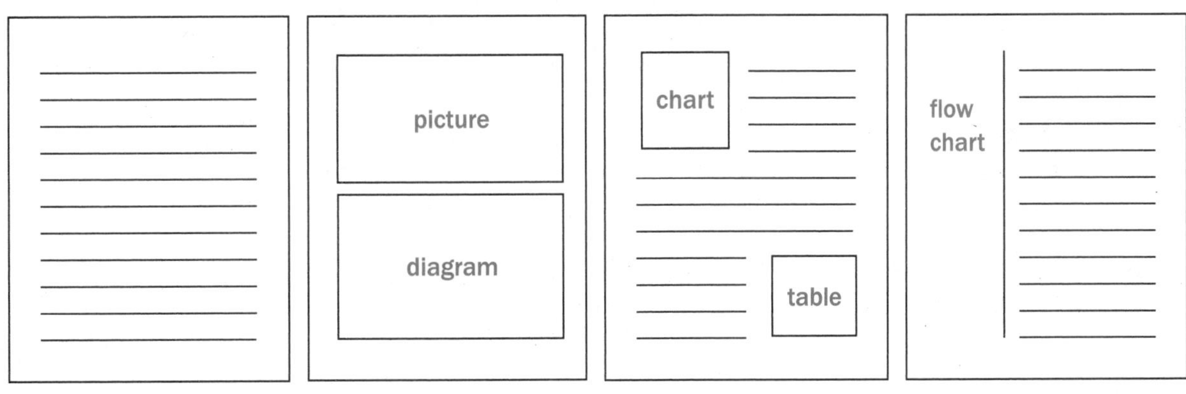

Page with no graphics — Page with no text — Page with two graphics — Page with flow chart

VISUALIZE: Add headings, boldface, frequent paragraphs, numbered steps, and graphics (if they apply) to the report you wrote on the previous page. Compare your new version with the one in which you used words only.

Writing Investigative Reports

So what's the scoop? Is research just for mad scientists and giant drug companies? Is investigation just for private eyes and overworked police detectives? The investigative report is a special report in which the writer digs up the facts for some purpose. In a way, the investigative report is the workplace version of the school research paper.

DEFINE: Turn to "What is information literacy?" (325) in your handbook and read the dialogue between James Pond and Stephanie Jerkyl. Then answer the following:

1. What does Stephanie learn from James Pond? Can you support his claims with examples from everyday life?

2. Define investigation. Use a dictionary, but also use what you know yourself and what you have learned from others.

BRAINSTORM: Below are two situations where research is needed. After each situation, list two examples of places or people that could help.

Everyday Life:

A couple expecting their first child shops around for the best high chair they can afford.

The Workplace:

An administrative assistant investigates hooking up her company's computers to the Internet.

Beginning with Key Questions

READ: Investigative reports always begin with questions that need answers. Turn to the "How do we work with information?" section of your handbook (326) and read through the next four pages, noting in particular the examples used in the "shoptalk" sections.

IMAGINE: Choose two of the following situations and, with a partner, brainstorm a list of key questions that the report writer needs to answer.

- A welder on a large construction job has injured his left leg. The site supervisor must report the incident.

- A marketing team investigates lagging sales for "Fleagone," a pill for dogs that helps control fleas.

- A medical clinic investigates patient requests for a midwife and home-birthing services.

- A scientist performs an environmental impact study on extending a road through a state forest.

- The Better Business Bureau investigates complaints about a restaurant's treatment of minorities.

Writing Your Own Investigative Report

CHOOSE one of the situations below and write an investigative report. Begin by reviewing "Writing Short Reports" (227) and "Discovering Information Pathways" (360) in your handbook. Make sure you work through the report-writing process fully:

- Brainstorm your key questions.
- Think about your report's purpose and reader.
- Consider your main topic's subtopics.
- Research your topic using the most appropriate methods.
- Make sense of your information.
- Draft the report using the most logical organization and outline.
- Get feedback. Revise and edit the report, being careful about documenting your sources.

OPTION #1: Investigate your options for postsecondary education (apprenticeship, tech college, etc.). Investigate methods of financing your education.

OPTION #2: Investigate volunteer opportunities in your neighborhood, town, or city. Try to find ones that connect with your career plans.

OPTION #3: You and your classmates are considering what personal computer to purchase for college use. What do you need and what can you afford?

OPTION #4: You will be moving out of your parents' house in a few months. Investigate housing options in the community you plan to live and work in.

OPTION #5: You need to buy insurance (car, health, renter's). Investigate your choices.

Writing Proposals

Change can be productive and positive—or downright aggravating. But how does change happen positively in the workplace? It happens through proposals—detailed plans that map out suggested changes. If proposals are creative, thoughtful, and well written, they can change the way things work—for the better.

READ & REACT: Check out the memo proposal below, written by a social worker. Discuss the changes the writer recommends and his attitude toward change.

Rivendell Services
Eugene, Oregon

Date: 10 August 1996
To: Mary Noresto, Director of Operations
From: Brad Brintley, Programs Supervisor
Subject: Promotion of Lisa Goodhands to full-time physical therapy aide

For the past two years, Lisa Goodhands has been an excellent member of the Programs team. I propose that she be promoted to a full-time position with the necessary $3.50 per hour wage increase plus full benefit package.

I recommend this promotion not just because of her exemplary work (most recent evaluation report attached), but because of anticipated needs at Rivendell.

1. In the past two weeks, Rivendell's Admissions Committee has reviewed the files of 16 people on the waiting list. Of these, 12 would need regular physical therapy. The present therapists would be overwhelmed by these additions.

2. Making Lisa full-time would give her a regular and consistent patient load. Patients would benefit from having her alone do their therapy.

Concerning the increased wages and benefits, I checked with Erin Ledoe in Accounting. She assured me that the increase would keep us within our wages and salaries budget for this year, since the replacement for Bob Barkley was hired at a lower pay scale.

If you find this proposal acceptable, please contact me and I will discuss the position with Lisa.

follow-up Join two other students and talk about recent changes that have taken place in your community, your school, or a local business. Have those changes been positive? Which of these changes might have begun with a proposal?

Guidelines for Proposals

READ & ANALYZE: Turn to "Writing Proposals," 225 in your handbook, and read through the four guidelines for putting together a proposal that works. Then, with a partner, analyze the policy-revision proposal on the next two pages. Give examples that show how the writer implemented the four guidelines.

1. **Problem:**

2. **Reader:**

3. **Workable Plan:**

4. **Organization:**

follow-up Workers write different types of proposals for different situations. Here are four main types:

justification—seeks to persuade members of an organization to approve a project or investment (for example, a new product or service)

research—seeks to persuade managers or funding organizations that a line of research makes sense for a specific reason

client or sales—seeks to persuade clients (individuals and organizations) to accept a product, service, plan, or project (for example, a construction bid)

troubleshooting—seeks to solve a problem within an organization (for example, poor customer service)

Date: 17 April 1996
To: Fay and Doug Wells
From: Mike Ellis
Subject: Proposal to Revise Hair Policy for Dairy Production Facility

As you requested, I have investigated our present hair policy to see if it is (1) adequate and (2) working well.

To complete this study, I did the following:

- carefully reviewed the present policy
- checked hair-related complaints with Customer Service
- observed present activities on the plant floor
- consulted the Food and Drug Administration's current health guidelines for food production
- surveyed staff, both plant management and the employee committees, concerning the policy (survey and results attached).

The information I gathered revealed two problem areas:

1. Facial hair. The present policy is unclear about whether facial hair is acceptable or not.
2. Visitor requirements. While regular plant staff do observe the present policy by wearing hair nets, management and visitors frequently tour the production areas without the protection of the nets.

Recommendation to Add Beard and Visitor Restrictions to Policy:

Given these two problems, I recommend that the hair policy be revised to read as follows:

Facial Hair and Hair Nets

As a food processor, we must do everything we can to ensure that our customers get quality products. For this reason, plant employees need to restrict facial hair in these ways:

1. Beards are not allowed.
2. Mustaches may be grown, but not beyond the outer edges and bottom of your mouth.
3. Sideburns may be grown, but they should not extend below the bottom of the ear.

Important Notes:

1. If an employee has a special reason for growing facial hair, such as scars, deformities, or a medical condition, he may be exempt from the no-beard policy. Such an employee should contact the Personnel Office.

2. All other employees, customers, vendors, and factory representatives must wear hair nets and beard nets (if needed) whenever they are in plant production areas. All hair, including sideburns, must be completely covered.
3. Both plant employees and plant visitors must wear the hair and beard nets provided by the company.

Implementing the New Policy:

Putting this new policy into practice should prove simple. As the survey showed, both management and the employee committees can accept the no-beard and visitor-restriction clauses. The results showed 100% support for requiring all visitors to wear nets and 90% support among males for restricting beards.

If we take the following steps, the policy changes should prove successful:

1. Distribute a copy of the policy changes to all employees.
2. Meet immediately with production staff to explain the changes, and follow up at department meetings for other staff.
3. Allow a two-week grace period for those production workers who must shave their beloved facial hair.
4. Put up large signs reading "HAIR AND BEARD NETS REQUIRED BEYOND THIS POINT" at the three main entrances to the production area.
5. Install hair-net and beard-net dispensers near the new signs.

These changes will be low-cost. Jillian O'Hara in Maintenance has given me the following estimates:

Signs (one time expense)	$150.00
Dispensers (one time expense)	240.00
Hair and beard nets (annual increase)	95.00
TOTAL:	$485.00

Conclusion:

These policy changes should prove acceptable to staff and beneficial to customers. Although complaints about hair in our dairy products have been rare, the new policy would make it even less likely that a customer will have a yogurt break interrupted by a stray hair.

Please call me when you have had time to consider this proposal. We can then discuss the details and make plans.

Writing a Proposal

RESPOND: Now that you have explored proposal planning, analyzed models, and reviewed proposal guidelines, it's time to write your own proposal. With two other students, choose one of the options below and write a proposal to effect change.

Propose to your school principal or an appropriate teacher one of the following:

- that the school day be extended an hour and the school year a month
- that bungee jumping become a regular physical education activity
- that the school mascot be changed to a platypus

Propose to a parent or adult relative one of these:

- that he or she lend you a car for two weeks during the summer to drive across the country
- that your family change their family name to (your choice)

Propose to a friend that the two of you do one of the following:

- start a worm farm
- start a support group for TV or computer addicts
- organize a basketball league for short people

Propose to your principal that he or she make one of the following changes:

- replace old or nonexistent equipment (lab, sports, computers, art)
- expand the range or depth of course offerings
- add extracurricular offerings (sports, music)
- update lunchroom offerings/facilities
- bring the career-planning process into the twenty-first century

Propose to your employer that he or she do one of these:

- change the image of the business to (your choice)
- improve a procedure according to your recommendation
- add a particular product or service
- change the company policy on tardiness, substitutes, or schedules
- improve benefits for part-time employees

Writing News Releases

Have you ever aced a test, made a great shot in volleyball, or helped someone through a tough problem and thought, "I wish I could share that with the whole world!" When a business or other organization does something that it wants to share with the world, someone within the organization writes a news release and sends it to the media. Why? Because the organization knows that if the media chooses to publish the news release or use the information to write its own story, the organization will receive good publicity.

READ "Writing for the Media" (230-231) in your handbook and answer the questions below.

1. How is the media useful to organizations?

2. In what sense is the model from Burlington High School (231) newsworthy?

3. How is the model a self-portrait of Burlington High School that pictures the school as it wants to be seen?

4. Look at the Burlington model and find details that answer each question.

a. What kind of event or activity took place?

b. Who was involved—individuals and organizations?

c. Where did it happen?

d. When did it happen?

follow-up Choose an event that's taking place in your school or community, such as an upcoming athletic event, school play, or awards night. Write a news release (follow the form in your handbook, 231). Send it to two local media.

Choosing a Newsworthy Subject

What makes a news story newsworthy? Why does one story make it on the radio waves, in the paper, or on the tube—when so many other stories do not? While individual stations, networks, newspapers, and magazines have different editorial policies with which they decide what's newsworthy, in general, a story must have four qualities to pass the test:

- *timely*—The event must have happened recently, or be about to happen.
- *local*—The event must have happened close to home, or have a "hook" (like the involvement of a local person) that connects the story to the media's audience.
- *human*—The audience must feel empathy for or identify with those whom the story is about.
- *important to the audience*—The story must be relevant to the people it reaches.

CHOOSE a business or nonprofit organization (school, hospital, club, religious center) that you know well. Brainstorm to identify two newsworthy events related to the organization.

1.

2.

GATHER, ORGANIZE, & WRITE: Choose one of the two events above and research (or make up) the necessary details for a news release. Organize the information by thinking about an upside-down pyramid like the one below. Remember, when an editor cuts a story, the final background info (the tip of the pyramid) is cut first—so always begin with the most important information first. Review the form of the news release shown in your handbook (231). Then write your news release.

- **Who? What? When? Where? How?** Starting from the top of the picture, first give the broad base of factual details telling who, what, where, when, and how.
- **Supporting Details** Then offer more specific details that give the reader a clearer picture of exactly who was involved and what happened.
- **Examples** Next give details that provide a close-up look at one thing, group, or person.
- **Background** Finally, provide background material. Keep in mind that this material will be cut first, so don't put any information here that is vital.

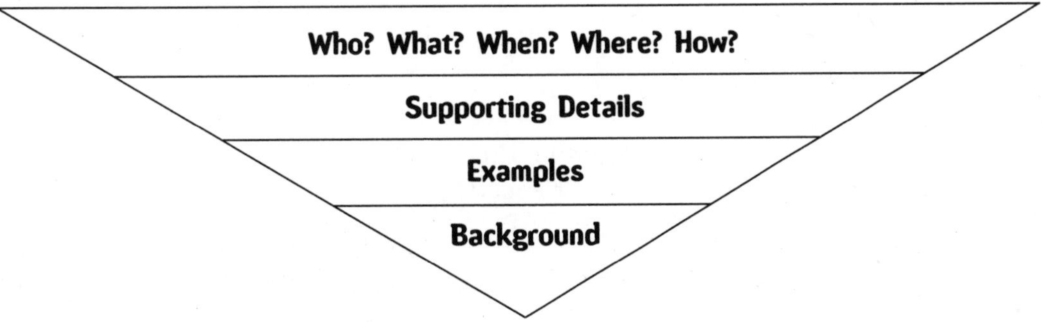

Sending Formal Faxes

In informal situations, faxes can be sent without a cover letter; but in business situations, a fax should always be sent with a cover sheet. (For an explanation of fax technology, see 336 in your handbook.) Besides a company's letterhead (which should contain its address, phone and fax numbers), a cover sheet provides space for the following information:

- the recipient's name, title, department, and company
- the recipient's phone number and fax number
- the sender's name, extension number, and fax number (in many companies today, these are different from the company's main phone and fax numbers)
- the date of transmission
- any special instructions or other handwritten information
- the number of pages sent, including the cover sheet (This is an important detail because fax machines have a nasty habit of coughing in the middle of a transmission or running out of paper. This way the recipient knows to call you for the missing pages.)

REACT: Pretend that Joyce Denisenko, an employee of Cribs and Crayons Child Care Center, and also the recipient of the application letter (209) in your handbook is faxing an enrollment form and two pages of information to Anne Maatman, a manager at the Travel Center. (See the letter at 196 in your handbook.) Complete the fax cover sheet below, using information from the two handbook letters just mentioned.

FACSIMILE COVER SHEET

Cribs and Crayons

1010 Brown Street
West Columbia, SC 29167-7644
(803) 961-2773 FAX (803) 961-4338

To:		From:	
Phone:		Date:	
Fax:		Pages including this cover sheet:	______

Understanding Electronic Mail

Sending and receiving electronic mail (or e-mail) is becoming increasingly common in many offices. (See 336 in your handbook for a brief summary of e-mail's advantages and disadvantages.) Cheaper than a phone call, e-mail has become an important form of business communication. While whole books have been written about e-mail, the basics are simple. One computer user writes to another computer user or dozens of computer users at the same time, using simple, typed messages like the one below.

```
To: herman, joyce, bsmith, rdouglas
From: phylicia
Subject: marketing meeting
Cc: mmoore
Date: 21 Sep 1996 08:20:55 AM

The next marketing meeting will be held Thursday at 2:30 p.m.
in the 5th floor conference room.  If you cannot attend this
meeting please e-mail me back.

Topics to be discussed include:

1. Winter 1997 marketing overview
2. Feedback from telemarketing survey of Robusto Pro consumers
3. Review new 15- and 30-second TV spots for Astro Clear
4. Discuss future of print vs. electronic advertising

If there are any items you would like discussed at this meeting
please send me e-mail.
```

ANALYZE: You can communicate information in five basic ways. See 335 and 336 in your handbook. Though there are no hard-and-fast rules about when to use one form or another, you'll want to make the best choice in any situation. Match the numbered situations below with the best forms of communicationn.

a. in person **b.** by telephone **c.** in writing **d.** by fax machine **e.** by e-mail

______ **1.** You have two articles from magazines that you need to send across town as soon as possible, and you don't have a messenger.

______ **2.** You need an answer immediately from someone in another company.

______ **3.** You have a legal document that will later need to be notarized.

______ **4.** You have a problem with your boss.

______ **5.** You want to bounce some ideas off several of your coworkers, and you don't have time for yet another meeting.

Using E-Mail

When you're using e-mail, you can develop your own style. Most people try to keep e-mail short, informal, and very direct; but that doesn't mean that everything you have ever learned about grammar, usage, and mechanics should fly out the window. Most of what you've learned can be transferred to this medium. Read the guidelines that follow.

- Remember the inverted pyramid? Write short messages, but put your most important information first.
- Reread every message before you send it. Though e-mail is informal, your message should be complete and accurate.
- Reply promptly. Check your e-mail two or three times a day and respond to all incoming messages. Otherwise you defeat the main advantage of this medium—its speed. If you don't have time for a full reply, write something like this: "Hold on, Adam, I'm checking on this for you." You'll keep everybody happy that way.

E-mail Shorthand

Although you don't need to know e-mail acronyms or "smileys" to send e-mail, it's fun to know a few of them. (If you're sending e-mail to the president of your company, you may want to hold off. E-mail is informal, but you still need to be aware of your audience.) Below is a list of some of the most commonly used acronyms.

OTOH	On the Other Hand	F2F	Face To Face
BTW	By The Way	FYI	For Your Information
IMHO	In My Humble Opinion	TIA	Thanks In Advance
WRT	With Respect To	IOW	In Other Words
GMTA	Great Minds Think Alike	FWIW	For What It's Worth

Smileys help computer communicators indicate moods—and have fun doing so. To see the "face" of a smiley, it helps to tilt your head to the left. All of the smileys can be made with common strokes on your keyboard. See if you can guess the meaning of the following smileys.

:)	______________	:D	______________
:(	______________	:X	______________
:-<	______________	:-o	______________
:-\	______________	:-/	______________
8-)	______________	X-(	______________

Part III

Writing Workshops

Searching and Selecting

Taking Stock of Your Writing

This is a chance for you to take stock of your writing experiences and abilities at the beginning of the year. Consider each question carefully before answering it, and word your answers clearly and carefully. This information will make it easier for you to evaluate your writing progress later in the year when you refer back to this survey.

1. What are the last pieces of writing you have completed? (Identify two or three.)

2. What forms of school-based writing are you most familiar with? (*Reports*, *essays*, *paragraphs*, *reviews*, *stories*, *poems*, *essay-test answers*, and so on.)

3. What forms of workplace writing are you most familiar with? (*Letters, memos, messages, instructions, summaries, proposals, reports,* and so on.)

4. What is the most successful piece of writing you've done in the past year or two? Briefly describe it.

5. What is your greatest strength as a writer? Explain.

6. What stage in the writing process gives you the most trouble? (*Getting started, focusing my efforts, organizing, drafting, revising, editing*, etc.) Explain.

7. Do you follow a set revising strategy? What sorts of changes do you normally make when you revise?

8. What type of writing gives you the most problems? What type of writing would you like to learn more about? What specific writing skills do you need to practice?

INSIDE

Review this survey each quarter to see how your writing attitudes, skills, and interests evolve throughout the year.

The Write Approach

READ: Read and enjoy the following quotations from a variety of people about the process of writing.

"Writing a business letter should be like having a conversation with a friend—it needs to be honest, open, and accurate."

—Shirley Born, Loan Officer

"To write about people you have to know people, to write about bloodhounds you have to know bloodhounds, to write about the Loch Ness monster you have to find out about it."

—James Thurber, Author

". . . as soon as you connect with your true subject you will write."

—Joyce Carol Oates, Author

"Ambiguity has no place in writing that is trying to convey information, and a clear style eliminates ambiguity."

—Marjorie Reitsma, Librarian

"The real writing takes place between the first miserable, crude draft and the finished thing."

—Gloria Naylor, Author

"You always feel when you look it straight in the eye that you could have put more into it, could have let yourself go and dug harder."

—Emily Carr, Author

REACT: Select one of the quotations that matches up well with your own writing experience. Explain the connection in a freely written exploratory draft. (Use your own paper.)

follow-up Write your own personal statement about writing to be posted in the classroom. If you're having trouble coming up with ideas, refer to "The Writing Process in Action" (003-009).

Selecting Strategies That Work

"There are few experiences quite so satisfying as getting a good idea . . . You're pleased with it, and feel good. It may not be right, but at least you try it out."

How do you get good ideas for your writing? Are they just waiting to be picked like so many heavy, ripe peaches? Or are they the result of your conscious effort, the process of putting pen to paper (or fingers to the keyboard)? Unless you think, eat, and sleep writing, selecting a subject is undoubtedly more work for you than it is play, more searching and sorting than plucking.

REVIEW: Review the "Guidelines for Selecting a Subject" (011-013) in your handbook. Identify two or three old reliables—activities listed in this section that you regularly use when searching for a writing idea. Also identify any *unreliables*—activities that you have tried once or twice without much success. And lastly, note any additional selecting practices you use that are not included in the list. (Share your results.)

- Old Reliables

- Unreliables

- Additional Selecting Practices

APPLY: Let's suppose you are assigned to write an essay of advice in which you offer advice (of course) on any subject you wish, to any audience you wish (classmate, parents, employers, yourself, . . .). Select a subject for this essay using the "Essentials of Life Checklist," 013, the last piece of information presented under the "Guidelines for Selecting a Subject." This checklist provides an incredible variety of writing possibilities. Unfortunately, too few writers use it. Now's your chance. (Do your sorting and thinking on another sheet of paper. List the subject you select on the line provided here.)

Subject: ....

follow-up Write nonstop for 8 to 10 minutes on this subject, recording whatever comes to mind as you go along. Afterward, take note of any ideas that surprise you, that seem perceptive and clear, that would be worthy of further development if you were to continue working with this subject.

Talking Heads

Creating **imaginary dialogues** can help you develop or explore possible ideas for writing projects. It's a way to get thoughts out of your head and onto paper where you can roll them around and build on them. Give this strategy a chance! You'll be surprised at the way your ideas (and possible subjects for writing) will begin to develop.

DIALOGUE: Complete the following storyboard by filling in the dialogue bubble in each frame. (Also consider drawing additional frames.)

follow-up Begin a short personal essay on a writing idea that has emerged from your dialogue. If, for example, your dialogue turned out to be about getting along or working together—like how it's necessary in families, or in the workplace, or how you're terrible at it—that can be your starting point. (Share the results of your writing.)

Generating Texts

Taking Shape

You know by now that there are quite a few steps in the writing process. You can't go from picking a subject to writing a final draft with no work in between. Most successful writers spend time shaping their writing subjects, and they also have their own preferences about the activities they use along the way. In this workshop, you are going to take stock of your own writing preferences when it comes to searching and shaping a subject.

REFLECT: How do you narrow a subject down? How do you gather supporting details? How do you decide what to focus on and how to start the first draft? In short, how do you usually work a subject into proper shape? Explain your searching and shaping process on your own paper.

RETHINK: Your handbook offers many suggestions for shaping a subject. Review the handbook section "Guidelines for Searching and Shaping a Subject," 015-016, and see what we mean. Think about how you might incorporate some of the activities listed there into your own process of working with a writing subject.

REACT: Use an activity from the handbook and respond to either *Offbeat Questions* or *Audience Appeal*. These two activities are sometimes overlooked as ways of shaping a subject, but they're surprisingly effective. Say you're writing an essay of reflection about an important decision in your life. See what you can discover about your subject using one of the activities mentioned above.

Note: If you're having trouble identifying a subject, try completing the sentence starter that follows.

My most important work-related decision during the last year was ....

....

INSIDE

Essays of reflection require reflective details, but you should incorporate other types of details as well. (For more information about the different "Types of Details," refer to topic 110 in your handbook.)

Cube It

READ: If you've already picked a topic, use the writing method called "cubing" to search your mind for more of what you already know. How many sides on a cube? That's easy: six. (Think of dice. The sides are numbered for you.) You can use the six sides of a cube to remind you of six major ways to explore your topic. Suppose you've decided to write about the TV coverage of a major sporting event. Here is how you might "cube" your topic.

Side 1: Describe It

For 5 minutes, write at top speed about the sights and sounds (and maybe the tastes, smells, and physical feelings) that you connect with the TV broadcast. Describe it so that a reader feels he or she has been there.

They put a camera right on the woman's skis while she was doing the slalom. I could hear the ripping sound of the edges of her skis through the ice crystals. The snow was spraying onto the camera lens and making circle rainbows . . .

Side 2: Compare It

For 5 minutes, write a comparison between the telecast you watched and something comparable to it: for example, a related personal experience or another channel's coverage of the same event.

Because of the way the camera got down to the snow level and made you feel and hear every cut and hump and whoosh and stuff, I got more excited watching this broadcast than I did the one time I went skiing in person. When I went skiing, I couldn't hear much because I had a rotten earache from the wind, and I couldn't feel much because the boots and stuff were killing my feet. I was totally numb . . .

Side 3: Associate It

For 5 more minutes, write about something that in some odd way you connect in your mind with the telecast. Maybe it reminds you of an afternoon nap, or a carnival sideshow, or a really bad play.

The telecast was like, let's see, okay, like a half-dream, when your mind is swirling with wild images part of the time but somebody keeps breaking in talking the rest of the time and spoiling the mood. These jerky announcers thought their jokes were worth more airtime than the skiing, but I wanted to stay caught up in the dream . . .

Side 4: Analyze It

For 5 more minutes, write about the different identifiable parts of the telecast.

I could count about four or five parts to the broadcast. Or maybe not parts but layers. There was the obvious commercial layer, which kept breaking in about every seven or eight minutes. Then there was the chitchat layer, where the announcers talked about themselves, mostly . . .

Side 5: Apply It

For 5 more minutes, write about what the telecast is good for, what its results are, how it could be used, etc.

Parts of this broadcast would work well for a ski school, since they showed some of the fine points about how a skier balances and absorbs shocks with the knees. Or a tape of the broadcast could be used in journalism school, to analyze the structure (and the faults!) of a typical sports broadcast . . .

Side 6: Argue for or Against It

For 5 more minutes, make a case pro or con—to keep the telecast or to dump it, to change it or to leave it the same. Argue for its style of presentation, or against its length, or whatever.

I want to argue that sports broadcasters should change the ratio between their talk and the amount of footage they show of the actual sport in action. The ideal, from my perspective, would be about five minutes of action footage for every one minute of talk. And the talk should concentrate on what the athlete is doing and why, not on who went to what college, who's from what Swiss village, who's got a collection of beer coasters, and that kind of junk.

There. That's a little over one half-hour's work. By the time you're through, you'll know a lot more about what you already knew. You're practically guaranteed to come up with some new ideas in the process of cubing. You'll be surprised! Then you can take that new material and channel it into an improved draft of your writing.

WRITE: Select an appealing topic from the "Essentials of Life," 013, in your handbook. First, free-write about this topic for about 5-8 minutes. Then search your mind for more ideas about your topic by cubing it. Or, if you have already written a poem, a story, an editorial, or an essay, cube that for new ideas. (Refer to "Guidelines for Searching and Shaping a Subject," 015-016, in the handbook to help you get started.) Underline any thoughts or phrases you especially like in your free writing and cubing.

Making Choices

Are you just about ready to write? Have you listed facts, details, examples, or key words? Have you tried clustering or free writing? Have you noted your best ideas?

At this point, some writers blast ahead. They write the first thing that comes to mind. Who knows? That might work for you. But if you want to get the feeling, the form, and the thrust of your writing more under your control, here is something that may help: a **Choice Chart**. Apply it to your next writing project.

Choice Chart

My broad subject:

My specific topic:

Type of writing: Comments:

.... Personal Narrative ....

.... Subject (Expository) ....

.... Creative Writing ....

.... Persuasive Writing ....

.... Academic Writing ....

.... Workplace Writing ....

If new or experimental, then

New angle .... What? ....

New form .... What? ....

New method .... What? ....

New style and language .... What? ....

I want to focus on Comments:

.... Emotion ....

.... Ideas, Facts, etc. ....

.... Convictions ....

If focusing on emotion, then

.... Fear .... Pride .... Love .... Other (Specify)

.... Compassion .... Anger .... Frustration

Comments: ....

....

What to do with the emotion:

.... Relive it .... Relieve it .... Build it .... Transform it

Comments: ....

....

If focusing on ideas, facts, etc., then

.... Narrate .... Analyze .... Evaluate .... Explain

.... Describe .... Classify .... Argue .... Combine several approaches

.... Define .... Compare .... Illustrate

Comments: ....

....

Start from

.... Conventional .... Unconventional .... Truly offbeat .... Other (Specify)

Comments: ....

....

If focusing on convictions, then

(........ My usual ones (or) .... Some new ones)

.... Consider .... Test .... Reject .... Recommend

Postscript: Well, have you made as many choices for your writing as you can? If some of them don't come easily, save them for later. They'll come to you, along with plenty of other choices. But if you're ready, why waste time talking? Get writing!

Hocus Focus

The focus of a piece of writing may be plainly stated near the beginning, or it may be postponed until later—or it may not be stated at all. How can a person tell what the focus of a piece of writing is? And how can you create a clearer focus in your next piece of writing?

Start with this general formula. A focus is the specific combination of the following elements:

1. A central subject
2. A specific topic or aspect of the subject
3. An idea and/or a feeling about that aspect

For the writing to be clearly focused, all of these elements should be present, although they may not need to be directly stated. (*Note:* Compare this formula with the formula for a topic sentence found in your handbook. See "The Topic Sentence," 108, in the handbook.)

READ & REACT: Read over the beginnings of the essays that follow. All come from an issue of *Life Magazine* that focused on the American family. Each has the same general subject, but each has a different focus. Some state their focus more openly than others. Try to identify the different elements that make up the focus in each passage. (You won't necessarily be able to comment on each element; just do the best you can.) Afterward, share your results.

Dozens of cereal boxes. Piles of unread mail. Stacks of magazines. Toilet paper tumbling from the linen closet. And a family room with no room for the family. Such was life at the Raffels' suburban New York home.

—Naomi Cutner, "Now You See It . . . Now You Don't"

Central Subject: ....

Specific Aspect: ....

Idea: ....

Feeling: ....

Our child is due in six weeks. A host of our friends have told us that we should start now, singing lullabies. They mean it. Babies hear things in the womb, they say. My husband, who finds this silly, has nonetheless lit upon a ritual all his own. At night with a fairly straight face, he whispers the rules of baseball to my belly. "You'll be wanting to know about tagging up," he says.

—Lisa Grunwald, "Family Talk"

Central Subject: ....

Specific Aspect: ....

Idea: ....

Feeling: ....

In my family most of the people are storytellers. Combine that with growing up in Hampton, Virginia—small towns make you aware of your ties to a place—and my romantic quest to find out more about my family makes sense. William Roscoe Davis, my great-grandfather, was the first African American on the Davis side. His father was an English sea captain and his mother, Liza, an African-born slave. My father's older brothers knew their great-grandmother; their memory was that she had a taste for French finery, especially things like perfume. In 1861 William's family became free when they escaped to the Union Army's Fort Monroe, near Hampton. William soon traveled to New York, under the auspices of the American Missionary Association, to lecture and raise money for the 1,500 blacks who were living around the fort. I found a January 14, 1862, story in The *New York Times* describing him as "a fine, intelligent-looking mulatto."

—Thulani Davis, "American Album"

Central Subject: ....

Specific Aspect: ....

Idea: ....

Feeling: ....

REFLECT: Which of these paragraphs do you enjoy the most? Which one seems most clearly focused? Which one states its focus most plainly? Which one has the most implicit (unstated) focus?

INSIDE

As you write about your own family life, or any other subject, keep the basic elements of a focus clearly in mind.

Write Angles

READ: Newspaper and magazine writers often talk about the importance of finding an angle for each of their stories. They know from experience that their readers are impatient. If a story doesn't immediately catch their attention with an interesting or engaging angle, they will quickly move on to another one.

The same holds true for the essays, reports, and many forms of workplace writing you produce. If you don't find that special angle or focus for a particular writing project, your readers will have a hard time maintaining interest in your work (not to mention the fact that you will have a hard time developing it).

REVIEW: Review what your handbook has to say about developing a focus, or an angle, for writing. (Refer to the section on **focus** [018-019] in the handbook.) Also study feature articles in magazines and newspapers to see how professionals focus their efforts into effective finished pieces.

REACT: Let's suppose you were assigned to write a profile of a specific enterprise or business. (A profile is the product of a writer's in-depth investigation.) This business happens to make and sell authentic East Indian gourmet meals to specialty stores. Review your notes on this business listed below. (These notes are based on a newspaper article about an actual business.)

- Indian Groceries & Spices, which started as a small shop selling spices, has started a line of frozen dishes.
- Thirteen dishes (all vegetarian) were quietly put on the market last month.
- One of the dishes is lentils and eggplant.
- A main feature of many of the dishes is curry, a popular Indian spice that at times can be very hot.
- The dishes are spicy and sometimes fiery.
- All of the dishes are microwavable.
- The meals retail for about $2.99 each.
- In New York the first shipment of 300 cases sold out in six weeks.
- The recipes for the dishes were developed by Shirish Sanghavi, who has been involved in the business since it was the small grocery store.
- In addition to frozen foods, the company sells 150 other products including mint chutney and mango pickles.
- Annual sales now top $10 million.
- One hundred employees work in the operation.
- The two brothers who run the business were originally chemical engineers.
- Many smaller competitors are starting in the field.
- The brothers are confident about their products because of the fine quality of ingredients the products contain.

WRITE: Now decide on a special angle, or focus, for your writing so you can begin developing your profile. (List two or three potential angles for your work.)

Hint: The leads (openings) in the subject-writing section of your handbook (146-157) might trigger some ideas.

Angle 1 I could focus on ....

....

Angle 2 ....

....

Angle 3 ....

....

EXTEND: Write the first part of your profile, focusing on one of the angles you've just written. Make sure that your opening grabs your reader's attention. (Write a number of versions of your opening until you hit upon one that you like.) Share your results. Then, if you're so inclined, write the complete profile, adding details of your own making if necessary.

INSIDE info

Always write with your readers in mind. Satisfy their need to learn something and to enjoy themselves by giving proper attention to your subject and the way you write about it (the angle).

Hooking Your Reader

Consider the fishhook. Why does it work? It's got a curve to make it catch, a point to make it sink in, and a barb to make it stick. Oh yes, and there's the bait.

What can fishhooks teach you about writing? Many writers speak of the need for a "hook" in their writing. The audience is the sea in which they fish. The reader is the fish they want to catch. The subject is the bait. The angle of approach is that curving hook. The surprise in the opening is the point that sinks in. And that little extra touch, that idea left open or that hint of things to come, is the barb that won't let the "hook" slip out.

READ: Here are the opening sentences or paragraphs from a number of published essays. As you read through these openings, see if you can catch on to the hook and barb in each one. (Share your thoughts.)

According to the projections, crime was supposed to be under control by now. The postwar baby-boom generation, which moved into its crime-prone years during the early 1960s, has grown up, yielding its place to the (proportionately) less numerous baby-bust generation. With relatively fewer 18-year-olds around, we should all be walking safer streets.

—James Q. Wilson and John J. DiIulio, Jr.,
"Crackdown: Treating the Symptoms of the Drug Problem"

Hint: What is the effect of the word "should" in the last sentence?

My, my, girls, what's all the fuss over the new "mommy test"? Hundreds of eager young female job seekers have written to me in the last few weeks alone, confident of being able to pass the drug test, the polygraph test, Exxon's new breathalyzer test—but panicked over the mommy test. Well, the first thing you have to grasp if you hope to enter the ranks of management is that corporations have a perfect right to separate the thieves from the decent folk, the straights from the druggies, and, of course, the women from the mommies.

—Barbara Ehrenreich, "The Mommy Test"

Hint: Can you tell that this opening is sticky with sarcasm?

In government circles it's called the "NIMBY problem." Whether the proposal is for AIDS clinics, halfway houses for prison parolees or dumps for toxic and nuclear waste, it is usually met by the opposition of citizens' groups who shout NIMBY—"not in my backyard!"

—Ted Peters, "The Waste-Disposal Crisis"

Hint: What is your emotional response immediately after you read the final phrase?

The end of the world is coming—again: 989 years ago, as the odometer of Western history approached its first millennium, the whole of Europe was seized by a paroxysm of preapocalyptic shivers.

—Bill Lawren, "Apocalypse Now?"

Hint: What is the tone of the word "again" in the first line?

So, you're walking tall out of high school thinking NOW-thoughts, dreaming NOW-dreams, and preparing for . . . WHEN? What are you preparing for with a head so full of "what's cool now" that there's no brain space left for a career plan?

—Technical college's recruiting letter sent to high-school seniors

Hint: Where do you suspect that the writer is leading? What makes you think so?

REFLECT: How do you think the writers go from these openings to the next paragraphs? In many cases, there is some kind of turn—a *but*, or *yet*, or *nevertheless*, or *still*. (The writer does that when she or he knows the "hook" is set, and it's time to start reeling in the fish.)

WRITE: Here is a chance to practice writing "hooks" for three different kinds of essays: personal, subject (expository), and business.

1. **Personal** Write an opening sentence or two with a "hook" about an aspect of your life that you think might be fascinating to a reader.

2. **Subject** Write a "hook" opening to an essay in which you communicate some specialized knowledge you already possess.

3. **Business** Write a "hook" opening to a sales letter that you address to your classmates. Be sure you have a worthwhile product (CD, concert tickets, calculator, car, or so on).

Let Me Tell You

When one of my many, many relatives wants to give me advice (something they all love to do), I'll get the infamous introductory remark: "Hey, kiddo, let me tell you something." Based on my experiences as a writer and as a member of a large family, I'd have to say that the essay of advice is a basic essay form.

REACT: When writing an essay of advice, you not only speak *of* an experience, you also speak *from* experience and provide your readers with helpful advice and tips. Let me show you how it's done . . . kiddo.

Essay topic: Getting a job

Narrowed topic: How to get your first job

Angle (Advice): Use life experience as a résumé

Three points of experience that support my angle:

1. I was oldest in a large family and had lots of responsibilities.
2. I helped in my parents' business once I was in middle school—ran errands, answered phone.
3. I volunteered to help with a park recreation program. (reference from director)

APPLY: Now that you are nearing graduation, you should be qualified to give advice about getting through high school. Suppose you were asked to advise next year's incoming freshmen on that subject. Plan your writing in the space provided below. (Use the model above as your guide.)

Essay topic: High school

Narrowed topic:

Angle (Advice):

Three points of experience that support your angle:

1.

2.

3.

Crunch Time

Some impromptu writing is free, fast, and wild. The only mistake you can make is to quit. But some impromptu writing has to be focused, organized, and clear. And you might be graded on it when you're through! GULP.

What should you do? You could go in there with fourteen #2 pencils, rub their erasers down, gnaw on your wrist bone, and blast out a half hour later, heavy with sweat. Or you could do this workshop to get a better idea of how to clear your head and make the best of your short writing time.

Suppose your teacher has asked you to write an essay in class for a grade. You may prepare for it outside of class, but you may not use notes while writing the essay. You will have 40 minutes to write and revise the essay. One way to prepare for those crunch times would be to train a little voice in your head to kick in with the right suggestions at the right time. Whether you're writing a memo to co-workers, reporting on a meeting, or responding to an unexpected situation, you'll benefit from having an impromptu writing strategy.

REACT: With the help of a classmate (or writing group) plan an impromptu writing strategy, an essential checklist of helpful hints and reminders that you could refer to for this type of writing. Include some of the ideas listed on this page as well as additional ideas you find in the handbook or create on your own. (Make sure that the items in your list are arranged in a logical order. The length of the list is up to you.)

Impromptu Writing Strategy

....
....
....
....
....
....
....
....
....
....
....
....
....

give details
connect the parts
consult your memory
check your work
stick to your topic
start where you feel the most power
avoid wasting time
follow through with what you start
make each word count
have every sentence do something
stay calm
stop and plan
go back later and fix it
jot an outline on scratch paper
keep parts in proportion
get to the point
ask what your reader wants
say it clearly
hang in there

Developing Texts

Hold Your Position

If everyone agreed on all important questions, we wouldn't have to explain or defend our positions. We could walk around uttering blanket statements. But since we don't all buy the same ideas, we have to develop our points using the best methods of development at our disposal. We can, among other things, describe, analyze, compare, or classify our ideas as we go along. (Refer to "Selecting a Method of Development," 026, in the handbook for more information.)

READ: Kara Watkins, the student who wrote the position paper below, uses many different methods of development to explain her thoughts about the gradual destruction of the oceans. Read the paper carefully to appreciate the position she builds.

Take a swim in the ocean. Chances are you'll come across pop cans, bottles, assorted plastics, maybe even a syringe or two. We have made the sea our dumping ground, thinking its great expanse will absorb whatever we put in it. Unfortunately, most of what we put into the oceans stays there. We have not taken out the garbage, just rearranged it. The ocean is part of our world, just as the land is. Anything that we "throw away" stays with us, often coming back to haunt us.

Consider the tons of toxic, factory-produced waste dumped into our rivers, streams, and oceans every day. This manmade, nonbiodegradable waste is carried into the open sea and is often eaten by fish and other small creatures. The fish are eaten by animals such as dolphins, whales, and seals—and human beings. Settling in the fat tissues, the toxic material stays in the animals' bodies for life, causing cancer, ulcers, and respiratory diseases which ultimately kill them.

Perhaps most frightening (aside from the fact that we also eat the fish and it has the same effect on us) is that female marine mammals pass the toxic waste to their young while the young are being produced, and through milk. Even if these young survive the birth defects caused by toxins, these babies grow up eating contaminated fish, increasing the levels of toxins in their bodies. And so on. Eventually, the level of toxins will become so great that the animals will no longer be able to survive. Mass extinction of sea life will result. This is the case because we insist that industrialization, with all of its waste products, is the way to success.

People don't realize how important a healthy, thriving ocean is to life on land. The entire food chain depends on the tiny organisms called phyto-plankton at the bottom which are eaten by fish, which in turn are eaten by animals including us. If any link of that chain is disturbed, the whole system collapses.

As I learn more about the environment and the oceans, about the damage we've caused, I grow more determined to make a difference by practicing conservation and educating others. I just hope we all wake up in time to help our oceans. The consequences of hesitation and ignorance are too frightening for me to imagine.

REACT: Can you spot the different methods Ms. Watkins uses to develop her position? Does she, for example, use any of the following methods?

- **Examples** (proving points with specific references)
- **Narration** (telling mini-stories in support)
- **Classification** (dividing large and complex things into smaller groups)
- **Prediction** (providing possible outcomes)
- **Analysis** (breaking points down)
- **Definition** (distinguishing what certain things are)
- **Comparison** (measuring one thing against something else)

Note below any methods of development that Ms. Watkins clearly seems to use. Be able to cite specific passages to support your choices. Also note anything you might have done differently in this paper. (Afterward, share your results.)

follow-up Write freely and rapidly for at least 5 minutes on a subject you feel strongly about. As you write, prompt yourself to use at least three of the development methods in the list above.

Tying It Together

Transitional words between sentences and paragraphs reassure and steer readers along, giving writing a more pleasing flow. Let's see how a professional writer uses transitional words and phrases to link ideas . . . and smooth out the writing.

READ: Here is a passage from an article on allergies that appeared in *Time* magazine. The capitalized words in the passage create effective transitions between sentences and between paragraphs. You can learn quite a bit about transitions simply by noticing them and thinking about how they work.

Acute attacks of asthma occur when the bronchial tubes become partly blocked. FOR REASONS THAT ARE NOT ENTIRELY CLEAR, the lungs are overstimulated by viral infections, allergens, or pollutants. The body RESPONDS by activating various defense cells from the immune system. THEIR MOBILIZATION causes the airways to swell. AT THE SAME TIME, the muscles surrounding the airways contract, cutting off airflow. WHEN THAT HAPPENS, asthmatics must inhale an adrenaline-like substance to stop the muscle spasm and reopen their airways.

IF THE ATTACKS RECUR enough times, HOWEVER, the lungs do not return to normal. THEY CONTINUE to act as if they are being invaded by parasites. THIS constant STATE of inflammatory alert damages the bronchial walls, creating scar tissue. AS A RESULT, the airways can no longer clear the mucus that forms deep in the lungs. The ENSUING buildup reduces the flow of air and sets the stage for the next attack.

RESPOND: Write thoughtful answers to the following questions. Afterward, share your answers with a classmate.

1. Do most of the transitional words appear toward the beginnings or the ends of the sentences? Do you think this pattern is a coincidence, or do you see a good reason for it?

2. What makes the word "responds" a transitional word? If you had to fill in some unwritten words after the word "responds" that would refer to the previous sentence, what would those words be?

3. Study the words "their mobilization": to what words in the previous sentence do they refer?

4. From what you can observe about transitions in these two paragraphs, write one or two of your own "rules for transition."

My Rules for Transition

Rule #1

Rule #2

Hint: You'll find a complete list of transitions in your handbook. (Refer to "Transitions and Linking Words," 114, in the handbook.)

follow-up Apply what you've learned about transitions in a two-paragraph passage in which you consider the effects that something new (3-D television, stricter requirements for college entrants, the changing employment picture, etc.) would have on you and your peers. Be able to explain to a classmate how you've used transitions in your writing.

Linking Paragraphs

"I began to see that writing, especially narrative, was not only an affair of sentences, but of paragraphs. Indeed, I thought the paragraph no less important than the sentence . . . Just as the sentence contains one idea in all its fullness, so the paragraph should embrace a distinct episode; and as sentences should follow one another in harmonious sequence, so the paragraphs must fit on to one another like the automatic couplings of railway carriages."

—Winston Churchill, *My Early Life*

The "couplings" Churchill referred to are better known as **transition** or **linking sentences**. They hook ideas together so that writing can flow along, like a train on smooth tracks.

REVIEW: Carefully review the writing scenario that follows. An idea for each of two paragraphs is given. The transition sentence that follows links the two paragraphs. (Transition sentences can come at the end of the first paragraph or at the beginning of the second paragraph.)

Paragraph A Main Idea:

The drive to the concert was a blast from start to finish.

Paragraph B Main Idea:

The concert itself was one disaster after another.

Transition sentence:

As soon as we got to the concert stadium, however, things took a major-league turn for the worse.

WRITE: Write transition sentences for the following sets of paragraph ideas. Concentrate on the relationship between the main ideas in the paragraphs. Consider using a transition or linking word listed in your handbook in each of your transition sentences. (Refer to "Transitions and Linking Words" in the handbook, 014, for this list.)

A. Working at Dog 'n' Spuds was a nightmare.

B. There were unexpected rewards for hanging in there.

Transition sentence: ....

....

....

A. Jesse was not what you would call a hunk.

B. Jesse was a great success as a leading man in school plays.

Transition sentence:

A. The first lesson the telemarketing salesperson learns is keeping the customer on the line.

B. Various techniques are used to keep customers from hanging up.

Transition sentence:

A. The men in cigarette ads look healthy, robust, and rugged.

B. A number of "Marlboro Men" of the 1950s sued because they developed cancer.

Transition sentence:

A. Some English teachers feel obligated to teach the classics.

B. Many young readers find a great deal of satisfaction reading more contemporary titles.

Transition sentence:

SHARE your transition sentences with a classmate. Did you both see the same relationships between paragraph ideas? Did you use the same transition words? Could you make your transition sentences even more effective? More striking? More lively?

Almost Human

READ: Here's a passage from Elie Wiesel's *Night*. Take special note of his use of personification. (Don't know what personification is? Look up this "Figure of speech" in your handbook, 486.)

> I lay down and tried to force myself to sleep, to doze a little, but in vain. God knows what I would not have given for a few moments of sleep. But, deep down, I felt that to sleep would mean to die. And something within me revolted against this death. All round me death was moving in, silently, without violence. It would seize upon some sleeping being, enter into him, and consume him bit by bit. Next to me there was someone trying to wake up his neighbor, his brother, perhaps, or a friend. In vain.

REACT: Here are some questions that will help you react to the passage. (Share responses with a classmate.)

- Where does the personification occur in the passage? (Underline it.)
- What exactly is being personified?
- Does the personification seem natural? Believable?
- What other characteristics of this writing do you like? Dislike?

WRITE: Try clustering on your own paper with an abstract noun as the nucleus word, perhaps a word like "happiness" or "courage." As you cluster, think in terms of human traits that relate to the noun. After three or four minutes of clustering, write a paragraph in which your abstract noun is in some way personified. (Refer to "Clustering," 011, in the handbook if you need help getting started.) Share your results.

INSIDE info

Your handbook lists a number of figures of speech, like personification, that you should practice using in your writing. (Refer to "Figure of speech," 486, for this information.) You've probably worked with metaphors and similes already. How about hyperbole or antithesis?

Grand Central Metaphor

If a piece of your writing needs expanding and clarifying, how are you going to come up with the necessary details? One way is to invent an appropriate **central metaphor** and then s-t-r-e-t-c-h it. Refer to "Metaphor" listed as a "Figure of speech," 486, in the handbook.

- Here is a short paragraph that could use some enrichment:

> The sales team would have broken up long ago were it not for the veteran saleswoman who was their leader. She kept the team together with words of encouragement and ready decisions about what to do next. When she gave an approving nod after each sale, she had the bearing of a queen.

- One way to expand and clarify this paragraph metaphorically is to work with the last word, "queen." Notice all the words and phrases in the revised paragraph below that in some way can be associated with a queen or royalty, although the word "queen" is not used—it is the hidden metaphor.

> With a regal nod, the sales team leader surveyed her whole showroom kingdom. She enthroned herself behind an old metal desk. From there, she was able to oversee her team as they moved in and out of the showroom with customers in tow. All the while she appeared to be thinking about other car lots, other sales teams, other kingdoms. It was because she alone saw beyond the showroom that she ruled.

REWRITE: Write a different paragraph of your own about the sales team, using a circus as the hidden central metaphor. (Compare your results.)

Hint: Stretching metaphors works best for special effects. If this technique is overused, it will draw attention to itself and sound artificial. Sometimes, however, a metaphor will work as the powerful central thread of an entire piece of writing.

(Example)

The sales team paraded around under the big top during the spring tent sale. Like a trapeze artist, the newest recruit swung nervously back and forth between two mildly interested customers. Meanwhile a veteran paced up and down the rows of cars, watching for the manager's nod over the head of a cowering client, much as a lion waiting for the crack of the ringmaster's whip.

follow-up → Find a paragraph or short essay that you've previously written that could be improved if developed around a central metaphor. Revise it accordingly and share your results.

Over and Over Again

READ: In this passage from *The Land Remembers*, Ben Logan notes specific images that come to his mind when he thinks of his childhood farm.

> Let the smell of mint touch me. I am kneeling along a little stream, the water numbing my hands as I reach for a trout. I feel the fish arch and struggle. I let go, pulling watercress from the water instead.
>
> Let me see a certain color and I am standing beside the threshing machine, grain cascading through my hands. The seeds we planted when snow was spitting down have multiplied a hundred times, returning in a stream of bright gold, still warm with the sunlight of the fields.
>
> Let me hear an odd whirring. I am deep in the woods, following an elusive sound, looking in vain for a last passenger pigeon, a feathered lightning I have never seen, unwilling to believe no person will ever see one again.

REACT: Ask yourself the following questions as you think about the passage. (Discuss the passage with a classmate. Read it out loud to each other.)

- What three ideas or phrases seem to tie the many images together in this passage?
- What do these three ideas have in common? How do they differ?
- What feeling or tone is established in this passage? Does the writing have a matter-of-fact quality to it or is it more poetic and dreamlike?
- What does the repetition of the three leading ideas contribute to the tone of the passage?
- What images or mental pictures do you especially like in the writing?

WRITE: Write freely about any subject, but try to begin as many sentences as you can with "Let me." See how long you can keep this going before it becomes tiresome. Afterward, review your writing to see if your "Let me" statements had a positive or negative effect on your writing. (Use your own paper.)

INSIDE

Much power or beauty in writing comes from the repetition of words, phrases, and ideas. Repetition is also an effective unifying or organizing device, as in the sample passage above.

Transformations

READ: If you were an alien visitor from another galaxy and had no idea what H_20 was, I would show you not only a glass of liquid water but also an ice cube and a kettle blowing off steam. To get a full idea of what water is, you would have to see it in all its forms.

You can use this same principle to improve or revise your writing. One of the major forms of writing is fiction. Another is poetry. Another is expository prose. Still another is business writing. See the chart "A Survey of Writing Forms," 134, or "Workplace Writing Tasks," 183, in your handbook to get an idea of the great many forms available to you.

To get a better appreciation of your writing, try changing it from one form to another. Switching forms will help you develop fresh perspectives and new approaches to your subject that you can apply when you revise.

- Here is a sentence of expository prose describing a house where an old cat-lover lives:

  Cats sun themselves on the fences, peep out the windows, and disappear around corners as I walk by.

- Here is how a professional writer transformed this idea into poetry:

  The house's eye appears to blink
  as a cat in a picture window
  parts a curtain.
  Suddenly, fences sprout
  whiskers, sidewalks run away.
  I am watched from shadows
  as I pass.

- Here is a reworking of the idea (by the same writer) into story form:

  I don't think I was paranoid, though my older sister had called me worse things before. But whenever I passed the neighbor's house where, at last count by my snoopy friends, there lived 24 cats, the feeling of being watched made me twitch and shrug.

- If this writer would transform the writing back into expository prose, the writing would surely be different because of the ideas that had arisen during the excursion into other forms.

WRITE: Write a fairly long sentence (or a short paragraph) about any subject that comes to mind. Then transform it into at least two of the writing forms listed in "A Survey of Writing Forms," 134 or "Workplace Writing Tasks," 183. Show your work to a writing partner.

follow-up Transform one of your compositions (or a good chunk of it) into a new form. Share your experiment with a classmate or your writing group.

Real-World Writing

What you want to write and what you actually write often have to be two different things, especially when you write in real-world situations. Your adrenalin might tell you to blow off steam, letting all your strongest feelings show in the words you use. But your head might tell you to calm down, be realistic, focus on results, and watch your language.

Watching your language means controlling your **diction** or tuning your words to the ears of your audience. (For some handbook help on ways to adjust your language to real-world situations, refer to "Using the Right Level of Language," 034.)

WRITE: Consider the following scenario: Bob and Johnny's Ice Cream Co. is accepting applications for individuals to work at the new ice-cream parlor they are opening in your town. Since you need a job (desperately), you decide to write a letter of application. As you write, keep in mind that Bob and Johnny's is a growing, upbeat, socially conscious, all-natural company with an excellent nationwide reputation. They want completely honest, pleasant, and dependable employees. Write a letter of inquiry showing enthusiasm, honesty, respect for the company, and positive qualities consistent with the company's needs. (For guidelines and a model, see "The Letter on Inquiry (or Request)," 194 in the handbook.) Address your letter to

Bob and Johnny's Ice Cream Co.
123 Berry Garcia Ln.
Stoughton, ME 01812

Important: As you write, avoid slipping into an inappropriate level of diction.

follow-up Now write a letter of application (209 in your handbook) to a local ice-cream parlor speaking very, very informally, as if the owner were a close friend. Compare the two letters.

Reviewing and Revising Texts

A Cold Eye

READ: One of the most important things you can do to make a piece of writing better is to stand back—not physically, but in your mind. After you've completed an early draft, you must step back from the work and view it with a cold eye. Here are some sentences you can practice saying to yourself so that you can successfully stand back from an early draft with a cold eye.

I didn't write this, a stranger did.
This piece is ancient history.
This is just a chunk of language.
Something crucial is missing here.
Thank goodness, I have another chance.
My best writing is still to come.
I've got a better idea.

REACT: If you have a piece of writing that is still in its early stages of development, turn your cold eye on it and plan a revising strategy. Use the handbook as your guide, referring specifically to the section on revising (028-032). When you've finished this cold-eyed strategy session, make a list of "Things to Do" to make your next draft better. (Use the space below or your own paper for your work.)

APPLY: Now you're ready to get dirty hands by working with the messy parts of your writing. First, set aside time for your work: a half hour to three hours is normal for a piece from one to five pages long. Next, gather all of your writing tools. Third, follow your "Things to Do" list and get to work.

The Write Instincts

READ: Study the short essay of comparison below. Read it over once and react to it instinctively. How does the writing work for you? In what ways? Then read it again in light of what your handbook says about effective writing style.

My sister and I have absolutely opposite personalities. I'm methodical, cautious, organized. Jennifer's impulsive, scattered, and fun-loving. I live for the future. She lives in the moment. When we were kids, I used to exploit these differences in our personalities—using them as a weapon against her. Basically, I teased her to death. For instance, she has always loved food and used to scarf down anything sweet at the speed of light when she was little. Every time we went for a ride in my father's classic 1956 Riviera sedan, something we did most every Sunday, my parents would give us one treat apiece. Usually we'd get a candy bar, sometimes an ice-cream bar. She'd eat her treat in about 10 seconds. I'd peel the wrapper real slow-like, and then eat my treat in stages. The outside of the peanut butter cup first, of course, and then the peanut butter. I'd spend a quarter of an hour on the outside chocolate alone! And of course, she'd have to sit there, and watch me eat the treat she no longer had—hers was eaten, mine was a weapon of torture. One day when she had eaten her Rice Krispie treat, and I was eating mine one Krispie at a time, my parents cured me of my urge to tease. They made me give her half my treat! I'm still the most methodical person I know, but no longer when it comes to dessert.

REACT: How does this writing stack up against the traits or characteristics of an effective style? We've listed a number of common traits below with space to write a brief response to each. Mention strengths as well as weaknesses in the style of the writing. (Work with a classmate if your teacher allows it.)

Concreteness ....

....

....

Focus ....

....

....

Vitality ....

....

....

Originality ....

....

....

Grace ....

....

....

Commitment ....

....

....

INSIDE

Remember: Your writing style comes from a series of writing choices you make. It is composed of your words, your sentences, and your paragraphs—nobody else's.

The 5-R's Revising Strategy

Writing authority Peter Elbow describes the results of first drafts in this way: ". . . a person's best writing is often all mixed up together with his worst. It all feels lousy to him as he's writing, but if he will let himself write it and come back later, he will find some parts of it are excellent. It is as though one's best words come wrapped in one's worst."

READ: To keep an open mind when you read what you have written, you need to put some distance between yourself and your writing.

- Whenever possible, put your writing aside for a day or two.
- Read it out loud.
- Ask others (family, friends, classmates) to read it out loud to you.
- Listen to the language you have used: How does it sound? What does it say?

REACT: These six questions will help you react to your own writing on your second or third read-through:

- What parts of my writing work for me?
- Do all of these parts work together?
- Do all the parts point to one idea? What is the main idea?
- Do the parts say exactly what I want them to say?
- Have I arranged the parts in the best possible order?
- Where do I need to go from here?

REWORK: Reworking your writing means rewriting and refining it until all of the parts work equally well. There is usually plenty of rewriting and refining to do in the early stages of writing.

REFLECT: One of the best ways to keep track of your reactions as you read, react, and rework is to write comments in the margins of your paper. Here are some guidelines:

- Explore your thoughts freely and naturally.
- Keep track of any suggestions for improving your writing.
- Note what you plan to cut, move, explain further, and so on.
- If you are unsure of yourself, write down a question to answer later.

REFINE: Refining is putting the final polish on your written copy—your thoughts and words. Here's what you can do to help:

- Read your paper out loud again to make sure that you haven't missed anything.
- Listen for both the sense and the sound of the writing.
- Make your final adjustments. Follow the 5 R's (read, react, rework, reflect, refine) each time you revise.

follow-up Select a work in progress and apply the 5-R's strategy. Write your reactions and reflections on another piece of paper.

Cut, Clarify, Condense

Here's an easy and effective strategy for fixing problems with wording. We call it "The 3 C's of Editing."

Editing Code:

CUT [brackets]

If you find a part that's unnecessary or wordy, put brackets around it. If you decide that section is really unneeded, cut it!

CLARIFY ～～～

If you see something confusing, unclear, or incomplete in your writing, put a wavy line under that section. You should rethink it, reword it, explain it, or add detail to it.

CONDENSE (parentheses)

If you come across a section of your writing that is wordy or overexplained, put a set of parentheses around it. Refer to "Wordiness," (095) "Deadwood," (090) and "Flowery language"(091) in the handbook for help.

READ & REACT: Here is a marked portion of a student's in-progress essay using the 3-C's editing code. Rewrite the essay following the coding used. *Hint:* Start by reading the entire paragraph first; then cross out those sections in brackets and consider how to improve the sections in parentheses.

My most memorable experience was the first time I drove my dad's car. I was twelve years old [at the time], and we had just gone up to Saxon, Wisconsin, for the summer. My dad had to go into town [for something], and he let me drive his (pride and joy). (As I was going along, I could see out the corner of my eye that he was trying to be cool, but I could tell that he was [getting] tense) [and uptight]. Every time I would come to a stop, I could see him unconsciously trying (to put the brakes on). As we (were coming into town), we passed Old Dan's Bar. Everything was going great. [What a trip!] Then I noticed that he had his hands on the dashboard to brace himself. As I was watching him, I suddenly drove into a fire hydrant and totaled the front of my father's brand-new Buick station wagon. (Dear old Dad almost had a canary). He was so mad at me that he couldn't (say a word). [He was speechless.] After that he decided to turn around and go back to camp. When we got there, he got a root beer from the cooler, and he didn't talk to me until the next day. [Needless to say] the rest of our trip was (a real bummer) for me.

follow-up Compare your revisions of the above paragraph with a classmate's. What do the two of you agree on? Where do you disagree?

On the Run

READ & REACT: Carefully read the first draft of "Soft Bones" below. It is the result of an in-class writing activity.

When I was growing up, my parents never quite agreed on my participation in contact sports or on what kinds of physical activity were good or not. My mom felt that there were plenty of ways to get hurt in life without deliberately going out to do something that could result in physical injury, like playing tackle football. To make sure I understood where she stood on this issue, my mom sat me down one afternoon and talked about a rare hereditary ailment that ran in her family called "soft bones." It was a condition that made strenuous physical activity really risky, especially for boys. I had a picture of my bones twisting like pretzels and hardening in strange positions. Mom just didn't understand about tackling and stuff like that.

My dad thought of "getting hurt" as something you sort of took for granted. You see, my dad was sort of a definite sports fanatic. My dad started playing ball at an early age. From the time I was able to stagger around on my own, he was always throwing some sort of ball at me.

Whether I would play peewee football at age seven became a real bone of contention between my parents. My mother didn't want me to play, while my dad did. This put me in a difficult situation. I wanted to make my dad happy. I didn't want to make my mom unhappy.

So, when I told my father I had decided to wait a while before attempting to play organized football, I could tell he was disappointed, but took it pretty well. It was a couple months later as we were playing on the lawn and twisted my ankle. Worried, I told Dad, "I hope my bones will get back into the right shape okay." Without thinking I blurted out about the "soft bones" that ran in Mom's family and affected males. He looked at me for a second and started to laugh, and laugh, and laugh.

REACT: Revise this first draft using the "Revising on the Run" (030) guidelines listed in your handbook. Make your changes on this sheet. (Share your results.)

Bridging the Gap

Writers need to practice using transitions to become skilled at moving smoothly and clearly from one point to the next in their writing. Need a list of transitions? Refer to "Transitions and Linking Words" (114) in the handbook.

READ: The following paragraph contains plenty of good details. But all is not well. The paragraph needs work in the transition department. (Some of the transitions are too abrupt and noticeable.) Read it carefully and see for yourself.

"One, two; kick, jump; five, six, seven, eight! Oh come on, you look like a bunch of slobs! This is jazz ballet! You're supposed to look graceful, not like soggy pieces of bread! All right, take a quick break!" Miss Nitchka roared. My name is Karen and Miss Nitchka is my jazz ballet disciplinarian. By the sound of it, you'd probably think I'm crazy if I said, "I love jazz, the discipline, the hard work, even the yelling!" Well I do; let me tell you why. To begin with, jazz is fun. I've always loved dancing. I was in gymnastics and I loved it. I wasn't exactly a champion at the tumbling part, but I was absolutely marvelous at the dance floor exercises. Since jazz has a combination of gymnastics—splits, leaps, kicks, high jumps, etc.—and dancing, I took to it. And am I glad I did! Secondly, I love all the hard work, all the sweat. It gives me a sense of accomplishment. I have more confidence in myself because I'm doing something I love and I'm working hard at it. I'm saving discipline and yelling for last because I feel they are the most important. They also have the same meaning. If she didn't yell, we wouldn't work as hard. In fact, we probably wouldn't find much interest in it and would give up. In conclusion, without the discipline we couldn't learn as much, so we wouldn't go on to bigger and better things.

REACT: Circle every transition that draws undue attention to itself. Also note details and ideas that you would like to cut, move, or reword. Then rewrite the paragraph, making sure it reads more smoothly and clearly.

Refining: Sentence Strengthening

When Complex Is Simpler . . .

READ: As you revise, you may want to combine some of your short, simple sentences into more mature, efficient sentences. To join two ideas that are not equal in importance, you may use a **complex sentence**. A complex sentence contains one independent clause and one (or more) dependent clauses. The complex sentence is used to show the relationship of one idea to another.

The complex sentence helps you tell the reader which of the two ideas expressed in the sentence is more important. The more important idea (main idea) is placed in the independent clause; the less important idea is placed in the dependent, or subordinate, clause. Since the purpose of all writing is to communicate ideas clearly, the complex sentence is especially valuable to the writer.

An adverb clause is one kind of subordinate clause. Loosely speaking, it modifies a verb or another modifier in the sentence. It is easier to use adverb clauses effectively when you understand what they do in a sentence and become familiar with the subordinating conjunctions used to introduce them.

- Some subordinating conjunctions introduce adverb clauses of **time:**
  before after when until since while
- Some subordinating conjunctions introduce adverb clauses telling the **reason why:**
  because since
- Some subordinating conjunctions introduce adverb clauses telling the **purpose or result**:
  so that so that in order that
- Some subordinating conjunctions introduce adverb clauses telling the **condition:**
  whereas if unless though although as long as while

COMBINE: Combine each set of simple sentences into a complex sentence by placing the less important idea in an adverb clause. An asterisk (*) is printed after the more important idea in the first few sets. In parentheses after each of your new complex sentences, explain what your adverb clause tells.

1. Eagles will usually kill animals lighter than themselves. Some fast-moving species have been known to carry off much heavier prey.*

   Although eagles will usually kill animals lighter than themselves, some fast-moving species have been known to carry off much heavier prey. (condition)

2. The writhing, talon-pierced carp weighed 13 pounds.
The sea eagle flew low and was almost pulled underwater by its prey.*

3. The young eagle is heavier than its parents by as much as one pound.*
It leaves the nest.

4. The hunters looked up toward the mountain crest.
They saw an American bald eagle descending with a mule deer fawn in its talons.*

5. The lurid and suspicious stories continued to be printed.
Worried mothers lived in fear of their babies being carried off by eagles.*

6. Arthur Bowland once persuaded a Verreaux's eagle to snatch a 20-pound pack while in flight. He could test the bird's supposed tremendous strength.

7. Scientific tests for muscularity and power will not be a true guide for the species.
They are done with wild, not captive, eagles.

8. Eagles can kill prey four times their own size. They ordinarily cannot carry a load much more than their own body weight.

It's All Relative

Another way to show which idea in a sentence is more important is to use an adjective clause for the less important idea. An adjective clause modifies, or describes, a noun or a pronoun.

Adjective clauses are usually introduced by the **relative pronouns**: *who, whom, whose, which, that*. Such clauses are called "relative clauses." *Who, whom,* and *whose* are used to refer to people. *Which* refers to nonliving objects or to animals. *That* may refer to people, nonliving objects, or animals.

Please note: An adjective clause can also be introduced with the words *when, where,* and *how*.

COMBINE: Combine the following simple sentences into complex sentences by using an adjective clause. Place the less important idea in the adjective clause. An asterisk (*) is printed after the more important idea in the first few groups of simple sentences. You decide which of the two ideas is more important in the rest of the groups.

1. The whale shark is the largest fish in the world.*
The whale shark is found in the warmer areas of the Atlantic, Pacific, and Indian oceans.

The whale shark, which is found in the warmer areas of the Atlantic, Pacific, and Indian oceans, is the largest fish in the world.

Note: Commas surround the adjective clause if it is a **nonrestrictive clause** (as in the example above). "Nonrestrictive" means the clause is not required to identify the noun or pronoun. Nonrestrictive clauses give extra information that is not necessary to the basic meaning of the sentence. **Restrictive clauses**, or those clauses that restrict or limit or are required to identify the noun or pronoun, are not set off by commas. (See 586 in your handbook for more information and examples.)

2. Dr. Andrew Smith examined the first recorded whale shark specimen in 1828.*
Dr. Smith was a military surgeon with the British army.

3. The fishermen harpooned the shark.
The fishermen had noticed its unusual gray coloration with white spots.*

4. The dried skin is preserved in the Museum d'Histoire Naturelle of Paris.*
Dr. Smith originally purchased the dried skin for $30.

5. In 1868 a young Irish naturalist studied the whale sharks in the Seychelle Islands.*
He had heard the natives speak of a monstrous fish called the "Chagrin."

6. He saw several specimens.
The specimens exceeded 50 feet in length.

7. Many men reported sharks measuring nearly 70 feet in length.
These men had always been considered trustworthy.

8. The largest fish ever held in captivity was a whale shark.
It was kept in a small bay rather than in an aquarium.

9. The only other exceptionally large fish is the basking shark.
It compares in size with the whale shark.

10. A fish frightened millions of viewers during the movie *Jaws*.
The fish was a replica of the carnivorous great white shark.

Clauses in Review

How much do you know about using adverb and adjective clauses? How do they help a writer? Do you use them in your own writing? This activity will help you answer these questions. Some important points to remember about adverb and adjective clauses are as follows:

- An **adverb clause** at the beginning of a sentence is set off by a comma; an adverb clause at the end of a sentence is generally not set off by a comma.
- An **adjective clause** that is nonrestrictive is set off by commas; an adjective clause that is restrictive (required) is not set off by commas. (See 586 in your handbook for additional information.)

COMBINE: To continue your practice of subordination, combine each of the following sets of simple sentences into one complex sentence by following the directions in parentheses.

1. A. Insects have three pairs of legs, one pair of antennae, and usually one or two pairs of wings.
B. Insects comprise the largest group of arthropods.
(Use B. in a nonrestrictive adjective clause.)

Insects, which comprise the largest group of arthropods, have three pairs of legs, one pair of antennae, and usually one or two pairs of wings.

2. A. It has been suggested that one day insects may inherit the earth.
B. This statement seems exaggerated to us humans.
(Use B. in an adverb clause telling the condition.)

3. A. This prediction may one day be realized.
B. The insects' small size, great variety, and fast rate of reproduction have made them nearly indestructible.
(Use B. in an adverb clause at the beginning of the sentence.)

4. A. Farmers like certain pollinating insects.
   B. Farmers despise the insects that destroy their crops.
   (Use A. in an adverb clause telling condition.)

5. A. The insects can be a serious threat to humanity.
   B. Some insects carry diseases such as typhus, malaria, and yellow fever.
   (Use B. in a restrictive adjective clause.)

   (Use B. in an adverb clause telling why.)

6. A. Butterflies and moths have wings covered with tiny overlapping scales.
   B. The scales provide their color.
   (Use B. in a nonrestrictive adjective clause.)

7. A. The worker honeybee will generally die after stinging someone.
   B. The barbed stinger stays in the wound, pulling the poison sac and other organs out of the bee.
   (Use B. in an adverb clause telling the reason why at the end of the sentence.)

Keeping Things Parallel

Parallel structure is the balanced or coordinated arrangement of sentence elements that are equal in importance; in other words, it is the arranging of similar ideas in a similar way. The use of parallel structure can add a sense of rhythm and emphasis to your writing style that makes it more appealing to your reader. (Refer to 440 in your handbook for more information on parallel structure.)

REVISE: To better understand parallel structure, look carefully at the sentences below. Each sentence contains two ideas or items that are equal in importance, but are not expressed in equal or parallel form. Those sentence parts that are not parallel and should be are underlined. Substitute a parallel expression in the place of one of those that are underlined. Revise each sentence as necessary so that the new expression fits in well and adds a sense of balance and rhythm to the overall sentence.

1. Swimming is an excellent exercise for strengthening your heart and one that will increase your lung power.

   Swimming is an excellent exercise for strengthening your heart and increasing your lung power.

2. Swim for 10 minutes, dividing the time between the breaststroke, the crawl, and doing the backstroke, and you will have had a good workout.

3. Swimming improves the mobility of major joints and is strengthening for the muscles.

4. There is a rather odd myth that swimming in freezing water is beneficial and you will enjoy it.

5. At best, plunging into cold water may give you a kick; at worst, you may have a heart attack.

6. Some people get less exercise at the pool than they intend; they talk to friends, tread water, and are hanging onto the side while watching others.

7. Faithful practice will result in a smooth swimming style and your breathing pattern will be efficient.

8. A steady ten-minute swim would probably comprise a good workout while swimming furiously for three minutes would not.

COMPLETE: Complete each of the following sentences by adding a word, phrase, or clause that is parallel to the underlined portion of the sentence. (Each addition must be sensible as well as parallel.)

1. Sitting in the middle of his new apartment were a suitcase, a box of books, and

2. He hopes to get a job either working as a limo driver or

3. This Saturday night some of my friends want to go to the hockey game, some want to go out for pizza, and

4. This time should really be spent planning for the future, not

5. We drove all morning to get to the job site, and we drove all afternoon

Saving the Best for Last

Here's a writing tip you may find useful: by postponing the crucial or main idea until the end of a sentence, you can build tension and draw your reader into the development of your thought. This kind of sentence, known as the **periodic sentence**, packs a nice punch—one that is not easily forgotten. (Refer to "periodic sentence" in "Arrangement of a Sentence," 760, in the handbook for more.)

READ: Read the samples below, paying particular attention to the location of the crucial or main idea (in regular italics).

> ***When the mountains and the pines turned into blue oxen, blue dogs, and blue people,*** *the old couple asked me to spend the night in the hut.*
>
> —from *The Woman Warrior*, Maxine Hong Kingston

> ***In the roads where the teams moved, where the wheels milled the ground and the hooves of the horses beat the ground,*** *the dirt crust broke and the dust formed.*
>
> —from *The Grapes of Wrath*, John Steinbeck

WRITE: Rewrite the following sentences so that the most crucial idea is postponed until the end of the sentence. (Share your results.)

1. The house stood at the top of the hill, surrounded by weeping willows and lilac bushes, punctuating a winding driveway that looked like an upside-down question mark.

....

....

2. Sean ran headlong into traffic, ignoring his own safety and chasing the renegade dog that held his only baseball.

....

....

INSIDE

Should you go out of your way to use periodic sentences in your writing? No. Should you try to use them often? Same answer. They should be used with care, when it seems right, when an important point demands more dramatic treatment.

Refining: Improving Style

What Makes "Good" Good?

Everyone has his or her own individual tastes. While I really like Mexican food (earthy and healthy), you might like Irish food (homey and hearty) or French food (bon appétit!). I like purple; however, you may go for chartreuse. I really dig blues, but you may prefer heavy metal. With writing style, it's the same. Everyone has opinions about what makes for good writing.

REACT: What do you value in writing? Do you prefer writing that is fast paced, or highly descriptive, or a bit hard edged and sarcastic? And what do you strive for when you write? On the lines below, list five things you like to see in writing (including your own). (You might, for example, enjoy writing that sounds friendly and unpretentious, like one person talking to another person.)

1. ....

....

2. ....

....

3. ....

....

4. ....

....

5. ....

....

RECONSIDER: Review your list in light of what the handbook says about the traits of good writing. Turn to the section "Traits of an Effective Style" (059) in the handbook. Review this section and note at least two things that you would add to your personal list of traits of effective writing. Share with a classmate the results of your personal inventory.

INSIDE

Though there are certain traits of effective writing that are commonly recognized, each writer's style is different—that uniqueness is the ultimate element of an effective style!

I Could Write Like That

READ & REACT: Select a piece of writing—preferably a passage from a magazine article—that you consider to be good in terms of both what it says (content) and how it says it (style). Then in a brief essay try to figure out what makes the writing work for you. Make references to specific words, phrases, and ideas you actually see and hear in the writing. (Attach a copy of the passage to your writing.)

Points you might want to consider in your writing:

- Does the writer have a clear purpose in mind?
- Does the writing sound sincere and honest? Do you hear a distinctive voice in the writing?
- Is the subject of the writing presented effectively? Is there a form or design to the writing? Does it move logically from one point to the next?
- Does the writer include anecdotes, figures of speech, effective details and examples, etc?
- Does the writing make you react in some way?

Hint: Also refer to your comments in the workshop entitled "What Makes 'Good' Good?" for ideas for your writing.

EXTEND: In a writing of your own, try imitating the style of the passage you selected. (The content of your writing should be original. The way you express your ideas should reflect the sample passage.)

INSIDE

Read as much as you can from a variety of sources if you are truly interested in developing your writing abilities. There's really no other way to expand your writing horizons. You have to see how other people are doing it.

What Comes Naturally

READ: User-friendly writing is writing that is concise and natural. "Natural" means it flows along the way we normally think and speak. "Concise" means that none of the words are wasted—they all contribute to the purpose of the writing. None are dead, none are flowery, none are aimless, and none are needlessly repeated. The opposite of natural writing is stilted writing, writing that is stiff, awkward, impersonal, and forced.

Stilted Thought:

The cool, free breeze in the learning center, which came like a storm in the night, was an extremely exhilarating change from the sultry confines of Ms. Brown's classroom.

Revised for Naturalness and Conciseness:

The cool breeze in the learning center was a refreshing change from Ms. Brown's muggy classroom.

Lubbos Publishing House

Date: February 5, 1996
From: James L. Blather, Shipping Department Manager
To: All shipping clerks

It has come to my attention during the past number of weeks that an inordinate amount of precious company time is being expended by shipping personnel in the task of preparing orders that require U.P.S. next-day-air delivery service. Because it is essential that we utilize all our resources of time in such a way that Lubbos Publishing House garners the greatest potential benefit from all its investments in personnel, this set of events contributing to a lack of productivity is an issue that requires our urgent and undivided attention.

Therefore, please be advised that on Friday of this present week, February 9, at 3:00 p.m. in the afternoon, the entire cadre of shipping clerks will meet together along with me in the Conference Room for a thorough and comprehensive discussion of this particular matter at hand.

follow-up The above memo is neither concise nor natural. In the space above or on your own paper, revise the memo so that it's clear, brief, and reader-friendly.

Be Concise

Your handbook lists the main causes of stiltedness (or unnaturalness) in writing and shows you how to overcome this problem. (Refer to "Writing Natural Sentences," 089-096, in the handbook.) Apply what you've learned in the following activity.

READ: Carefully read the following letter to the editor that happens to be full of stilted language. Afterward, note at least five examples of stilted language in the spaces we've provided below. (Work on this with a partner if your teacher allows it.)

To the Editor:

Allow me to register my opposition to the little gasoline-powered contrivance that is commonly referred to as a leaf blower. Most members of our honorable citizenry appear to view it in the aspect of an implement for good lawn grooming and landscape maintenance. But to me it's a big pain in the neck. It blows pollen particles into the air. It blows a whole bunch of dust around. Probably, the unsanitary leavings of pet animals are blown around, too. Gas fumes are not to be ignored, either. Then when I come down with a killer case of an allergic reaction, thanks to the dust and stuff, I, wouldn't you know it, can't sleep. The roaring of the leaf blower makes too much noise. I'm ticked. Let's go back to brooms and rakes and similar premodern implements.

Lila

1. Wordiness: Most members of our honorable . . . and landscape maintenance.
2. Deadwood: ....
3. Flowery language: ....
4. Triteness: ....
5. Euphemism: ....
6. Jargon: ....
7. Cliche: ....
8. Awkward interruption: ....

follow-up Remove as many of the symptoms of stiltedness in Lila's letter as you can, and rewrite it so that the main thoughts come through naturally and gracefully.

Low-Fat Writing

READ: Most writers can leave out a great deal more in their writing than they think. For example, all of the words in parentheses in the following paragraph can be removed or simplified:

At the game (which was played) last night between St. Thomas High and its archrival, Union High, (the players who were considered the best on each team) (were injured) (in the course of the action). Marty Grunwald, (who plays for) St. Thomas, (received an injury to) her shoulder (when she collided) (without warning) with an opposing player (from Union High School). (Regrettably,) (the force of the collision was responsible for) dislocating (her) right (shoulder). (Likewise, in a surprising coincidence), Cassie Ribero from Union High (also suffered a dislocated right shoulder) (in an accidental collision). (The loss of their top players was a disappointment to both teams). [106 words]

When all of the useless words are removed, the thought can be fully expressed in one smooth-reading sentence:

At last night's game between archrivals St. Thomas and Union high schools, Marty Grunwald and Cassie Ribero, team leaders for their respective schools, both dislocated their right shoulders in collisions with opposing players. [33 words]

REWRITE: With a partner, study the following paragraph adapted from an article in *Scientific American*. Then trim the fat by cutting or simplifying all of the words and phrases that are unnecessary. Rewrite the paragraph on your own paper. Compare your results with other teams.

Imagine in your mind, if you will, a pinball-type machine that actually propels tiny photons of light instead of the usual steel marble-like objects and that uses things like mirrors to function as bumpers. If you watch very carefully the path taken by a photon as it is fired with considerable force into play, it ricochets off the mirrors as if it were a solid object, like a rock. But if, as all this is going on, you stop observing with your eyes, things begin to get strange and unusual. Unlike a hard, metallic, round steel ball, the photon shatters into many wavelets, each wavelet taking a different route or path through the imaginary machine on which the game is being played.

Refining: Editing

Editing Checklist

Have you ever used a shopping or study list? Isn't it helpful to have your thoughts organized? The following checklist should help you each time you review and edit your writing. You might think of it as a "chopping" list, but it's really more: chopping, connecting, rearranging, polishing . . .

.... 1. Read your final draft aloud to test it for sense and sound. Better yet, have someone read it aloud to you. Listen carefully as he or she reads. Your writing should read smoothly and naturally. If it doesn't, you have more editing to do.

.... 2. Does each sentence express a complete thought? Does each paragraph have an overall point or purpose?

.... 3. Have you used different sentence types and lengths? Are any sentences too long and rambling? Do you use too many short, choppy sentences?

.... 4. Have you used a variety of sentence beginnings? Watch out for too many sentences that begin with the same pronoun or article (*I*, *My*, *The* . . .).

.... 5. Check each simple sentence for effective use of modifiers, especially prepositional phrases, participial phrases, and appositives. Have you punctuated these modifiers correctly?

.... 6. Check your compound sentences. Do they contain two equal ideas, and is the logical relationship between the two ideas expressed by a proper conjunction (*and* versus *but* versus *or* . . .)?

.... 7. What about your complex sentences? Have you used subordination effectively? Does the independent clause contain the most important idea? Are less important ideas contained in dependent clauses?

.... 8. Make sure your writing is clear and concise. Have you omitted jargon, slang, redundancies, and other forms of wordiness?

.... 9. Is your writing fresh and original? Have you avoided overused words and phrases? If not, substitute nouns, verbs, and adjectives that are specific, vivid, and colorful.

.... 10. Replace any words or phrases that may be awkward, confusing, or misleading.

follow-up Add points of your own so the list truly becomes a personal editing checklist. Then put the list to work. Choose a piece of unfinished writing from your folder and work with it, using the checklist as your guide.

Agreement: Subject & Verb

READ & REACT: Study the guidelines for subject and verb agreement in your handbook. In the exercise below, underline the subject and circle the correct verb choice in the parentheses.

1. Half of the dorms on campus (is, are) coed dorms.
2. Most of the students (is, are) upperclassmen.
3. The faculty (present, presents) a freshman orientation to school every year.
4. Some of the students (is, are) commuting to school every day.
5. The campus news (include, includes), among other items, a list of activities for the week.
6. Personal computing is one of the new classes that (is, are) being offered for the first time this semester.
7. None of the freshmen (realize, realizes) where the student union is located.
8. All of the campus organizations (is, are) looking for new members among the incoming freshmen.
9. This is one of the books that (is, are) required for the freshman English course.
10. Mathematics (is, are) a requirement for almost any field of study.
11. The cause of the bad grade (was, were) poor study habits.
12. Of the tests that (is, are) used for evaluating college applicants, the ACT test is used most frequently.
13. Some of the students (request, requests) a specific instructor for each course they take.
14. Business is one of the majors that (is, are) becoming more popular.
15. Some of the students attending college today (is, are) required to attend all classes.
16. Any of the students missing classes (is, are) required to report the reason for the absence.
17. The room and time slot that (was, were) assigned to this class have been changed.
18. The increased enrollment for the class (was, were) the reason for these changes.

Agreement: Pronoun & Antecedent

READ & REACT: Study the rules in your handbook concerning agreement of pronouns and antecedents. Then underline the correct pronoun in each of the following sentences. Circle the antecedent.

1. For the job hunter to get the best possible job, (he or she, they) needs to have three or four job offers from which to choose.
2. Everyone looking for a job should be aware of the different methods of searching available to (him or her, them).
3. Every job hunter owes it to (himself or herself, themselves) to become acquainted with all phases of the job-hunting process.
4. Both Ashley and her friend, Shelli, use newspaper ads for new job leads that (she, they) then follow up with a phone call and a letter.
5. Neither Ashley nor Shelli expects to find the perfect job on (her, their) first attempt.
6. Sometimes job hunters try to make (his or her, their) availability known by placing ads about themselves and (his or her, their) job skills in newspapers.
7. Most colleges have especially good placement services because (they, it) understand that finding a good job is the major reason (their, its) students came to college in the first place.
8. Some colleges offer (its, their) students a complete job placement service, including placement help years after the students have graduated.
9. Other college offices, however, think they have done (its, their) job when they place the student once after graduation.
10. The private employment agency charges (its, their) customer only when (he or she, they) get(s) a job.
11. When employers use an executive search firm, (he or she, they) want the firm to hire people presently employed by other companies.
12. Both the employer and the job hunter can send (his or her, their) listings to a clearinghouse.
13. The U.S. government offers all (its, their) citizens a free employment service.

Indefinite Pronoun Reference

A writer must be careful not to confuse the reader with pronoun references that are ambiguous. (*Ambiguous* means *indefinite or unclear.*) Indefinite pronoun reference results when it is not clear which word is being referred to by the pronoun in the sentence.

REACT: Circle the pronoun in each sentence below that is ambiguous or indefinite. Then rewrite each of the sentences so that the error in reference is corrected.

1. As he drove his car up to the service window, (it) made a strange rattling sound.

   As he drove up to the service window, his car made a strange rattling sound.

2. They moved the file cabinet out of the office so they could wash it.

3. Take the apples out of the bowls and wash them.

4. Sarah put her album on the stereo that she had gotten as a graduation gift.

5. Jerry asked Jack if he needed a raincoat.

6. The hawk spied the rattlesnake nearing its eggs.

7. When the hail hit the skylight, it exploded into hundreds of little pieces.

follow-up Conduct a 5-minute minilesson with a classmate or small writing group about another sentence-related problem. Ideally this will be a problem that shows up in your own writing every now and then. (Refer to "Writing Sentences," 069-101, in the handbook for ideas.)

Postscript: In your minilesson, identify the problem, show how it can be fixed, and provide at least one sample sentence to be corrected and discussed.

Dangling Modifiers

READ: You know what happens when you drag your feet along the bottom of a lake. Things become murky and obscure. That's what happens in your reader's brain when you accidentally use misplaced or dangling modifiers. To ensure clarity, you must be able to recognize misplaced modifiers so they can be moved or reworded accordingly. (Refer to "Misplaced modifiers," 087, in the handbook for more information.)

REACT: Each of the sentences below contains a misplaced modifier, a modifier that is incorrectly placed, causing the meaning of the sentence to be confusing or misleading. Locate and underline the misplaced modifier in each sentence. Then revise each sentence by moving the misplaced modifier to its proper location. (Make other changes to the sentence as needed.)

1. The books are piled in stacks for the new students <u>with course-identification numbers</u>. (The phrase "with course-identification numbers" appears to modify "students"; it should modify "stacks.")

The books for the new students are piled in stacks with course-identification numbers.

2. Athletes must train hard to make the Olympic team for many years.

3. When young women began riding bicycles, they were told it was not a feminine thing to do in the 1890s.

4. We will be visiting several four-year colleges that I am considering attending over the summer.

5. My father has gone to the library every Sunday to check out a book for years.

REVISE: Many of the sentences below contain a dangling modifier, a modifier that appears to modify the wrong word. Locate and underline the dangling modifier in each sentence. Revise each sentence so that the modifier clearly modifies the word it was intended to modify.

1. After swimming in the lake nearly all afternoon, Bill's mother called him.
(The phrase "After swimming in the lake nearly all afternoon" appears to modify "Bill's mother"; it is intended to modify "Bill.")

   After swimming in the lake nearly all afternoon, Bill heard his mother call him.

2. While printing out my newest report, someone came to the door.

3. Having never ridden on a plane before, the attendant was especially nice to me.

4. Though only fourteen years old, my father gave me my first driving lesson.

5. After preparing two versions of the presentation, the sales team leader signaled us to take a break.

6. Coming in late for work, the supervisor gave me a lecture on common courtesy.

7. Failing to see the stop sign, the car rammed into the side of an oncoming truck.

Writing Acceptable Sentences

Careful attention is necessary when revising your rough drafts to make sure each sentence is "acceptable." That means you want to avoid *substandard language* and *double negatives*.

CORRECT: Rewrite each of the sentences to correct the clarity problem. After the revision, identify in parentheses the type of problem you corrected. (Refer to "Writing Acceptable Sentences," 097-101, in the handbook, for help.)

1. Jim's supervisor had to ask him to get off of the phone and wait on a customer.

2. Someone should have told Jim that gabbing with friends on the phone at work isn't the best way to earn brownie points.

3. Working the third shift is not no easy job.

4. If Martha would of checked the paper tray before she began making copies, she would not of run out of paper in the middle of the job.

5. Mark didn't hardly get no help from his partner.

6. You must try and understand other people's feelings and beliefs.

Common Sentence Errors

REACT: Place RO in front of each run-on sentence, CS in front of each comma splice, F in front of each fragment, and C in front of each correct sentence. Make any changes necessary to correct each faulty sentence. (For handbook help, see "Writing Complete Sentences," 078-082.)

CS **1.** I never really enjoyed science; math is my favorite class.

...... **2.** By the time we arrived, the show was nearly over, we missed everything but the credits and the cartoon.

...... **3.** Don't touch that chair it has just been painted.

...... **4.** Last summer during our camping trip to Canada.

...... **5.** My room is a real mess, but I like it that way.

...... **6.** Most students would rather goof around than study, most adults went through the same thing when they were in school.

...... **7.** The rain which continued for seven straight days.

...... **8.** Some run-on sentences are easy to recognize, others are much more difficult.

...... **9.** Maria's mother works at the hospital her father works at the school.

...... **10.** John had to go to his violin lesson however he will stop by when he is through.

...... **11.** Karen enjoys shopping for clothes, especially when someone else is paying for them.

...... **12.** After I had squeezed on my stiff, heavy boot.

...... **13.** I got an "A" on my English test I've never gotten one before.

...... **14.** Time goes slowly when you are working, it seems to fly when you are playing.

...... **15.** Luis will meet us at the skating rink later he has to go home to pick up his skates.

...... **16.** Never leave your bike outside at night, it might not be there in the morning.

...... **17.** Even though we sprayed twice a day with a strong disinfectant.

...... **18.** I can't go with you tonight unless you can be back by nine.

Complete & Mature

REACT: Carefully review the following paragraph, correcting any sentence errors as you go along. (You will find examples of sentence fragments, comma splices, and run-on sentences in the paragraph.) Cross out incorrect punctuation marks and add punctuation and capital letters as needed. (Refer to "Writing Sentences," 069-101, in the handbook for help.)

As a small child, he had always eaten jelly doughnuts for breakfast. Now, however, at a plump and rather easily winded 29. He has switched over to granola and skim milk. Along with his new eating habits, his looks are also beginning to change. He wears his hair a bit longer in back, and thinner on top and his shoes are those flip-flop kind. That are good for lower back pain. He thinks about this as he sits gazing out at the backyard, which the neighbor kid with the nose ring mows every Saturday for a sawbuck. He wonders if the kid knows that a sawbuck is a slang term for ten dollars. Maybe his younger brother Kevin is right in his appraisal, maybe he is old-fashioned and far, far out of step. They had just gone out with their parents the night before, a monthly guilt-abating ritual. Kevin had walked into the restaurant and had scanned his brother's clothes and posture, in addition, he had even seemed to scan his brother's thoughts, with slow-mounting amusement, Kevin had said, "You look so . . . granola." Trying to disguise his obvious embarrassment, the older brother had grabbed his keys and had headed for the Subaru pickup in the parking lot.

follow-up Professional writers occasionally break the rules in their work. A writer might, for example, purposely use a series of sentence fragments or express a long, rambling idea. Find a passage from a magazine article in which the writer has obviously broken one of the rules regarding the correct use of sentences. Discuss the passage with your classmates. Does it work in the writing as a whole? (Try breaking the rules yourself in one of your upcoming pieces of writing, but do so carefully, with a desired effect in mind.)

Refining: Proofreading

Proofreading Checklist

The following guidelines will help you put the finishing touches on your writing before you share it with your audience. (As you use this checklist, add points of your own to truly make it a personal checklist.)

Spelling

1. Have you spelled all your words correctly? Here are some tips:
   - Read your writing backward and aloud—one word at a time—so you focus on each word.
   - Circle each word you are unsure of.
   - For help, consult the list of commonly misspelled words in your handbook. (For additional help, check a dictionary, or ask the "designated speller" in your classroom.)

Punctuation

2. Does each sentence end with a punctuation mark?

3. Are coordinating conjunctions (*and*, *but*, *or*, *so*, etc.) in compound sentences preceded by a comma? Have you used commas to set off items listed in a series, after introductory clauses, and so on?

4. Have you used apostrophes to show possession or to mark contractions?

5. Is all dialogue, or written conversation, properly punctuated?

Capitalization

6. Do all sentences, including dialogue, begin with a capital letter?

7. Have you capitalized the proper names of people, places, and things?

Usage

8. Have you misused any of the commonly mixed pairs of words: *there / their / they're; accept / except?* Refer to the section "Using the Right Word" in your handbook.

9. Have you used any words, phrases, or sentences that may confuse the reader?

Grammar

10. Do your subjects and verbs agree in number?

11. Do your pronouns agree with their antecedents?

12. Have you used any sentence fragments, run-ons, or rambling sentences?

Form

13. Have you chosen an appropriate title if one is needed?

14. Is your paper labeled correctly with the author's name and class?

Test Yourself

IDENTIFY: In the following sentences, groups of words with one or more punctuation or usage errors are underlined and numbered in parentheses. Copy the underlined words on the blank spaces making the necessary corrections as you go along. (Be careful to show the exact location of each punctuation mark.)

Plato an (1) ancient Greek philosopher and educator was (2) the first to write about the lost continent of Atlantis. Most scholars agree that Plato book (3) entitled Critias (4) includes legendary events not (5) real history. In his book, Plato was writing about events that he claimed happened over 9000 (6) years before his own lifetime. When Plato described atlantis he (7) painted a picture of a people of fabulous wealth who ruled over a great and wonderful empire. He said the royal palace was "a marvel to behold for size and beauty. Plato (8) also claimed that the continent of Atlantis sank beneath the sea in one days time. (9)

If Atlantis really existed where (10) was it located? Many places have been candidates for the honor however the (11) following locations are most commonly listed the (12) Atlantic Ocean the (13) Sahara Desert, the island of Crete, Spain, England, Greenland, and Mexico.

Is their lost (14) treasure waiting for someone to discover or (15) was Atlantis only the product of Plato's imagination? Wouldnt it (16) be marvelous if someone found the fabled land of gold and silver where Plato said kings gathered every five years to administer the laws hunt (17) bulls and (18) make sacrifices to the gods? Atlantis has been many things to many people but mostly (19) of all it is what it will always be a (20) mystery.

1. Plato, an
2. ....
3. ....
4. ....
5. ....
6. ....
7. ....
8. ....
9. ....
10. ....
11. ....
12. ....
13. ....
14. ....
15. ....
16. ....
17. ....
18. ....
19. ....
20. ....

Comma Practice

READ & INSERT: Read and study the handbook rules on using commas. Then insert commas where they are needed in the sentences below. Circle each comma you insert. Some sentences may not need commas.

1. Last week in our first-aid class, we learned the Heimlich maneuver, a method of clearing a choking person's blocked airway.
2. The Heimlich maneuver not artificial respiration is used to save a choking victim.
3. Unless you act to save him or her a victim of food choking will die of strangulation in four minutes.
4. When using the Heimlich maneuver you exert pressure that pushes the diaphragm up compresses the air in the lungs and expels the object blocking the airway.
5. A friend of mine who had apparently paid attention to her first-aid class saved the life of a choking victim.
6. The victim who had been eating steak was forever grateful that my friend had learned the Heimlich maneuver.
7. That is why it is important for everyone to know how to perform this maneuver or to get quick professional help.
8. Whenever you think a situation is life threatening don't hesitate to call an ambulance or the rescue squad.
9. After calling for emergency help be prepared to state your name the injured person's name the address or place where the injured person is located and a brief description of what happened.
10. This is necessary so that the emergency personnel know exactly what they have to do when they arrive.
11. Also remember that your objective to help save a life can be better accomplished when you remain calm and follow suggested procedures.

follow-up Commas are used to separate a *vocative* from the rest of the sentence. Do you know what that means? If not, look in your handbook (589).

Using Commas

INSERT: Insert commas where they are needed in the sentences below and circle each. After consulting your handbook, write the rule (or rules) for each comma you insert.

1. Although the brain requires 25% of all oxygen used by the body, it comprises only 2% of a person's total body weight.

   Use a comma after an introductory adverb clause.

2. Did you know John that a whale's heart beats only nine times a minute?

3. Hey please turn the music down! I'm trying to get some sleep!

4. If it would make you feel any better I'd be happy to come along and drive you home from the dentist's office.

5. "One-fourth of the 206 bones in the human body" explained Mr. Brown the paramedic "are located in the feet."

6. Although it is a mind-boggling fact the body does indeed have 70000 miles of blood vessels.

7. James Rudan D.D.S. will be extracting all of my wisdom teeth.

8. It is the female bee not the male that does all the work in and around the hive.

9. I have taken art and science courses all through high school and I expect to major in landscape design at the Madison Area Technical College; my classes will begin September 3 1996.

10. Sarah who is planning to major in psychology has already enrolled at the University of Maryland.

11. The tiny delicate hummingbird weighs less than a penny and is the only bird believe it or not that can fly backward.

12. The hummingbird has a body temperature of 111 degrees Fahrenheit beats its wings more than 75 times a second and builds a nest the size of a walnut.

Black Holes

INSERT: Place commas and semicolons where they are needed in the paragraphs below. Circle punctuation marks you add. (Remember to refer to your handbook if you have any questions about the rules for using commas and semicolons.)

One of the most remarkable and brilliant scientists of our time is 50-something Stephen Hawking, physics professor, author, and theorist. His studies concerning the nature of the universe and black holes have advanced our understanding of space. More importantly Dr. Hawking has done more than any other physicist in describing and detailing his life's work in language understood by the average person. In short he has brought the outer limits of the universe "down to earth."

These accomplishments alone merit our praise and respect that Dr. Hawking has accomplished them despite disabling personal setbacks is almost incomprehensible. In 1962 when he was only 20 years old Stephen Hawking learned he had amyotrophic lateral sclerosis or ALS. ALS gradually destroys the nerves and muscles needed for moving. Doctors told him that he would probably die before he finished his doctoral degree however Stephen didn't let their prognosis stop him. With the support of fellow Cambridge student Jane Wilde whom he later married he continued his studies and received his Ph.D.

During the course of his doctoral work Dr. Hawking became interested in the work of scientist Roger Penrose an early theorist in the study of black holes. Black holes are spaces that Penrose and Hawking believe exist in space. These spaces possibly formed when a star burns itself out and collapses are areas in which gravity is extremely strong anything pulled into the black hole cannot get out. Even time stops!

Stephen Hawking's work on black holes and the nature of the universe was published in a book entitled *A Brief History of Time: From the Big Bang to Black Holes*. The book was written for people who do not have a scientific background. It is a remarkable book. What makes it even more remarkable is that it was written by a man unable to move his arms and hands to write unable to speak and unable to communicate normally. The book is a testament to one person's determination to succeed to be heard and to overcome personal tragedy.

follow-up One semicolon rule in your handbook states, "A semicolon is used to separate groups of words that already contain commas." Provide an example sentence illustrating this rule without looking in your handbook (598) until after your sentence is written. Then refer to the handbook to check your work.

Using Semicolons

READ & INSERT: Read and study the semicolon rules in your handbook. Afterward, insert semicolons where they are needed in the following sentences. Circle your answers. (Some sentences may not need a semicolon.)

1. Lightning had struck the old willow tree one too many times; now and then one could hear an ominous cracking sound.
2. Before the morning was out, Dad noticed an ever-widening crack in the trunk unless the tree was cut down, it seemed inevitable that the tree would soon fall on the roof.
3. The tree began to split on a Saturday after a strong, furious windstorm the night before and Dad knew that getting fast, dependable, and reasonably priced tree service on the weekend would be a difficult job.
4. He called number after number from the phone book and finally found someone willing to come and look at the old willow.
5. We had always loved that willow tree it saddened everyone to talk of cutting it down.
6. Mom asked the man several questions about bracing the tree however, he was forced to speak honestly with her about the necessity of taking the tree down.
7. The willow certainly held fond memories for us nevertheless, we could not risk the property damage and personal injury the fast-splitting tree might cause.
8. As the work began and progressed, our small yard seemed to brim with workers, neighbors, and family members ladders, power saws, and ropes leaves, branches, and pieces of the willow's trunk.
9. Finally the job was finished the tree had been safely cut down.
10. We no longer look out the back door to see our stately, old willow tree instead we see the back of our neighbor's not-so-stately garage.

Remember: When two independent clauses are connected with a conjunctive adverb (*however*, *also*, *moreover*), include a semicolon before it and a comma after it.

Using Colons

REVIEW & INSERT: Review the colon rules in your handbook. Then insert colons where they are needed below. (Some sentences may not need a colon.) Circle the punctuation marks you add.

1. Rob has sent for information about schools in these states: Wisconsin, Illinois, California, and Florida.
2. Dear Registrar

   Please send me your latest catalog. I am also interested in . . .
3. One question is very important to anyone seeking an education How much is it going to cost?
4. Rob made his decision after carefully considering the information about tuition, housing, programs, and financial aid.
5. Here is another important, two-part question for prospective students to ask Will I receive a quality education, and will the degree I earn be recognized as valid in the career area I have chosen?
6. My father had important advice he never tired of repeating "These days, you've got to get a good education."
7. As a new student, Rob plans to take courses in several subjects communication, lettering, graphic design, market research, and drawing.
8. New students soon learn that you sometimes have to leave your noisy apartment in search of two important ingredients for productive studying peace and quiet.
9. It is no wonder that during final exam time the school libraries are filled with students doing one thing studying.
10. All things considered, the first year at school can be exciting, challenging, and fun.

follow-up Identify and learn one colon rule in the handbook that wasn't covered in this activity.

Punctuating for Style

IDENTIFY: Carefully read the short essay below. Then, on the lines that follow the essay, explain the specific function of each underlined punctuation mark—a dash, a hyphen, or a set of quotation marks. (Consult your handbook for help.)

Along with the fitness and exercise craze that has swept America have come sore muscles, pulled tendons, and torn ligaments. Many of these injuries could be avoided if proper warm-up and conditioning routines were followed. Most beginners start out exercising too hard and too fast. A thorough warm-up before any exercising is a must. The warm-up serves two important functions—stretching the muscles in preparation for a workout and getting the heart pumping.

The stretch should begin at the top of the body and work slowly down to the ankles. The routine should consist of basic stretches such as head rotations to relax the neck, arm circles to loosen the shoulders, and trunk rotations to stretch the back and stomach muscles. Stretching out the leg muscles is also very important as most exercising involves much use of the legs. Toe touches, calf stretches, and ankle rotations—these are just some of the exercises that can be used to loosen the leg muscles. It is important to remember that these are muscle-stretching exercises. Stretching does not mean bouncing or jerking the muscles. Such action could easily lead to pulls, sprains, or tears.

The second half of the warm-up consists of getting the heart ready for a full workout. This can be done with any of a number of activities such as jumping jacks, jogging, or even running in place. You must remember to start out slowly and increase your pace gradually until the body feels ready to begin the full-scale workout. Throughout the warm-up period, you should try to breathe regularly. There is a tendency for beginners either to hold their breath during certain exercises or to greatly increase breathing—both are serious mistakes.

Another common mistake beginners often make is to stop exercising suddenly. Warming "down" after a workout is just as important as warming up. This final phase can consist of the same stretching exercises used in the warm-up. A warm-down, or cooldown as some call it, gradually returns the body to a normal state. This helps prevent muscle injuries and brings the heartbeat back to its normal rate.

1. ....

2. ....

3. ....

4. ....

follow-up Identify and learn one rule in your handbook for using dashes, hyphens, or quotation marks that wasn't covered in this activity.

Using the Right Word

SELECT: As you carefully read through the following sentences, underline the correct word in each set of parentheses. (Refer to "Using the Right Word," 692-701, in the handbook for help.)

1. Elisha attended the (annual, perennial) career fair at the local college.
2. She and her classmates had to (accept, except) (their, there, they're) invitations four weeks in advance in order to attend the fair.
3. (Already, All ready) the (amount, number) of people attending was (all together, altogether) too many.
4. Even though the (sight, site) of the fair was a large auditorium, (their, there) was (hardly, not hardly) room for all those who came.
5. Elisha found she had no (personal, personnel) interest in the main speaker's topic, "Let astrology be (your, you're) career guide."
6. (Among, Between) the speakers at the fair were some very eminent members of the business community.
7. Still, (there, their, they're) were (fewer, less) speakers (than, then) Elisha anticipated.
8. At one point, Elisha had to (chose, choose) (between, among) visiting a college recruiter and a vocational counselor.
9. The vocational counselor presented her material (good, well) (accept, except) for those few times she was (to, too, two) (quiet, quite).
10. The booths of the college representatives were set up (beside, besides) the vocational representatives' booths.
11. (Further, Farther) down were the booths of the two-year and specialty schools.
12. The (continuous, continual) activity made Elisha very tired; still, she had to (compliment, complement) the organizers on a job well done.

All Right Already

CORRECT: Correct any usage errors below by drawing a line through each word that is used incorrectly and writing the correct form above it. There are a total of 15 usage errors in the passage. (Two of these errors have been corrected for you.)

The ~~berth~~ birth of my baby sister Tasha had a strange ~~affect~~ effect on my mother. Until that "blessed" day, my mother had always been a calm, excepting person. She endured my pranks and teasings as a matter of coarse; it was the territory that came with having a son. The day Tasha was born, however, my world came tumbling down.

The first indication I had that things wood never be the same was my mother's command to wash my face and hands before dinner. Dirty hands and face had always been excepted as a young boy's write. Now, everything was different. I never new from one minute to the next witch old habit would come before the examination bored. After the "Clean Appendages Act" came the "Healthy Foods Declaration." Donuts, pizza, and corn dogs were outlawed; salads, fish, and fruit were adapted as our dietary mainstays. Nothing was sacred. My Nike high-tops suddenly inherited new white shoelaces. My favorite blew jeans disappeared.

I tried blaming Tasha, but she hardly looked the criminal type. It was hard to be mad at nine pounds of diapers, dribble, and baby powder. I finally asked my father what he thought had happened to Mom. He smiled and ruffled my hair. "Its not the first time this has happened," he replied. "You should have scene her when you were born. We had to carry our shoes in the house and tiptoe even when you were awake. Lawrence, eventually things will return to normal."

Unsinkable!

CORRECT: Proofread the essay below. Draw a line through any errors you find in capitalization, numbers, abbreviations, punctuation, spelling, and usage. Write the correction above each error. Add (and circle) punctuation as necessary. (*Hint:* Numbers are used frequently in this piece. Refer to the rules on "Numbers" (678) in your handbook.)

About 450 miles off the coast of Newfoundland in 12,000 feet of water scientists have recently discovered the remains of the great ocean liner the S S Titanic. The seventy-three year search for the Titanic, which went down in what is considered the worlds' greatest sea disaster has been a challengeing one. It concluded finally in September 1985. Because of this discovary interest in this legendary ship is stronger then ever.

In part this interest may be due to the titanics reputation. When it was first launched in 1912, the british steamer was the largest ship in the world. An incredible 882 ft. long and 175 ft. high, The Titanic was comparable to 4 city blocks in length and 11 stories in hieght. It was proclaimed the most expensive most luxurious ship ever built. It was said to be "unsinkable".

The later claim was the result of special features. The Titanic was equiped with a double bottom and the hull was divided into 16 separate watertight compartments. These added features, it was felt, would make the Titanic unsinkable.

Despite its reputation, the mighty Titanic did sink; and on its maiden voyage too. Carrying approximatly 2 2 0 0 passengers and over $420,000 worth of cargo, the Titanic set sail from England in April, 1912, bound for New York. Just a few days out of port, however on the night of April 14 the Titanic collided with an iceberg in the north atlantic, ripping a 300 ft. gash along its starboard side. The mighty "floating palace" sunk in a matter of 2 1/2 hours, taking with it all of its cargo and 1 5 2 2 of its passengers

The Index

A

B

C

D

L

M

N

O

P